English Literature and the Disciplines of Knowledge,
Early Modern to Eighteenth Century

Textxet

STUDIES IN COMPARATIVE LITERATURE

Series Editors

Theo D'haen (*University of Leuven*)
Karen Laura Thornber (*Harvard University*)
Zhang Longxi (*City University of Hong Kong*)
C.C. Barfoot (*University of Leiden*)
Hans Bertens (*University of Utrecht*)

VOLUME 84

The titles published in this series are listed at *brill.com/tscl*

English Literature and the Disciplines of Knowledge, Early Modern to Eighteenth Century

A Trade for Light

Edited by

Jorge Bastos da Silva
Miguel Ramalhete Gomes

BRILL
RODOPI

LEIDEN | BOSTON

Cover illustration: A depressed scholar surrounded by mythological figures; representing the melancholy temperament. Etching by J.D. Nessenthaler after himself, c. 1750. Reproduced by kind permission of the Wellcome Library, London.

Library of Congress Control Number: 2017042304

Typeface for the Latin, Greek, and Cyrillic scripts: "Brill". See and download: brill.com/brill-typeface.

ISSN 0927-5754
ISBN 978-90-04-34935-3 (hardback)
ISBN 978-90-04-34936-0 (e-book)

Contents

List of Figures

Introduction

Jorge Bastos da Silva and Miguel Ramalhete Gomes

This collection of essays focuses on the relationships between English literary culture and the sciences (in the broad sense of the word) from the Early
Modern Period to the late eighteenth century. The volume highlights the connections that link both literary discourse and the discourse about literature
to the conceptual or representational frameworks, practices, and cognitive
results (the "truths") of disciplines such as psychology, medicine, epistemology,
anthropology, cartography, chemistry, and rhetoric. On the whole, literature
and the sciences emerge as fields of inquiry and representation which share
an important number of assumptions and are determined or constructed by
several modes of cross-fertilization, not least because of the dynamics and the
morals of social interaction involved in their production and circulation.

The title of the collection draws upon a passage in Sir Francis Bacon's *New
Atlantis* (written around 1623–24, published posthumously in 1627). This fable
of the cultivation and preservation of knowledge is itself a good example of
the formal dialogue and interconnectedness of fields of learning and creative
practices the present volume is meant to investigate. Bacon offers a scientific
programme cast in the guise of a utopian narrative, thereby making a plea for
knowledge as the nerve centre of a virtuous and advanced society – a plea
which is both rational and passionate, for the wise ancient king Solamona, law-
giver of the island of Bensalem and founder of Salomon's House, "had a *large
heart*".[1] Salomon's House is "the very eye of this kingdom", the travellers are told,
and the narrator imparts the wonder of the discovery by saying: "we were come
into a land of angels".[2] Aware of its superiority, and wishing to remain safe from
envy and corruption, the people of Bensalem does the utmost not to reveal
itself to the world, while keeping abreast of developments elsewhere by send-
ing Fellows or Brethren of Salomon's House abroad on secret missions with the
sole purpose of collecting information, instruments and books. The governor
of the House of Strangers, one of the European visitors' main interlocutors,
describes such undertakings with the help of a mercantile comparison:

---

1   Francis Bacon, *The Advancement of Learning and New Atlantis*, ed. Arthur Johnston (Oxford,
    Clarendon Press, 1974), 228.
2   *Ibid.*, 222, 221.

But thus you see we maintain a trade, not for gold, silver, or jewels; nor
for silks; nor for spices; nor any other commodity of matter; but only for
God's first creature, which was *Light*: to have *light* (I say) of the growth of
all parts of the world.[3]

Crucially, by turning on the word "light", which became classic in descriptions
of the eighteenth century but is here derived from a text from the Early Modern
Period, the present volume foregrounds the shifts and continuities traversing
the two periods, aspects which are all-too-often concealed by the apparatus
of cultural chronology into airtight paradigmatic blocks or metanarratives
with their corresponding teaching units in university curricula and with their
respectively assigned slots in the institutional organization of research. Moreover, the word "trade" points usefully to the notion of exchange (to trade *for*
and *with*) as well as to the specialization and eventual professionalization of
the disciplines and their practitioners (to trade *in*), thereby suggesting both
transdisciplinary connections and discrete disciplinary formations.

In particular, the contributors' emphasis on discursive aspects foregrounds
the fact that the work of science produces discrete *texts*, i.e. that its workings
and findings do not exist as abstractions, rather that their expression, circulation, scrutiny and influence are inextricable from their embeddedness in specific historical circumstances (in Stephen Shapin's words, science is "produced
by people with bodies, situated in time, space, culture, and society, and struggling for credibility and authority"[4]). It is concurrently emphasised that science,
like literature, is a discursive field endowed with and susceptible of being
defined through language- and protocol-specific possibilities and constraints.
The recognition of this fundamental affinity, which determines the range and
nature of the cognitive contents of the sciences together with the appropriate
modes for formulating and conveying such contents, underlies the contributors' stress on the ways in which the sciences have been centrally engaged with
the precepts – and have endeavoured to engage the resources – of rhetoric and
social interaction.[5]

---

3   *Ibid.*, 230.

4   Steven Shapin, *Never Pure: Historical Studies of Science as if it Was Produced by People with
    Bodies, Situated in Time, Space, Culture, and Society, and Struggling for Credibility and Author-
    ity* (Baltimore, Johns Hopkins University Press, 2010).

5   The comparative novelty of the approach deserves prominence. As has been observed,
    "rhetoric *per se* has been a legitimate area of inquiry since the ancient Greeks, but the distinc-
    tion in Aristotle between rhetoric and science has meant that a 'rhetoric of science' seemed
    an impossibility, because the very distinctiveness of science as a body of valid reasoning
    came from its difference from rhetoric. With the development of the sociology of scientific

Hence, the authors' concentration on the performative aspect of scientific inquiry and thus on the specific discursive forms involved in the practical and institutional make-up of the disciplines of knowledge amounts to the common thread uniting the essays in this collection, which therefore may be seen as so many contributions to a "social history of knowledge" or a "social history of truth", in Peter Burke's and Steven Shapin's phrases.[6] Some of the essays in the volume additionally trace prevailing attitudes to science as reflected in literature, and broaden the scope of the survey to include the visual arts. Moreover, although case studies focus on literature written in Britain, the potential wider significance for the understanding of cultural modernity of a number of the issues discussed is also suggested. The range of authors examined includes Richard Brome, Margaret Cavendish, Aphra Behn, the third Earl of Shaftesbury, Daniel Defoe, Jonathan Swift, Samuel Richardson, and Tobias Smollett. Emphasis is placed throughout on how authors of literature regard the practices, practitioners and findings of science, as well as on how the actual modes of knowing and depicting the world operative in literature (that which since Antiquity has been called "mimesis") intersect with those which are characteristic of the several disciplines of science.

The author of *New Atlantis* may have been a pioneer in the theoretical conception of the epistemological and institutional devices of modern science, but he was far from alone in his confidence that knowledge would lead men to progress, both technical and moral; indeed, the practical exploits of his contemporaries, such as navigators, experimenters and inventors, was often infused with that faith. Nor was he the only author to relate progress to transactions of other sorts. In the preface to his translation of *The Odyssey* in 1675, Thomas Hobbes – a far more conspicuous transgressor of disciplinary boundaries than Bacon himself – prescribes that the heroic poem should give delight and profit to the reader, i.e. it ought to provide pleasure which is neither idle nor corrupt. "By Profit", he explains, "I intend not here any accession of Wealth, either to the Poet, or to the Reader; but accession of Prudence, Justice, Fortitude, by the example of such Great and Noble Persons as he introduceth speaking, or

---

knowledge (SSK), scholars started to investigate how the contents of well-accepted scientific knowledge could be examined using the tools of rhetorical and literary analysis. If science was to be regarded as a social construct, then it was surely constructed in part by literary and rhetorical means" (Trevor J. Pinch, "Rhetoric", in *Reader's Guide to the History of Science*, ed. Arne Hessenbruch (London / Chicago: Fitzroy Dearborn Publishers, 2000), 653).

6   P. Burke, *A Social History of Knowledge: From Gutenberg to Diderot* (Cambridge: Polity Press, 2008 [2000]), and *A Social History of Knowledge II: From the* Encyclopédie *to Wikipedia* (Cambridge: Polity Press, 2012); S. Shapin, *A Social History of Truth: Civility and Science in Seventeenth-Century England* (Chicago / London: University of Chicago Press, 1995 [1994]).

describeth acting".[7] Like Bacon, Hobbes resorts to language which is evocative of mercantile values, at once ascertaining and undermining them by suggesting both the importance of exchanges and the inadequacy of purely material pursuits. Significantly, his espousal of the epic is in tune with the Early Modern apologetics of science: the sphere of the latter, like that of literature, is bound up with the practical issues of living a better life.[8] Conversely, as it strives to elevate the human mind, literature is, like science, a trade for light.

• • •

Both Literary Studies and the History of Science are fields of research which have proved to require ever-widening perspectives over the past few decades. By undergoing the so-called "cultural turn", Literary Studies have encouraged scholars to take extratextual aspects increasingly into consideration. The History of Science – and, indeed, the history of knowledge more broadly – has evolved from a study of the principles, methods and institutions of science into more inclusive approaches, thereby deepening our awareness of the embeddedness of scientific inquiry in significant cultural, epistemological and sociological features of specific historical moments.

In this spirit, *English Literature and the Disciplines of Knowledge, Early Modern to Eighteenth Century: A Trade for Light* acknowledges the ways in which Literary Studies and the History of Science have become broader and revitalised academic fields by addressing the space(s) of their intersections. The collection provides a body of readings which are not only interdisciplinary but also balanced, insofar as it covers major alongside lesser-known authors. It also suggests a particular timeframe (c. 1500-c. 1800) as the period of the rise of modernity, focusing on contrasts and continuities across an era which is too often seen (both by scholars of the Early Modern Period and by those who specialise in the long eighteenth century) as split around the mid-1600s. By providing a panoramic view of some three centuries through a series of essays focusing on specific case studies, the volume combines a broad scope with an attention to detail as a means to characterise the shifting and productive

---

7   T. Hobbes, "Preface to *Homer's Odysses, Translated by Tho. Hobbes of Malmsbury*", in *Critical Essays of the Seventeenth Century*, ed. N.E. Spingarn, 3 vols. (Bloomington / London: Indiana University Press, 1968), Vol. ii, 67–68.

8   Science may accordingly be seen as a legitimate "road to fulfilment". Yet, surprisingly, it is virtually absent from Keith Thomas' fascinating and wide-ranging digest of sixteenth- to eighteenth-century values and attitudes, *The Ends of Life: Roads to Fulfilment in Early Modern England* (Oxford: Oxford University Press, 2009).

historical relations between different but mutually dependent fields during this period.

The collection is divided into two parts which trace different aspects of an ongoing process. The parts adopt a different rationale from the dominant chronological partition mentioned above. The two groups of studies are preceded by a forethought by George Rousseau, who provides a survey of the discipline(s) and of the interdisciplinary field which the present volume addresses, as well as an argument for the relevance of the specific contributions it entails. Rousseau offers an overview of developments that took place in the latter half of the twentieth century by which the Humanities and the exact sciences stepped out of their respective comfort zones to challenge, enhance and redefine one another. He stresses the relevance of interdisciplinary approaches as well as the difficulties posed to scholars by the negotiation of different idiolects and the sheer range of knowledge(s) involved, not least in the aftermath of the rise of the digital Humanities. Most interestingly in the present context, Rousseau evokes the age of the Enlightenment to stress the fact that "something analogous to these post-1960s cycles was occurring" in that era, and corrects the prevalent view that science influenced literature by underlining the fact that "the influence proceeds as preponderantly in the opposite direction: *from* literature *to* science".

The title of the first part, "ENGENDERING SPACE, CREATING MEANING", alludes to several forms of creating and opening up a space for scientific production, while at the same time using space itself either as the object of discussion or as a conceptual place through which one situates oneself in the world. The essays gathered under that heading evince the constructive and often contentious character of discourses which not only register reality but actively engender it through acts of discovery, elaboration and appropriation, whether fictional, experiential or scientific.

In the opening essay Bernhard Klein discusses how the mapping of African space by seventeenth-century Dutch and Flemish cartographers was accompanied by the visual representation of African bodies whose markers of racial and ethnic difference exist in a conceptual affinity with the clearly defined ethnic portrayal of a literary character such as Aphra Behn's Oroonoko. In order to do so, Klein relates Oroonoko to his clearest literary predecessor, Shakespeare's Othello, in order to describe not only their relation to space and placelessness, as well as the sexual decorum implied in them, but also to track the shift in the verbal description of ethnic difference from one end of the seventeenth century to the other, in which Othello's indefinable ethnic status is contrasted with the precise detail of Aphra Behn's description of Oroonoko. This is followed by a discussion of several seventeenth-century continental maps of

Africa which both supports and expands the argument developed in the first half of the chapter. Klein argues that maps were beginning to define "a nexus between people and land, race and space, ethnicity and geography" by means of strict spatial categories in which the human body increasingly became a part of the cartographic effort to rationalise the world. The submission of these bodies to the modern slave economy found its parallel in their submission to the mechanisms of natural history, of which the description of peoples and places formed an instrumental and hardly disinterested subgenre.

Miguel Ramalhete Gomes focuses as well on the imaginative production of space in Richard Brome's 1638 play, *The Antipodes*, a clever dramatisation of geography as an *idée fixe*. After an introduction which expounds a theoretical method – namely "presentism", a recent offshoot of Shakespearean historicism – Ramalhete Gomes deliberately engages with anachronism by reading Brome's play as a representative but unremarked upon part of the type of writings which were raided by Freud and Jung in the course of shaping psychoanalysis. *The Antipodes* is thus looked at as a text that Freud and Jung might have considered valuable, had they come across it, in that it contains instances of slips of the tongue, a case history, moments of analysis and extensive therapy, as well as allusions to sexual fears as one of the possible origins of mental disturbance. The anachronistic method is then folded upon itself in a series of considerations on the historicising neutralisation of Freud and the role of cultural poetics in silencing aspects of texts which do not conform to the current understanding of what such texts are expected to historically represent.

In a similar manner, Kate De Rycker's chapter explores links between Margaret Cavendish's questioning of the experimental method favoured by the Royal Society – an institution whose experiments Cavendish was invited to observe, but from which she was nevertheless excluded – and recent epistemological discussions in the humanities regarding the construction and communication of historical evidence. As De Rycker shows, Cavendish suggested that the Royal Society's experimental methods actually allowed them to construct their own proof. The previous gendered reading of her participation in seventeenth-century debates regarding what could be considered as truth and evidence is complicated by De Rycker, who explains that the hierarchical division between a superior "feminine" writing and a "masculine" one, allegedly attributed to Cavendish, should in fact be read along significantly different lines. Arguing rather that all writers were subjective, Cavendish suggests that, as a woman, she was more attuned to such subjectivity, whereas it was male scientists who did not accept their inability to be entirely objective. Cavendish therefore engendered a place of her own in a community and intellectual culture from which she was traditionally excluded.

Also bearing on issues of gender, Mihaela Irimia's chapter at the end of this part considers some of the imagology generated by British "Grand Tourists", by focusing on positive and negative evaluations of national difference and of the adoption, which was also an adaptation, of procedures from foreign cultures. This process implied an intertwining of the arts and the sciences which was obviously different for young male aristocrats and upper class women, their overall educational process alternating between painting and music, mechanics and transport, or fashion and landscape gardening. Irimia's chapter then goes on to explore the conjunction of *Francophilia* and *Italophilia* in the context of the British Grand Tour, namely in the areas of macaroni fashion, coiffures and gardening. Like Klein's, Irimia's contribution is enriched by illustrations which point to the relevance of taking into account the juxtaposition of the lived, the seen and the spoken.

It is in the wake of discussions concerning the permeability of the languages of art and science already introduced in the first part of the book, then, that the chapters in the second part, entitled "FORMS OF DISCOURSE AND SOCIABILITY", direct their attention to language and rhetoric as focal points in the interaction between the arts and the sciences. These essays are fuelled by a concern with the experiential dimension which is inextricable from the processes and products of learning, and their discursive, even stylistic, aspect, amounting to a moral, and therefore human, element referable to the persons of those who talk or write, and those who listen or read – or, in other words, those who teach and communicate, and those who learn or contest.

Maria Avxentevskaya comes back to one of the issues essential to Kate De Rycker's chapter, the uncertain binary opposition between the language of proof and literary rhetoric. Her chapter turns around John Wilkins, one of the founding members of the Royal Society of London and a populariser of science, best known for his project of inventing an artificial philosophical language which combined both logic and rhetoric, as well as cognitive and performative languages. In his *Mathematical Magick, or the Wonders that may be performed by Mechanical Geometry* (1648), Avxentevskaya argues, Wilkins employed humanist historicising and literary experiential testimonies to solve methodological problems within the contemporary art of mechanics. Striking a balance between the figural and the literal, Wilkins' performative techniques compensated for the contemporary lack of a mathematical proof for hypotheses on the physics of motion, as well as for the lack of special knowledge on the part of his readership. His attempt to bridge the gap between professional and popular science relied, however, on a concept of experience which, though necessary as a principle of intelligibility, constantly postponed the totalisation it promised.

Richard Nate also pursues the discomfort recurrently expressed towards rhetoric in the wake of the seventeenth-century Scientific Revolution. As Nate argues, even the defence of the "plain style", by such authors as Thomas Sprat and Robert Boyle, was obviously unable to abolish rhetoric altogether, ultimately producing only a new rhetorical decorum which used rhetoric to attack an understanding of rhetoric as a superfluous, artificial addition to "normal" language. His chapter then focuses on the impact such anti-rhetorical gestures had on English literature of the eighteenth century, first in the "circumstantial method" employed by Daniel Defoe's narrator in *Robinson Crusoe* (1719) but also in the parodies that make up Jonathan Swift's *Gulliver's Travels* (1726), both of which pretended to offer "factual" accounts in a straightforward manner. Later in the eighteenth century, anti-rhetorical postures were to become so widespread that they went beyond the borders of scientific discourse into the realm of political discourse, as was the case of the "War of Pamphlets", which engaged authors such as Edmund Burke, Thomas Paine and Mary Wollstonecraft. Unsurprisingly perhaps, the same tensions which led to the use of rhetorical tropes in the process of denouncing a rhetorically charged language were to be found here as well. Nate's chapter concludes at the very end of the eighteenth century, with Wordsworth's defence of a simple language in his preface to *Lyrical Ballads* (1800), regarding which Nate points both to the irony of using a book of poetry to criticise bookish learning and to the irony of resorting to anti-rhetorical arguments, elaborated during the course of the Scientific Revolution, in corroborating critical comments on the scientific worldview.

Jorge Bastos da Silva's chapter turns to what Anthony Ashley Cooper, the third Earl of Shaftesbury, deemed "True Learning", that is, knowledge of the self, specifically in terms of the strategies of explanation and argumentation developed in *Soliloquy: Or, Advice to an Author*, the treatise in Shaftesbury's major work, *Characteristicks of Men, Manners, Opinions, Times*, which most explicitly deals with the question of self-knowledge. Bastos da Silva examines the disparate frames of reference used by Shaftesbury and inquires into their consistency, ultimately focusing on the significance of their inconsistency. Drawing upon the distinction made by theorist of science John Ziman between *consensibility* and *consensuality*, the chapter analyses how Shaftesbury experimented with several languages of consensibility, because, it is argued, although certain of the ethical points he wished to make, he was sceptical regarding the modes for understanding human nature provided by physiology, metaphysics, religion, and even by his former tutor, John Locke. What becomes a positive epistemological predicament for Shaftesbury allows Bastos da Silva to link the author's convivial and non-magisterial style to the way in which scientific inquiry was enabled and problems of credibility were resolved by being encoded as gentlemanly behaviour within a culture of honour and rank in the seventeenth century.

Daniel Essig García, on the other hand, deals with the culture of sentimental reading in Daniel Defoe's *A Journal of the Plague Year* and Samuel Richardson's *Pamela*. Although, at first sight, this may not appear to be a scientifically inflected topic, Essig García points out that the performance of tears in the second half of the eighteenth century follows upon the demise of Galenic humoral medicine, so that one witnesses a shift of perception between an externally induced purgation, such as bloodletting, and the internal welling of the spirits conducive to crying. These tears additionally characterise a new, sentimentally charged sense of masculinity, so that literature, as well as diaries and correspondence, come to include men who cry. This tendency is contrasted with the regulated distance basic to the novel in letters, which reveals some of the theatricality of the act of shedding tears. Essig García turns his attention to the material conditions – the innovations in the Post – as well as literary conditions – the Ovidian and "baroque" traditions of epistolarity – behind this interest in the novel of letters, which, along with increasing representations of scenes of reading, became a metaphor for the paradoxes of distance and privacy, as well as for their theatricalisation.

In the final chapter, Wojciech Nowicki discusses portraits of quirky scholars in two novels from the second half of the eighteenth century, Tobias Smollett's *Launcelot Greaves* (1760–61) and an anonymous text called *The Philosophical Quixote* (1782), which he sets in a wider context of depictions of scientists as morally and/or psychologically unbalanced characters. Based on actual contemporary scientists, respectively John Shebbeare and Joseph Priestley, both of them practitioners of "chymistry", the new science of the day, the scholars in these two texts prove to be either quacks, selling fake medicine with the help of manipulative and prolix language, or irresponsible experimenters, whose eccentric dabbling in electricity has literally explosive results. Their "chemical" quirkiness has, however, a more metaphorical import, in that, besides its obvious criticism of scientific practices and actual scientists, it is made to comment upon their contemporary political reality. Hence, each of these figures is made to recall, on the one hand, the cynicism and prolixity of contemporary politicians, and, on the other hand, political explosiveness or radicalism.

Nowicki's essay may serve as a final reminder of the fact that literature and science share yet another important feature: they are both linked to, and are indeed dependent on, issues of power and accountability. What they reveal, and what they construe, is always subject to, and contingent upon, the judgment of individuals and of society, although they shape the latter in the process as well. To return to the beginning of this introduction, Francis Bacon was not unaware of these entanglements. The trade for light committed to the Fellows of Salomon's House in *New Atlantis* was a trade "for God's first creature".[9] This ambition is consistent with the calling of that remarkable scientific institution: "The End of our Foundation is the knowledge of Causes, and secret motions of things; and the enlarging of the bounds of Human Empire, to the effecting of all things possible", says one of the venerable Brethren.[10] The works of science are forward-looking by way of looking back, and looking into, the constitution of all things; they not only investigate the inner principles of substances and phenomena, but also their *primum mobile*, their maker, Him they are the creatures of. In this light – in this *light* – the "enlarging of the bounds of Human Empire, to the effecting of all things possible" points to more than a mere hankering for material or technological progress; rather, it postulates a combination of the lofty and the practical which matches the traditionally-avowed aims of literature as an agent in the fulfilment of humanity as a creature endowed with reason, conscience, and the ability to act in this world. As, indeed, the only species graced with such predicament, and therefore, most truly, "God's first creature".

Works Cited

Bacon, Francis. *The Advancement of Learning and New Atlantis*, edited by Arthur Johnston. Oxford: Clarendon Press, 1974.

Burke, Peter. *A Social History of Knowledge II: From the* Encyclopédie *to Wikipedia*. Cambridge: Polity Press, 2012.

Burke, Peter. *A Social History of Knowledge: From Gutenberg to Diderot*. Cambridge: Polity Press, 2008 [2000].

Hobbes, Thomas. "Preface to *Homer's Odysses, Translated by Tho. Hobbes of Malmsbury*", in *Critical Essays of the Seventeenth Century*, edited by J.E. Spingarn. Vol. II, 67–76. Bloomington / London: Indiana University Press, 1968. 3 vols.

Pinch, Trevor J. "Rhetoric", in *Reader's Guide to the History of Science*, edited by Arne Hessenbruch. 653–654. London / Chicago: Fitzroy Dearborn Publishers, 2000.

---

9   Bacon, *The Advancement of Learning and New Atlantis*, 230.
10   *Ibid.*, 239.

Shapin, Steven. *Never Pure: Historical Studies of Science as if it Was Produced by People with Bodies, Situated in Time, Space, Culture, and Society, and Struggling for Credibility and Authority*. Baltimore: Johns Hopkins University Press, 2010.

Shapin, Steven. *A Social History of Truth: Civility and Science in Seventeenth-Century England*. Chicago / London: University of Chicago Press, 1995 [1994].

Thomas, Keith. *The Ends of Life: Roads to Fulfilment in Early Modern England*. Oxford: Oxford University Press, 2009.

Forethought: *A Trade for Light* and the State of the Art

George Rousseau

Today it is less consequential that practitioners of the Humanities speak in different vocabularies and academic idiolects – historians, philosophers, literary and art historians all using different terminologies – than the *truths* they attempt to bring to light. And the status of truth itself may have globally diminished in 2016 when some of the world's most authoritative dictionaries enlist the word "post-truth" and assure us we now live in the era of "post-truth". An art historian and philosopher, for example, both invoke "the Renaissance" and "the Enlightenment", or "the Age of Genius" and "the Enlightenment Mind", and may even share common assumptions about the chronology of these movements, but each wants to extract different truths from the labels. Similarly for historians (whether cultural, political, social or whatever persuasion) and literary historians. Their language differs, as well as the aims pursued: "truth" in one discipline differs drastically from truth in another. All agree that the European Enlightenment existed, had some basis in historical reality, and extended chronologically from circa 1700 to 1790 (arbitrary dates).[1] Here ends the consensus: the Enlightenment's origins and causes, geographies and bio-geographies, whether it was beneficial, how it altered human history, and so forth. The point is so self-evident as barely to need iteration; yet overlook it, proceed as if "all of us working in the Humanities" are in this research pursuit together, for similar purpose and goal, and you encounter barricades as insurmountable as the current migrants in the Balkans. Historians of the nineteenth century know, for instance, how much genuine repulsion existed among Victorians for the eighteenth-century Enlightenment (however interpreted and not merely because it was viewed primarily as a French phenomenon). Yet toilers in other fields unaware of the antipathy blithely beaver away in the belief that *everyone* has endorsed "the Enlightenment" since its eighteenth-century arrival. Nothing could be further from the truth.

---

1 Distinguished American historian of early modern technology Lynn White believed the Enlightenment continued until the death of Queen Victoria in 1901; see Lynn White and American Council of Learned Societies, *Medieval Technology and Social Change* (London: Oxford University Press, 1962).

The implication of these truths is what underlies interdisciplinary studies. *Interdisciplinary*: the ability to glimpse the reality of the past from the perspective of *moving between different disciplines*, negotiating problems and solutions by consulting at least two disciplines. *Transdisciplinary* is more fraught and denotes working "across" or "through" more than two disciplines at the same time: literature, history, and art history, for instance. Add to the equation disciplines *outside* the Humanities (medicine, the sciences, technology, the law) and the enterprise becomes more tortured for a variety of reasons ranging from the need for deep-layer knowledge about each field to the use of the (above-mentioned) idiolects. What we have, then, is a *gradus ad parnassum* of interdisciplinarities from the rudimentary (in my first example above) to the more stratospheric when disciplines outside the traditional Humanities are invoked. It takes a capable scholar of the original field – philosophy, for example – to bring off what I am calling the elementary interdisciplinarity between just two disciplines. To accomplish the stratospheric transdisciplinary type between several disciplines is very hard to do, in addition to the ranges of required knowledge.[2]

Interdisciplinary approaches (of whatever grade of difficulty) arose because monodisciplinary knowledge was insufficient for problem solving. They especially arose in the natural sciences. Historically in the twentieth century, astrophysics, biochemistry, sociobiology, neurobiology, and dozens of others. Their trajectory in the Humanities was different because they arose in the West in response to specific sociopolitical developments: catastrophic war and holocaust in the twentieth century, mass migration, technology associated with warfare, colliding political systems, freedom and tyranny. By the 1970s the former linguistic and philological approaches of traditional literary study (i.e., learning languages, editing and annotating texts, verbal *explication de texte*) appeared inadequate to meet the post-1960s sociopolitical developments.[3] Frustrated that these older approaches were now insufficient, or at least circumscribed, academics working across the Humanities began to import the tools of social scientists. By the 1980s a revolution resulted in broadly based cultural studies across all humanistic fields, especially with presentist leanings. Cultural history differed from cultural studies by privileging the *historical*

---

2   See the debates between Stanley Fish and George Rousseau: Stanley Fish, "Being Interdisciplinary Is So Very Hard to Do", in *There's No Such Thing as Free Speech*, 231–242 (Oxford: Oxford University Press, 1994); and G.S. Rousseau, "Riddles of Interdisciplinarity: A Reply to Stanley Fish", in *Intercultural Encounters – Studies in English Literature*, ed. Heinz Antor and Kevin L. Cope, 111–130 (Heidelberg: C. Winter, 1999).

3   Of course it did not stop New Critics such as F.R. Leavis from writing their books.

component.[4] Also, the sense that some literary camps had armed themselves during the 1970s with sufficient theory to deploy arsenals of jargon bearing no resemblance to reality was pervasive in certain quarters. It was the view – as one critic melodramatically put it – that literary academia contained guerilla troops armed to the teeth with theory and jargon.[5] The charge? The new troops could not describe in concise English – this was the allegation – what they meant. Only the initiated could understand. Yet the indictment was paradoxically fair and unfair: fair insofar as the new idiolects were often impenetrable, unfair for failing to acknowledge that complex ideas can require specialized vocabularies embedded in convoluted rhetorical discourses to convey their meaning. After much paper warfare, pockets of deep resistance endured through the 1980s. Some fields refused to capitulate, others did what they could to deracinate theory, but it was nevertheless clear that the Humanities would not soon return to their pre-1960s profile let alone their pre-World War Two mold.

These developments posed colossal hurdles for many mid-stream career academics, ranging from readjustment of their view of the social sciences to retraining themselves in new fields (anthropology, economics, sociology, etc.). Others rejoiced at the breath of fresh air, asphyxiated, as they lamented they were, by the doldrums in which the Humanities had lingered for so many decades before the 1970s. Then, just when many academics thought they had made their peace with the new tide bringing in theory and the social sciences, something momentous occurred: the rise of virtual technology leading to the digital Humanities. This new arrival – the digital fix – proved far more tyrannical and invincible than its predecessor in theory and the social sciences. It represented a conceptual leap from the old Humanities (which had not been based on hypertextual or algorithmic principles)[6] as well as altered everyone's working routine, the volume of information that could be accessed with the click of a keystroke or depression of a mouse, as well as the psychological fallout of hyperlinking realism. The speed of human communication altered as well – smart telephones, Apple computers, the new Internet. Even projects in *medias res* needed to alter their modus vivendi and start over from scratch. The bottom line: c. 1990 you might still beaver away at the Humanities in disregard

---

4   For a successful example of the difference see Mihaela Irimia, ed., *Literary into Cultural History: International Colloquium* (Bucharest: Institutul Cultural Roman, 2009).

5   There is no point to citing single sources, as the notion was then widespread in the UK and USA.

6   George Landow was a pioneer in the field: see George P. Landow, *Hyper/Text/Theory* (Baltimore: Johns Hopkins University Press, 1994).

of the social sciences but you could do nothing apart from the new digital technology. There was nowhere to hide from the "techies" whose tribe swelled daily, unless you posed as a Miniver Cheevy pining for the past and writing with a quill on yellow pads. If, by 1980, the social sciences appeared here to stay, the digital Humanities, and their "techies", entrenched themselves more solidly, neither one a passing phase from which nostalgic purists would awaken.

The fallout for literary and cultural history in our time has been noteworthy. If the older philological methods – as mentioned – succumbed to the social sciences, and the instauration of transdisciplinary approaches summoned various sciences in a big way, the digital Humanities has taken an even more magisterial toll. First, it reversed the desideratum of most academics from too *little* – think of all those scholars in the Humanities compiling the first online bibliographies[7] – to too *much*. Today everyone I know is drowning in a surfeit of information. Yet in the 1990s the gathering of huge hulks of data grew so facile with just a few clicks of the mouse that it facilitated writing while also proliferating the forms and genres of communication. By the millennium, publications in print or electronic form were two of several options, and new Internet genres concurrently arose ranging from blogs and personal websites to videos and podcasts. The result has been exponential hyperactivity and a rampant increase in the numbers of words produced – to such extent that interdisciplinarity today is dauntingly complex. The earlier disciplinary concerns of Fish and Rousseau – about intellectual challenge and loyalty to the home discipline – are now obsolete.[8] The human brain, however plastic and malleable, today bellows in agony it cannot cope with the knowledge-explosion. Fidelity to some "home discipline" is low on any list of priorities.

On first glance these developments can seem extraneous to this book's concerns, yet nothing could be further from the truth. For something analogous to these post-1960s cycles was occurring in the era our contributors survey. This collection's chronology extends from approximately 1680 to 1760, capturing a swath of early Enlightenment life, its geography focused on just one island in northwest Europe – striving to become "Great Britain" but not yet so – and aiming to surpass richer countries still in possession of far-flung empires such as France, Spain and the Netherlands (the latter two in palpable decline). The Scientific Revolution underpinned many socioeconomic developments and artistic movements then, as thinkers from Bacon and Hobbes to Boyle and Locke brought forward their speculations. Nothing – it seemed to many in that epoch – would ever be the same, not the ways of believing,

---

7 Exemplified in the decades spent compiling the *Eighteenth-Century Short Title Catalogue*.
8 See n. 2.

knowing, or worshipping, the last still crucial in an agrarian society not yet secular. Today, little agreement exists about the manifested social roles of this late seventeenth-century Scientific Revolution, no more than about my disciplinary approaches above. Even so, most contemporary historical students concur that by the time Newton died (in 1727), something *faute de mieux* like "the modern mind" had arisen and "modernity" commenced, or, at least, pre-modernity had finished its work. This "something" was Cartesian thought, especially Descartes' dualism and physio-philosophical solutions to age-old impasses such as the body-mind riddle and its attendant consciousness (the same consciousness our neuroscientists grapple with today). The historical content gathered in this book deals with the collective and individual mind-sets steeped in the ways of knowing Descartes fractured and Newton sought to repair.[9] To describe its effects in literature the nine authors of *A Trade for Light* hover between science as metaphor and science as reality. Nevertheless, whether science connotes realism or representation, all recognize the figures they follow were being wrenched from their comfort zones. Science – even the Renaissance *scientia* on which some post-Cartesian science was predicated[10] – impressed these thinkers from Bacon to Newton as composed of both realism and representation, even if post-1900 science has often proceeded as if the two could be kept apart.

The historical transition from Cartesian dualism to Newtonian mechanism underpinned much Enlightenment thought but was never imagined as the whole story, certainly not in the eighteenth century. By approximately 1750 a competing view to Newtonian mechanism arose in the intellectual ferment of the Scottish Enlightenment. It was a paradigm about self-organization and organic form Adam Smith and his colleagues captured in *The Wealth of Nations* (1776) in the concept of "The Invisible Hand". This referred to dark, inscrutable and unforeseen forces that combine to influence the way societies form and self-regulate themselves, and ultimately enable the sociocultural benefits of human sympathy, sensibility, and sociability.[11] Smith's "Invisible Hand" did not occur in a flash of epiphanic insight (he only invokes the phrase a couple of

---

9   A masterful study of the subject is Stephen Gaukroger, *The Collapse of Mechanism and the Rise of Sensibility: Science and the Shaping of Modernity, 1680–1760* (Oxford: Oxford University Press, 2010).

10   The booklength study of the transition from Renaissance *scientia* to eighteenth-century science awaits to be written.

11   A new book adroitly studies the genesis of the concept; see Dror Wahrman, *The Making of the Modern Self: Identity and Culture in Eighteenth-Century England* (New Haven, CT: Yale University Press, 2004).

times in his works). The "Invisible Hand" nevertheless suggests how he (resting on the thought of other Scottish moralists such as David Hume and Adam Ferguson) amalgamated reason, passion, chance, certitude, and human nature in ways never dreamed of by Locke or Newton. This "other half" of Enlightenment thought, as I am crudely calling it – the portion Smith and his cohort described – leaned on the validity of mechanical knowledge while simultaneously rebelling against mechanism's most fundamental tenets. It placed in doubt the application of Newtonian mathematics and physics, especially as they related to society and state, self and selfhood, sentiment and sensibility. Thinkers extending from Hume to Hunt, Laurence Sterne to J.J. Rousseau, and virtually all the Romantic philosophers and poets, eventually embraced the Smithian view even if they did not associate it with Smith. The "Invisible Hand" was no minor counterpart to Newtonianism loosely conceived, or even its forebear in a broadly-based Cartesianism. The two trajectories – mechanical and sentimental, Newtonian and Smithian, or, more loosely, physical and social – account for the magisterial ideological breadth of Enlightenment thought whether or not one endorses Enlightenment's contributions to the *longue durée* of Western civilization. *A Trade for Light* features the former, the Cartesian-Newtonian passage and its literary representations. But I suspect the contributors to this collection would not recoil from the latter component if they had focused on it. Besides, attention to the former, the Cartesian-Newtonian, could not have been given without its companion state – the Smithian "Invisible hand" – having also been on the tip of these scholars' collective imaginations.

Moreover, the Cartesian-Newtonian legacy was fundamentally pluralistic for the way it embedded religion, philosophy, and politics, none of these spheres of knowledge then fractured from others in the way the academic disciplines have developed since 1800. And it would have been unthinkable that historians of the early modern world could have charted its rise from 1500 to 1800 without the history of science, a subject field as old as the Greeks and Romans yet professionally institutionalized as late as the twentieth century. The history of science as taught in universities and learned institutions during the last century demonstrated that facile assertions about this legacy were premature: they required the amassing of large bodies of knowledge about post-Cartesian and post-Newtonian legacies before generalities could be substantiated. When largely Anglo-American scholars proposed arguments, during the last century, claiming that the Newtonian revolution enabled the rise of modernity through technological prowess, they were challenged. Not until a huge archive of the history of science was integrated into larger cultural frames of reference could anything proximate to understanding of the transition from post-Cartesian to post-Newtonian mentalities be achieved. It

was here that the luminaries of the last generation were important: the great
Cartesian and Newtonian scholars, far-flung Enlightenment historians, the
German Marxists in the Frankfurt School, diverse sociologists, Foucault and
Foucauldians, and, of course, the countless literary historians absorbing and
assimilating their claims. All have contributed to an appreciation of the reasons why the transitions (in the plural) from Early Modernity to Modernity
cannot be grasped through the use of the tools of an individual discipline. To
call this enterprise "interdisciplinary" or "transdisciplinary" stamps it with a
flip label and minimizes its heroic challenges. The work entails the combination of many disciplines and sub-disciplines sharing the results of their research and pooling their forms of knowledge.[12]

Set the chronological dials to approximately 1950–60, when the whole globe
was beginning to recover from the Nazi holocaust, and you discover literary
scholars and historians of science resuming their work in the shared hope
they can carry on. But not without being reminded, daily, that recent horrific
experience on many continents would never again permit a naïve literary
history or history of science pictured as "discrete" or "pure". All scholarship –
they began to recognize more passionately than their forebears – embedded
agendas steeped in political bias and ideological predilection, no less than
post-Cartesian and post-Newtonian debates raging through Europe during the
eighteenth century.[13] This newly acquired sense after 1950–60 of the fundamental nature of the scientific enterprise was both invigorating and daunting.
Literary scholars could no longer take refuge in philological and rhetorical
approaches (for example) now appearing woefully narrow-minded. Nor could
historians of science proceed as if Pearl Harbor, Hiroshima and Auschwitz had
never occurred, even if eighteenth-century scholars from Richard Bentley to
Richard Hurd (two random representatives) had written as if famine, poverty,
and war were ancillary to their concerns. Modernity altered the conditions of
criticism. Henceforward, scholars active in all these disciplines after World
War Two proceeded as if the past had passed a barrier of no return. The
pre-1940 comfort zones were shattered. Cartesian-Newtonian fallout could

---

12   I spent the 1980s attempting to explain the variety of combinations in a trilogy of books:
      see G.S. Rousseau, *Enlightenment Borders: Pre- and Post-Modern Discourses: Medical,
      Scientific* (Manchester: Manchester University Press, 1991a); *Enlightenment Crossings:
      Pre- and Postmodern Discourses: Anthropological* (Manchester: Manchester University
      Press, 1991b); *Perilous Enlightenment: Pre- and Postmodern Discourses: Sexual, Historical*
      (Manchester: Manchester University Press, 1991c).
13   As demonstrated, for example, in the books of historical sociologist Robert K. Merton: see
      Robert King Merton, *Science, Technology & Society in Seventeenth Century England* (New
      York; London: Harper & Row, 1970).

seem equally jolting in the eighteenth century, even if the earlier Baconian revolution in knowledge had different valences and entailed philosophical principles rather than global wars.

The life and works of Michel Foucault (1926–84) epitomize the stakes and perils. Foucault was too young to comprehend the full force of the fascist menace before 1939 and was, besides, too engrossed is his burgeoning adolescent homosexuality and multiple suicide attempts to immerse himself in international politics. But by the 1950s he (provisionally) "came out", calmed down, stopped trying to harm himself, discovered "the miracle of" Nietzsche, Marxism, phenomenology, existentialism, and grew profoundly interested in the history of madness. But it was not until he traveled abroad, to Scandinavia, Germany, Poland, and finally North Africa, that his imagination coagulated and he began to realize the stranglehold sex and violence held over his early life. He enacted them in the underground world he frequented in Europe and Africa, persuading himself that freedom and its opposites – punishment and penalizing institutions such as prisons – had constituted one of history's grand matrices.[14] When Foucault eventually wrote about them, in books about mental illness, the history of madness, and the tyranny of intellectual disciplines, he adopted a view that the epoch of the Enlightenment had been transformative in all. This propensity fixed him in the eighteenth century – the *Age Classique*. His books ranged widely from Ancients to Moderns, Greeks to postwar Germans, but it was from his *Age Classique*, the transitory shift from Cartesianism to post-Newtonianism, that he constructed his controversial paradigms and epistemic breaks. For two decades, from c. 1975 to 1995, eighteenth-century studies reeled from his startling and prolific writings. Afterwards, a predictable negative reaction set in and academic scholarship turned more empirical and less ideological. But if Foucault had never written, eighteenth-century studies would not be in the robust state it exists today: heavily invested in the social sciences, digitally on the cutting edge, rarely in denial of the political realities that enable criticism and scholarship in the first place. Foucault did not initiate these tendencies but monumentally enhanced them. You could say that Foucaldism was a phase of maturity the field needed to pass through.

Now flash forward a few decades to 2017 and you find societies for the study of Literature and Science (SLS) globally flourishing. Composed of participants from both camps (although lorded over by those working in the Humanities), these groups are dedicated to demonstration that no area of the Humanities

---

14   For example, Michel Foucault, *Discipline and Punish: The Birth of the Prison* (London: Allen Lane, 1977). The semantic interplay of the tyranny of the academic *disciplines* and *disciplinary* institutions never ceased to amaze Foucault.

can be probed apart from science and technology. The dream of George Sarton, the Belgian founder of the history of science in America who also established the first department for the subject, in Harvard University, has been achieved. Sarton envisioned a "humanistic history of science" (his phrase) never capable of doing its work apart from the core Humanities disciplines: literature, philosophy, psychology, the social sciences. His manifesto made perfectly clear that a narrowly conceived history of science would impoverish the discipline and prevent it from attaining the place in the liberal arts it deserved.[15]

Today the names of university departments and faculties belie what they do: Department of English, Foreign Languages, Philosophy, History, Music, and so forth. Everyone within universities has known for two generations that the intellectual ferment occurs in centers, institutes, and special programmes, but for all sorts of reasons university departments are unable to alter their internal structures or change their names. Nor is there need: funding and opportunity now proceed directly to these beehives of activity rather than the often-moribund amalgams called "departments" and "faculties". Even the designation "English Literature", closer to home, which describes a body of writing rather more than academic departments in colleges and universities, has lost its former connotation, the only consensus about its ontological status being that it studies literature written in the English language, which does not say much. Little cause for concern should exist, either bibliographically or institutionally. What counts now is the *work* produced and the caliber and methods of that work.

The question to ask therefore is not "in what department do you *work*?" but "what type of *work* exactly do you do and how do you proceed to accomplish it?" The contributors to *A Trade for Light* are professional literary scholars who teach and research in departments of the Humanities. We must inquire, of course and as a curiosity if nothing more, why no historians of science, or philosophers of science, appear here. The reason surely is the sheer difficulty of enlisting their talents owing to the pressures of the workplace and the pace of modern life. Another question too is begged. Can the transitions *A Trade for Light* aims to cover be charted *apart* from these types of scholars? Would *A Trade for Light* have made a stronger, and indubitably a different *type* of case, if these fields were represented? The riposte exceeds the rhetorical imperative in reverse. The question put to historians of science should have been, how can you chart these passages from 1680–1760 without intrinsic knowledge of *literature*? Usually we pose the arrows of influence in the opposite direction:

---

15   See George Sarton, *The History of Science and the New Humanism* (Cambridge, Mass.: Harvard University Press, 1937).

from science *to* literature. In reality the influence proceeds as preponderantly in the opposite direction: *from* literature *to* science.

The Humanities contribute as much to contemporary life as do the sciences. It is not a proposition to be debated even if the sciences, especially the bio-medical sciences, are so much more lavishly funded than the Humanities. Our authors contributing to *A Trade for Light* aim to make this claim for literature, a further reason their collective effort should be applauded despite the absence of the just-mentioned disciplines. For good reason many pre-Newtonian theologies, not merely Christian theologies, believed that "In the beginning was the Word (...) and God gave the Word" as the greatest gift to Adam and Eve. Light preceded the Word in the Edenic garden, but the account of genesis would have been impossible without the Word. If my narrative has any validity it is that we cannot perform our work without recognition of the monumental value of language and literature, or accomplish it through the lens of one discipline only. The Word is what *all* the Humanities share, and most of the sciences too.[16]

Works Cited

Fish, Stanley. "Being Interdisciplinary Is So Very Hard to Do". In *There's No Such Thing as Free Speech*, 231–42. Oxford: Oxford University Press, 1994.

Foucault, Michel. *Discipline and Punish: The Birth of the Prison*. London: Allen Lane, 1977.

Gaukroger, Stephen. *The Collapse of Mechanism and the Rise of Sensibility: Science and the Shaping of Modernity, 1680–1760*. Oxford: Oxford University Press, 2010.

Irimia, Mihaela. *Literary into Cultural History: International Colloquium*. Bucharest: Institutul Cultural Roman, 2009.

Landow, George P. *Hyper/Text/Theory*. Baltimore: Johns Hopkins University Press, 1994.

Merton, Robert King. *Science, Technology & Society in Seventeenth Century England*. New York; London: Harper & Row, 1970.

---

16   Abundant scholars have spent their time documenting, for example, that the Royal Society's maxim *nullius in verba*, nothing in the word, was a smokescreen, a piety for what they hoped to accomplish in a better world based on a different edenic genesis and history of knowledge (*scientia*). See, for example: Margery Purver, *The Royal Society: Concept and Creation* (London: Routledge and Kegan Paul, 1967); and Barbara J. Shapiro, *Probability and Certainty in Seventeenth-Century England: A Study of the Relationships between Natural Science, Religion, History, Law, and Literature* (Princeton: Princeton University Press, 1983).

Purver, Margery. *The Royal Society: Concept and Creation*. London: Routledge and
    Kegan Paul, 1967.

Rousseau, G.S. "Riddles of Interdisciplinarity: A Reply to Stanley Fish". In *Intercultural
    Encounters – Studies in English Literature*, edited by Heinz Antor and Kevin L. Cope,
    111–30. Heidelberg: C. Winter, 1999.

Rousseau, G.S. *Enlightenment Borders: Pre- and Post-Modern Discourses: Medical,
    Scientific*. Manchester: Manchester University Press, 1991a.

Rousseau, G.S. *Enlightenment Crossings: Pre- and Postmodern Discourses: Anthropologi-
    cal*. Manchester: Manchester University Press, 1991b.

Rousseau, G.S. *Perilous Enlightenment: Pre- and Postmodern Discourses: Sexual, Histori-
    cal*. Manchester: Manchester University Press, 1991c.

Sarton, George. *The History of Science and the New Humanism*. Cambridge, Mass.:
    Harvard University Press, 1937.

Shapiro, Barbara J. *Probability and Certainty in Seventeenth-Century England: A Study
    of the Relationships between Natural Science, Religion, History, Law, and Literature*.
    Princeton: Princeton University Press, 1983.

Wahrman, Dror. *The Making of the Modern Self: Identity and Culture in Eighteenth-
    Century England*. New Haven, CT: Yale University Press, 2004.

White, Lynn, and American Council of Learned Societies. *Medieval Technology and
    Social Change*. London: Oxford University Press, 1962.

PART 1

Engendering Space, Creating Meaning

∵

CHAPTER 1

Oroonoko and the Mapping of Africa

Bernhard Klein

Abstract

This essay traces connections between the mapping of Africa and the character of Oroonoko in Aphra Behn's 1688 novella. Cartography never encompassed the physical environment without reference to the human body, a connection reinforced visually in the seventeenth century by portraits of local figures placed in the margins of maps. The essay argues that this juxtaposition of land and people affected not only the understanding of human diversity but also the creation of a literary character such as Oroonoko, whose fictional identity is owed to representational conventions developed in the mapmaking workshops of early modern Europe.

"[M]aps inspire literary creation",[1] Tom Conley argues, noting the frequent interweaving of cartography and fiction in early modern writing: maps were turned into poetic metaphors, used as stage props, and discussed in prose; they were held up as the potent symbols of a new geographical consciousness in

---

1 Tom Conley, "Early Modern Literature and Cartography: An Overview", in *The History of Cartography, vol. 3: Cartography in the European Renaissance*, 2 parts, ed. David Woodward (Chicago: The University of Chicago Press, 2007), Part 1, 401–411 (401). This standard reference work for the history of early modern cartography includes seven chapters devoted to the link between literature and cartography (401–476). For a selection of other recent critical works in the field, see D.K. Smith, *The Cartographic Imagination in Early Modern England: Re-writing the World in Marlowe, Spenser, Raleigh and Marvell* (Burlington: Ashgate, 2008); Andrew Gordon and Bernhard Klein, eds, *Literature, Mapping, and the Politics of Space in Early Modern Britain* (Cambridge: Cambridge University Press, 2001); Tom Conley, *The Self-Made Map. Cartographic Writing in Early Modern France* (Minneapolis: University of Minnesota Press, 1996); John Gillies, *Shakespeare and the Geography of Difference* (Cambridge: Cambridge University Press, 1994); and Richard Helgerson, *Forms of Nationhood: The Elizabethan Writing of England* (Chicago: Chicago University Press, 1992). For some influential theoretical approaches to the study of maps, see Christian Jacob, *The Sovereign Map. Theoretical Approaches in Cartography throughout History*, trans. Tom Conley (Chicago and London: The University of Chicago Press, 2006); and J.B. Harley, *The New Nature of Maps. Essays in the History of Cartography*, ed. Paul Laxton (Baltimore: Johns Hopkins University Press, 2001).

Europe, and their presence on the page cannot even be gauged through overt references to cartography alone. Below the visual surface of the map lurks the scientific work of observation, measurement, calculation and projection, fostering a particular kind of cartographic gaze that shaped the perception of space in imaginative writing as well as in many other realms of social and aesthetic practice. This gaze turned the tactile, sensory world of experience into flattened, two-dimensional scenes of visual contemplation by filtering spatial data through mathematically inspired formulae of graphic representation. Maps rely on numbers but cannot be restricted to the mathematical: "the measure of mapping", Denis Cosgrove writes, "may equally be spiritual, political or moral".[2] Or, indeed, social: since space is no scientific abstraction, maps never encompassed the physical environment without reference to the human bodies inhabiting that environment, a connection reinforced visually by those Dutch and Flemish cartographers of the seventeenth century who included portraits depicting representative local figures dressed in regional costume in the margins of their maps.

Such social "acts of mapping",[3] I suggest in this essay,[4] have left their traces in early modern fiction, especially in fiction dealing with the non-European world. Using Aphra Behn's *Oroonoko, or The Royal Slave* (1688) as a literary reference point, and contemporary European maps of the African continent as a cartographic context, I want to argue that the prominent juxtaposition of land and people on seventeenth-century maps affected not only the understanding of human diversity around the globe but also the creation of a literary character such as Oroonoko, whose fictional identity is grounded in patterns of racial and ethnic difference prefigured by the representational conventions developed in the mapmaking workshops of early modern Europe. The argument presented here will entail, first, a brief comparison between the respective geographical frameworks of Oroonoko and his most immediate literary ancestor in English literature, Othello, in the context of the sixteenth-century mapping of Africa, and second, a discussion of a sequence of continental maps of Africa circulating in Europe in the seventeenth century.

---

2   Denis Cosgrove, "Introduction: Mapping Meaning", in *Mappings*, ed. Denis Cosgrove (London: Reaktion, 1999), 1–23 (2).

3   The phrase is Denis Cosgrove's. See *ibid.*, 1.

4   This essay was completed in 2013 as a contribution to the present volume. Sections of it revisit (and substantially revise) some of the material included in my "Randfiguren. Othello, Oroonoko und die kartographische Repräsentation Afrikas", in *Imaginationen des Anderen im 16. und 17. Jahrhundert*, Wolfenbütteler Forschungen 97, ed. Michaela Boenke and Ina Schabert (Wiesbaden: Harrassowitz Verlag, 2002), 185–216.

Africa in Maps and Texts

Oroonoko has long been seen as a prime example of the way seventeenth-century literature processed changes in European spatial awareness mirrored in the visual advances of cartography. Catherine Gallagher has called the book "the first literary work in English to grasp the global interactions of the modern world",[5] a universal connectedness visualized in unprecedented graphic detail over a century earlier on the world maps of geographers such as Abraham Ortelius and Gerard Mercator. Behn's tale combines in its setting the three corners of a triangle – Europe, Africa and the New World – and stresses throughout the "mutual interpenetration"[6] of all three places: Coromantine, the seventeenth-century, English-built slave castle on the Gold Coast (modern Ghana) where Oroonoko is captured, supplies slave labour to the plantations in Suriname, on the other side of the Atlantic, and to the Caribbean more widely, from where raw materials such as tobacco, sugar, cotton, cocoa and coffee are exported to Europe, and specifically to England, where the book is written. World maps like Ortelius' hugely successful *Typus Orbis Terrarum* (first state 1570; in print for over 40 years), showed all the regions of the earth linked through one vast, navigable body of water, enabling the mental appropriation of this interlocking, transcontinental world order, and defining it visually as structured around the north Atlantic corridor, the key spatial axis holding the plot of Behn's novel together.

Africa appeared on the modern world map as a self-contained continent, situated as a spatially separate entity from other unified land masses. To represent Africa in this fashion is already the product of a gaze conditioned by modern cartography. For the classical geographers, who invented the division of the world into the three continents Asia, Africa, and Europe[7] – a notion later theologized and largely abstracted from empirical reality in the medieval period – Africa's northern regions were commonly connected to a broadly conceived Mediterranean, bordered further south by the torrid or uninhabitable zone. The early modern navigators refined this view by following the lead of the fifteenth-century Portuguese chronicler Gomes Eanes de Zurara who split Africa in his *Chronicle of Guinea* (1453) into the "land of the Moors"

---

5   Catherine Gallagher, "Introduction: Cultural and Historical Background", in Aphra Behn, *Oroonoko*, ed. Catherine Gallagher (Boston and New York: Bedford/St. Martin's, 2000), 3–25 (3).

6   *Ibid.*

7   See Martin W. Lewis and Kären E. Wigen, *The Myth of Continents. A Critique of Metageography* (Berkeley and Los Angeles: University of California Press, 1997), 21–46.

(northern Africa) and the "land of the Blacks" (Guinea), a kind of inhabited torrid zone, with the Senegal River as the dividing line.[8] This ethnic division held sway until well into a later period. John Pory, the English editor of Leo Africanus, for example, confirmed in 1600 that the Senegal river "maketh a separation betweene nations of sundrie colours: for the people on this side are of a dead ash-colour, leane, and of a small stature; but on the farther side they are exceeding blacke, of tall and manly stature, and very well proportioned".[9] By 1600 knowledge of Africa's southern coast had been considerably advanced in the wake of the late fifteenth-century circumnavigations of the Cape by Bartolomeu Dias and Vasco da Gama, but such endeavours were not immediately paralleled by explorations of the African interior.

Two maps of Africa printed in sixteenth-century Europe helped more than any others to give the continent its modern visual and conceptual shape.[10] The first of these was a map by Sebastian Münster, "the earliest, readily available printed map to show the entire continent of Africa"[11] (fig. 1.1), first published in 1540 and included in Münster's popular *Cosmography* between 1544 and 1578. The second appeared three decades later as part of an entirely new type of book: the cartographic atlas. The first edition of Ortelius' *Theatrum Orbis Terrarum* (1570) contained 70 regional, national, and continental maps, including "one of the cornerstone maps of Africa"[12] (fig. 1.2), which quickly supplanted Münster's old map in popular demand. (The latter's fate was to be eventually replaced by an Ortelian derivative in editions of the *Cosmography* from 1588 onwards.) Both maps shaped the image of Africa for European viewers throughout the second half of the sixteenth century, and both are representative examples of the "new geography" that had exploded the ancient geographical paradigms associated with the classical and medieval works of Herodotus, Pliny and

---

8   See Josiah Blackmore, *Moorings. Portuguese Expansion and the Writing of Africa* (Minneapolis: University of Minnesota Press, 2009), 15–16.

9   John Pory, "A general description of all Africa", preface to Leo Africanus, *A Geographical Historie of Africa*, trans. John Pory (London: Georg Bishop, 1600), 4.

10   The latest overview of early maps of Africa is provided by Richard L. Betz, *The Mapping of Africa. A Cartobibliography of Printed Maps of the African Continent up to 1700*, Utrecht Studies in the History of Cartography 7 ('t Goy-Houten: Hes & de Graaf, 2007). For related earlier works see Oscar I. Norwich, *Maps of Africa. An Illustrated and Annotated Carto-Bibliography* (Johannesburg: Ad. Donker, 1983), republished as *Norwich's Maps of Africa*, ed. Jeffrey Stone (Vermont: Terra Nova, 1997); Ronald Vere Tooley, *Collector's Guide to Maps of the African Continent and Southern Africa* (London: Carta Press, 1969); and Egon Klemp, *Afrika auf Karten vom 12. bis 18. Jahrhundert* (Leipzig: Ed. Leipzig, 1968).

11   Betz, *The Mapping of Africa*, 83. Betz discusses the map in full on pages 83–94.

12   *Ibid.*, 122. Betz discusses the map in full on pages 118–125.

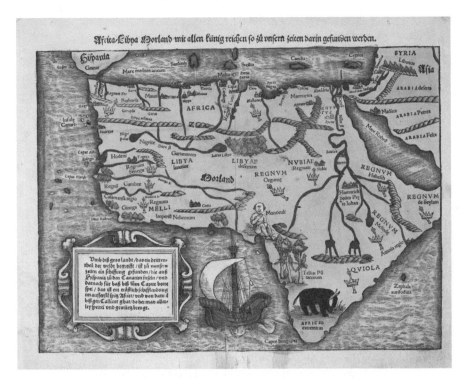

FIGURE 1.1   *Map of Africa by Sebastian Münster (1544).*

Mandeville.[13] Despite their evident novelty, however, both maps still invested
in the "old cosmography" and made it a residual part of the sixteenth-century
cartographic discourse about Africa.

On Münster's map (fig. 1.1) these connections are most directly visible.
Africa is cast as an imaginative visual blend of exotic animals, monster-like fish
and mythical rivers. Sub-Saharan Africa appears as little more than a shrivelled
appendix; the south is almost completely filled by a huge elephant. The names
of the ancient African kingdoms are scattered across the surface of the map
but toponyms are relatively scarce, and generically exotic creatures – parrots in
the Congo region; a one-eyed giant or cyclops cowering in the Bight of Biafra –
fill the map with content instead. The cyclops advertises the affinity between
this map and the ancient geographic imaginary through his kinship with the
league of monstrous creatures that Pliny had described in his *Natural History*:

---

13   See Gillies, *Shakespeare and the Geography of Difference*, 1–39.

FIGURE 1.2   *Map of Africa by Abraham Ortelius (1570).*
STADT- UND UNIVERSITÄTSBIBLIOTHEK FRANKFURT AM MAIN
(SHELF-MARK: WF 127).

the many-armed, double-faced or long-necked dwellers in the outer reaches of
the earth, staples of medieval works dealing in geography, cosmography and
travel. Such figures still populated many print versions of the Ptolemaic world
map published in the fifteenth century, and their persistence indicates that the
moral authority vested in the ancient sources was not easily disputed. Instead
it remained one of the geographer's principal duties to supply working definitions of cultural otherness: the margins of the world are zones of a diffuse ex-
oticism, beyond the borders of the *oikumene* or ancient "house-world", where
physical difference almost always serves as an indicator of moral transgression.

At first sight Ortelius' Africa (fig. 1.2) severs all these ancient connections.
The map is couched in the modern cartographic idiom of longitude and latitude, secure coastal borders and dense toponymic coverage. Its share in the
Theatrum Orbis Terrarum makes it part of one of "the new geography's most
monumental statements".[14] Yet even this map still features ancient legends
such as the realm of the mighty Christian king, "magnus princeps Presbiter
Iones", just north of the equator, and the "Amazonum regio" further south

---

14   *Ibid.,* 35.

in the African interior. These mythic flashes in the midst of the ostensible modernity of this map clearly inspired contemporaries, as the recorded response of one prominent early modern reader confirms. A character in Christopher Marlowe's second *Tamburlaine* play, imagining a triumphant march throughout the whole of Africa, delivers a 20-line speech in Act 1 that includes 14 different toponyms and geographical references to African locations, including direct mentions of Prester John and the kingdom of the Amazons.[15] When the critic Ethel Seaton matched this speech to Ortelius' map in 1924, she could show that the string of placenames Marlowe weaves together corresponds one-to-one to his cartographic source.[16] The map provides the launchpad for the imaginative appropriation of African space, as both the atlas (Ortelius' *Theatrum*) and the theatre (soon a "globe" in Southwark) generate visions of imperial power that enable Marlowe's character effortlessly to pass all temporal and spatial barriers. The map appears less as a medium of pragmatic orientation in space than as a catalyst for the electric experience of intoxicating expansion.

Marlowe's Tamburlaine is an eloquent witness to the lingering authority of the ancient geography in other respects as well. He still found it necessary, in 1592, to "confute those blind geographers" that divided the world, as Ptolemy and the medieval makers of the mappaemundi had done, into "triple regions"[17] (i.e., the three continents, Asia, Africa and Europe), arranged around the spiritual centre of Jerusalem. His aggressive denunciation of this world view only confirms the pervasive influence of such seemingly outdated geographical concepts.[18] Other examples of the continuing respect for the ancient sources include Sir Walter Ralegh, who reported in 1596 that headless men with eyes in their shoulders and mouths in their breasts, such as Herodotus and Mandeville had described, were living in Guyana, though he was careful to add that he had not seen any of them personally.[19] Even Münster's *Cosmography*,

---

15   See Christopher Marlowe, *Tamburlaine*, Part 2, in *The Complete Plays*, ed. J.B. Steane (Harmondsworth: Penguin, 1969), 1.6.59–78. See also my *Maps and the Writing of Space in Early Modern England and Ireland* (Basingstoke: Palgrave, 2001), 15–20.

16   See Ethel Seaton, "Marlowe's Map" [1924], in *Marlowe: A Collection of Critical Essays*, Twentieth-Century Views, ed. Clifford Leech (Eaglewood Cliffs, NJ: Prentice Hall, 1964), 36–56. See also John Gillies' criticism of Seaton's approach (*Shakespeare and the Geography of Difference*, 52–53).

17   Marlowe, *Tamburlaine*, Part 1, ed. Steane, 4.4.81–2.

18   See my *"Tamburlaine, Sacred Space, and the Heritage of Medieval Cartography"*, *Reading the Medieval in Early Modern England*, ed. David Matthews and Gordon McMullan (Cambridge: Cambridge University Press, 2007), 143–158.

19   See Sir Walter Ralegh, *Discoverie of the Large, Rich, and Bewtifvl Empire of Guiana* (London: Robert Robinson, 1596), 69–70.

which remained in print until 1628 (longer, in fact, than Ortelius' *Theatrum*), continued to present ancient and modern world maps side by side in its seventeenth-century editions, as did many other geographical works.

Shakespeare is another seventeenth-century witness to the force of the ancient geography. In the biographical fragment Othello offers up in front of the Venetian senate, when pressed to explain how a noble white lady like Desdemona could have possibly been won over by "what she feared to look on" (1.3.98),[20] he explains how his travels took him precisely through the marginal wastelands of a Plinian geography – "antres vast and deserts idle, / Rough quarries, rocks and hills whose heads touch heaven" (1.3.141–2) – a monstrous periphery beyond the civilized world where he stood face to face with "the cannibals that each other eat, / The Anthropophagi, and men whose heads / Do grow beneath their shoulders" (1.3.144–6). When Othello later in the play declares that "a horned man's a monster, and a beast" (4.1.62), he is not only describing himself as a cuckold and duped lover but also as a wild creature or beast with real horns growing on his head, advertising his affiliation with the deformed monsters he met in the fabled regions beyond the civilized world.

Othello has often been connected to *Oroonoko* in criticism, and for good reason: the two titular heroes are possibly the most famous African characters in seventeenth-century English literature, and the affinities between them far exceed assonance and alliteration. Central to the comparison between the two has been their "race", less often their "space".[21] The distinction between "race" and "space" is to some extent artificial, since neither concept can be entirely separated from the other. Ethnic difference blends into the geographic description of foreign or "exotic" lands as much as specific spatial properties are seen to define human character and temperament. Othello and Oroonoko are separated by over eight decades, yet the parallels between them are strikingly apparent: both Shakespeare's "moor of Venice" and Behn's "royal slave" share a "natural" nobility and dignity, both are military heroes, both tragically fall victim to European treachery, both begin as romantic lovers and end up murdering their wives, both finally relapse into "wildness", and neither survives

---

20   All *Othello* quotations are taken from William Shakespeare, *Othello*, The Arden Shakespeare, ed. E.A.J. Honigmann (Walton-on-Thames, Surrey: Thomas Nelson, 1997).

21   See Margaret Ferguson, "Transmuting *Othello*: Aphra Behn's *Oroonoko*", in *Cross-Cultural Performances: Differences in Women's Re-Visions of Shakespeare*, ed. Marianne Novy (Champaign: University of Illinois Press, 1993), 15–49; and Thomas Cartelli, *Repositioning Shakespeare. National Formations, Postcolonial Appropriations* (London and New York: Routledge, 1999), 123–146. For a comparative reading focused on the connections between character and geography, see Gillies, *Shakespeare and the Geography of Difference*, 26–30.

the tale that encompasses their imaginative existence. These similarities should not, however, obscure some important discontinuities between both characters: while Othello is filtered through the prism of an ancient Mediterranean geography, Oroonoko is conceived within a new Atlantic context;[22] while Othello starts the play as an African outsider in Europe in the service of a Christian ruler, Oroonoko is initially depicted in his own proper environment, heir to the throne of an African kingdom; while Othello makes a tragic mistake based on a moral misjudgement, Oroonoko remains morally blameless throughout; and while Othello is generically a traveller, Oroonoko would have never morphed into one had circumstances not conspired against him.[23]

Perhaps the principal difference between the two characters, as John Gillies has argued, is their choice of sexual partner: while Othello is "transgressively" paired with Desdemona, Oroonoko is "decorously"[24] paired with Imoinda, the "beautiful black Venus",[25] who shares Oroonoko's race and class. For Gillies, Othello's clandestine marriage is more than a breach of social decorum.[26] The moral imperative implicit in Othello's *errant* identity as an "extravagant and wheeling stranger / Of here and everywhere" (1.1.134–5) equates generic homelessness and promiscuity almost inevitably with the violation of moral, sexual and – importantly – geographical *limits*. Inherent in Othello's imaginative being is a tragic contradiction between his inner nobility and what Mary Douglas would have called the "pollution danger"[27] he represents to Venetian society. Oroonoko's fate, by contrast, is entirely unnecessary, as he falls victim to the racist system of a slave economy epitomized in the colonizers' failure to honour the dignity and *gravitas* of a natural born prince. That Oroonoko travels no longer through the "ancient poetic geography"[28] that governed Shakespeare's constructions of otherness, but through abstract, quantifiable space measured in distance, scale, number and time, is confirmed by his fascination for the "globes and maps and mathematical discourses and instruments"[29]

---

22   On *Oroonoko* in an Atlantic context, see Kate Chedgzoy, *Women's Writing in the British Atlantic World. Memory, Place and History, 1550–1700* (Cambridge: Cambridge University Press, 2007), 168–197.

23   See also Gallagher, "Introduction: Cultural and Historical Background", 17.

24   The terms are John Gillies' (*Shakespeare and the Geography of Difference*, 26).

25   Aphra Behn, *Oroonoko and Other Writings*, ed. Paul Salzman (Oxford: Oxford University Press, 1994), 12.

26   See Gillies, *Shakespeare and the Geography of Difference*, 26–27.

27   See Mary Douglas, *Purity and Danger. An Analysis of the Concepts of Pollution and Taboo* (London: Routledge, 1966). Gillies uses Douglas' terminology in ibid. 27–28.

28   Gillies, *Shakespeare and the Geography of Difference*, 28.

29   Behn, *Oroonoko*, ed. Salzman, 33.

that the English captain produces in Coromantine, which lure Oroonoko into thinking of the white man as an honest friend and partner in conversation, before he is revealed as a slave trader intent on nothing but profit. His maps are both cause and condition of Oroonoko's deportation into slavery.[30]

Othello, on the other hand, confirms in his wooing of Desdemona that he is entirely ignorant of the new geography. His geographic existence is that of an "erring Barbarian" (1.3.356), as Iago thinks, a wanderer between the worlds without a recognized home, destiny, or point of origin. His lack of a definable place in Venetian society – Othello's generic "placelessness", shifting essence, and transgressive being – is mirrored in his undefinable skin colour, which escapes all clarity of description: it is ungraspable, "impure", meandering between shades of light brown and dark or black, as Iago's and Roderigo's racist references to him in the opening scene of the play indicate: "thicklips" (1.1.65), "black ram" (1.1.87), "barbary horse" (1.1.110). This in-betweenness appears especially pronounced when compared to the precise definition, cultural fixity and appropriate ethnic classification of Oroonoko, reflected in his social class and decorum, as well as his extreme blackness of skin, described as exact, precious and pure, "of perfect ebony, or polished jet".[31] This striking shift in ethnic description, as I aim to show in what follows, has distinct cartographic resonances. Seventeenth-century maps of Africa, following on from Münster and Ortelius, similarly begin to fix people in space as well as in ethnicity, custom and skin colour, by turning the continent's spaces into compartmentalized zones, pushing into controlled visibility the obscure, wandering entities of human geography, "extravagant and wheeling stranger[s] / Of here and everywhere".

Marginal Figures

For more than a century after the publication of Ortelius' atlas, the toponymic surface of the African continent that Marlowe exploited showed few signs of change on European maps (with the exception of the coastal placenames that were crucial to European navigation). Much happened, however, to their representational frame. Probably the most significant event in the European cartography of Africa in the seventeenth century was the publication of Willem Janszoon Blaeu's wall map of 1608 (fig. 1.3), part of a quartet of wall maps

---

30   See my "Staying Afloat. Literary Shipboard Encounters from Shakespeare to Equiano", in *Sea Changes. Historicizing the Ocean*, ed. Bernhard Klein and Gesa Mackenthun (New York: Routledge, 2004), 91–109 (100–101).

31   Behn, *Oroonoko*, ed. Salzman, 12.

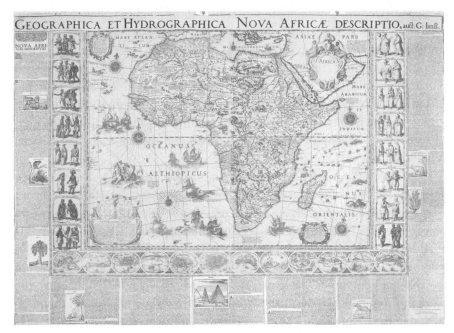

FIGURE 1.3 *Map of Africa by Willem Janszoon Blaeu (1624; first state 1608).*
DIMENSIONS: 1,70 M × 1,20 M. KLASSIK STIFTUNG WEIMAR, HERZOGIN
ANNA AMALIA BIBLIOTHEK, SHELF-MARK KT 030–32 R, PHOTOGRAPH: OLAF
MOKANSKY.

depicting the four continents, a work "of such importance that for the next
100 years numerous mapmakers throughout Europe diligently copied this map,
both in design and in content".[32] The purpose of the map is reflected in its
massive size (c. 1.20 m by 1.70 m): designed to hang in the houses of patricians,
wealthy merchants, clergy, etc, the map documents the sum of geographical
knowledge about Africa circulating in Europe at the beginning of the seventeenth century.[33]

Compared to Ortelius' map, its most obvious innovative feature is the
addition of decorative and explanatory frames: in a process of multiple
encasements Africa is surrounded by city views, figurative portraits, and a
descriptive geographical text. The element that most compels attention in
the context of this essay is the addition of sixteen mini-galleries depicting the
people of Africa on either side of the map image: standing under arches in

---

32   Betz, *The Mapping of Africa*, 217.
33   For a full documentation and analysis of all four wall maps see Günter Schilder,
      *Monumenta Cartographica Neerlandica v: Tien wandkaarten van Blaeu en Visscher / Ten
      Wall Maps by Blaeu and Visscher* (Alphen aan den Rijn: Uitgeverij Canaletto, 1996), 75–213.

groups of two, three or four, are not *monoculi* or elephants but the inhabitants of the various kingdoms, countries and regions that make up the African continent. In the cartographic culture of Europe, such *cartes à figures*, depicting people alongside "their" land, are prominent from the end of the sixteenth century onwards. Two Dutch cartographers, Jodocus Hondius and Pieter van den Keere, have been credited with the first use of this convention in 1595,[34] when they placed portraits of regional merchants and aristocrats into the margins of their wall map of Europe, thus turning it into a social space shared equally by trade and nobility.

Maps, of course, have never been devoid of decorative additions like arabesques, allegorical motifs, ornamental patterns or classical quotations. Oceans on maps frequently sport mythical sea creatures or ships. But such features are usually broad generalizations; they rarely make specific, targeted comments on the geographical space depicted. In *cartes à figures*, however, the rationale behind the inclusion of portraits is precisely to add local knowledge to the abstract contours of the land. When city views began to be included, the order of geographical space on such maps was constructed through the mental and material interaction between people, cities and nations or continents, resulting in a fusion of chorographic and geographical scales that caused widely disparate spatial data to coexist within the same frame of representation. Put differently, the map is a visual amalgamation of three separate genres: the costume manual, the city atlas and the national or continental map. This list could be extended in both directions: the earth as a whole is contained in the celestial globe, and even more detailed information on people and their bodies is available in the anatomical treatise. In his 1611 atlas of Britain, John Speed set the anatomically dissected and fragmented body in explicit analogy to the work of the mapmaker: "here [in this atlas] first wee will (by Example of best Anatomists) propose to the view the *whole Body*, and *Monarchie* intire ... and after will dissect and lay open the particular Members, Veines and Ioints, (I meane the Shires, Riuers, Cities, and Townes)".[35]

The best known contemporary city atlas, from which most of the twelve views along the bottom of Blaeu's 1608 map of Africa are taken,[36] is Georg

---

34   See Günter Schilder, *Monumenta Cartographica Neerlandica III* (Alphen aan den Rijn: Uitgeverij Canaletto, 1990), Chapter IIIb: "The Development of Decorative Borders on Dutch Wall Maps Before 1619", 115–146. The 1595 map referred to in the text is a wall map of Europe in 15 sheets.

35   John Speed, *The Theatre of the Empire of Great Britain* (London: Iohn Sudbury & George Humble, 1611), sig. E1r (Speed's italics).

36   See Schilder, *Monumenta Cartographica Neerlandica V*, 150, for a list of known models and sources of these 12 city views.

Braun and Frans Hogenberg's *Civitates Orbis Terrarum* (1572–1617), a six-volume collection of city views whose title already announces its conceptual affinity to Ortelius' world atlas, the *Theatrum Orbis Terrarum*. Indeed, although its frame of reference is clearly chorographic, the project of the *Civitates* atlas was cosmographic in intent: the overall aim of the collection was to show "how artful master builders have decorated *the entire earthly sphere* with cities and towns".[37] The purpose of the city atlas in the narrow sense was to furnish the visual proof of historical competence in civilization – cities testify to human-kind's ability to give undefined space a recognizable and socially meaningful structure. Like world and city atlas, the costume manual was a visual form that enabled the comprehension of geographical space through its regional varia-tion. Many of the sources for the portraits Blaeu included on this and the other three wall maps in his 1608 series have been traced to contemporary costume manuals,[38] and the engraver Hessel Gerritsz, who provided the etchings for Blaeu's map, followed their pictorial conventions very closely. The express pur-pose of the costume manual, as Caspar Rutz explained in the preface to one notable example of the genre, Jean-Jacques Boissard's *Habitus Variarum Orbis Gentium* (1581), was to annotate and illustrate maps: since the "painted world" of modern cartographers displayed many details of landscape, it is only appro-priate that man himself should be depicted "in his own costume and habit", so that "the mental dispositions and local customs can be represented and eas-ily recognized".[39] The abstract shape of the land should be read against the

---

37   Georg Braun and Frans Hogenberg, *Beschreibung und Contrafactur der vornembster Stätt der Welt* (Cologne: Heinrich von Ach, 1574), preface, n.p. (my translation and emphasis). "Wie ... kunstreiche Bawmeister den gantzen erdenkreiß ... mit Stäten und flecken verziert ...".

38   See Schilder, *Monumenta Cartographica Neerlandica* V, 105–106, 124–128, 147–152, and 160–168. Since the publication of Schilder's pioneering study, I have been able to identify several further sources (see note 52 below).

39   Jean-Jacques Boissard, *Habitus Variarum Orbis Gentium* (Cologne: Caspar Rutz, 1581), pref-ace: "Nachdem heytiger tag / vil / und mancherley Bücher beschrieben / auch zu Kupffer gestechen werden ... welliche auß denn Carttis / oder Mappen / von einer abgemalten Welt sich berichts holen / unnd lernen müssen / Gedünckt mich dasselb nit ein geringe / sonder notwendige nutzbare arbeit sein ... Wann denn Menschen / dem alle ding zu notturft / vnnd lust erschaffen sein / mit seiner selbst Kleidung / vnnd dracht fürbilden ... vnnd durch die Kleidung die gemütter / vnnd sitten / gemeinlich abgenommen werden / vnnd leichtlich zuerkennen ist". ["Since today many and diverse books are written and engraved in copper ... which need to gather information and learn from a painted world in cards and maps, it seems to me not a small but a necessary work ... if man himself, for whose use and pleasure all things have been created, is pictured in his own costume and habit ... so that through costume the mental dispositions and local customs can be repre-sented and easily recognized" (my translation).]

cultural and moral profile of its inhabitants; regional costume – understood as a fixed cultural code, not as a transitory fashion statement – offers a visually recognizable structure for this purpose.

On Blaeu's map the portraits link up with the image of the land in two distinct ways. On the one hand, they literally serve to re-inhabit the empty, depopulated space of the map, evoke certain regional forms of spatial practice, and gesture at what cannot be represented in maps: the lived social spaces of local "users".⁴⁰ For the abstract image of the continent is to a large degree the result of geometric calculation, the portraits of the people, however, imply an immediate and direct confrontation with the social spaces they both live and define. On the other hand, the technology of cartographic representation is transferred from the surface of the land to the people themselves: just as the entire continent can be pressed into a coherent visual form, people can be ordered, classified and exhibited in discrete taxonomies and ornamental galleries. In contrast to Münster's cyclops, Blaeu's bodies do not form part of the image of the land but define their own discursive space in relation to this land. They are no longer symbolic projections of a diffuse periphery onto the land but socially and geographically clearly defined individuals: the captions describe them, for instance, as "women from Guinea with servants", a "Congolese soldier with wife", "inhabitants of the Cape of Good Hope", "Moroccans", or – encoding a classic patriarchal motif found in several costume manuals – "virgin, widow, wife" in Ethiopia (with a turbaned male figure standing just to the right of the trio).⁴¹ The figures are thus defined through their gender, their marital status, their regional roots (like Oroonoko; unlike Othello), and their social identity and rank: merchants, dukes, pilgrims, soldiers, even a king (of Madagascar) are among the social types represented.

One notable feature is the predominant arrangement of these figures into groups of three or four people of varying gender and age (four babies and one child are included in total) – out of sixteen images, only five portray couples.⁴² The significance of this arrangement arises from its relative rarity; subsequent

---

40   On the concept of social space see Henri Lefebvre, *The Production of Space* [1974], trans. Donald Nicolson-Smith (Oxford: Blackwell, 1991); and Michel de Certeau, *The Practice of Everyday Life* [1974], trans. Steven Randall (Berkeley et al.: University of California Press, 1988).

41   See galleries 3, 6 and 7 in the left margin, and 1 and 4 in the right margin (counting from the top). The original captions are: "Guinearum Mvlieres et ancilla", "Miles Congonensis cum femina", "Promontorii bonæ spæi habitatores", "Marocchi", "Virgo, vidva, mvlier Afra. Æthiops".

42   The five couples are: "Miles Congonensis cum femina"; "Promontorii bonæ spæi habitatores" (two men); "Fezani"; "Peregrini euntes ad Meccam" (two men); and "Abissini".

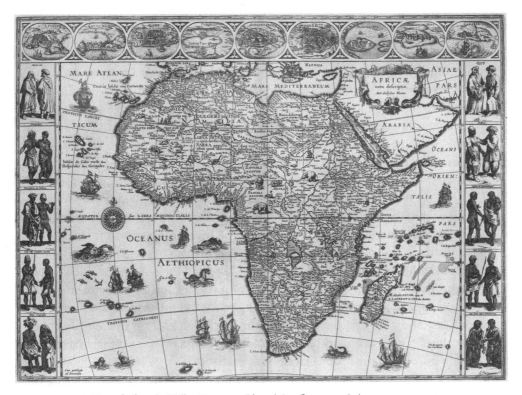

FIGURE 1.4   *Map of Africa by Willem Janszoon Blaeu (1630; first state 1617).*
            BIBLIOTHÈQUE NATIONALE DE FRANCE.

maps of this genre depict almost exclusively couples (mainly, but not always, male–female pairings). Figure 1.4 shows what was probably the most successful African map of the seventeenth century, also by Willem Janszoon Blaeu and clearly based on his earlier wall map.[43] Printed in many editions and variants from 1617 onwards, its third state is included, for instance, in the century's most expensive publication project, the 12-volume *Atlas Maior* (Amsterdam 1662/1665) by Joan Blaeu, son of Willem. In contrast to the 1608 wall map, all the marginal figures on this map appear as couples, leading Valerie Traub to see "a specifically *heterosexual* idiom"[44] at work in the map and a drive towards

---

43   For descriptions of this map see Günter Schilder, *Monumenta Cartographica Neerlandica VII* (Alphen aan den Rijn: Uitgeverij Canaletto, 2000), 116–119; and Betz, *The Mapping of Africa*, 225–228.

44   Valerie Traub, "Mapping the Global Body", in *Early Modern Visual Culture: Representation, Race, and Empire in Renaissance England*, ed. Peter Erickson and Clark Hulse (Philadelphia: University of Pennsylvania Press, 2000), 44–97 (71).

marital union as the normative visual paradigm for figurative portraits. (The point is astute but not quite accurate, since two of the ten couples on the map of Africa are actually male-male pairings.[45])

Equally significant is the new logic behind the general arrangement of the figures on the map. The 1608 wall map, from which all of these portraits are derived, foregrounds the Zuraran discourse of a continent split along ethno-religious lines into a "land of Moors" and a "land of Blacks", and prioritizes this division over the geographical connections between people and land: seven out of eight galleries on the right depict north and east African Muslim societies, with all figures shown fully dressed wearing kaftans, robes, cloaks or shirts, while only the bottom gallery ("Cafres in Mozambique") shows four black-skinned Africans (one a baby), of whom two are depicted naked, and two wear only a piece of cloth. On the left, all galleries feature sub-Saharan people, and all are depicted with large parts of their body exposed. The arrangement makes white dominate on the right, and black on the left (in the uncoloured version of the map). Within each column, the countries are shown in the geographical sequence suggested by the map (the trajectories are northwest to east and south on the right; west to south and east on the left), but this arrangement is secondary to the overriding division of Africa into two separate spheres, one Moorish, one Black.

By contrast, the 1617 map operates a model of geographical indexing in which the images from top to bottom correspond to the location of cultures and countries along Africa's north–south axis, resulting in a clear hierarchy of colour and culture: light-skinned North Africans in exquisite costume are placed at the top (Moroccans on the left; Egyptians on the right); down the frame on either side the nakedness, blackness and "wildness" of the figures gradually increase, with the "lowest" point reached at the Cape, whose inhabitants (the Khoikhoi) are shown eating the raw entrails of dead cattle.[46] The example of the 1608 wall map, on which the same image of the Khoikhoi was placed in the left-hand column, one image up from the bottom, demonstrates that while assumptions about "savagery" at the Cape had not changed, the carefully choreographed visual descent into darkness, exposed skin and revolting eating

---

45   These two are the portraits depicting merchants in Guinea and inhabitants of the Cape of
       Good Hope ("Mercatores in Guinea"; "Cap: bonæ Spæi habitatores").

46   Accusations of coprophagy against the Khoikhoi were frequently made by early Euro-
       pean commentators: "Numerous writers claimed that the Khoikhoi consumed the cattle's
       intestines raw, or nearly raw, along with the excrement inside". George Steinmetz, *The
       Devil's Handwriting. Postcoloniality and the German Colonial State in Qingdao, Samoa, and
       Southwest Africa* (Chicago: Chicago University Press, 2007), 83. See also Andrew B. Smith,
       "Different Facets of the Crystal: Early European Images of the Khoikhoi at the Cape, South
       Africa", *Goodwin Series*, VII (1993), 8–20 (10).

habits was a deliberate aesthetic choice, not a necessity dictated by the "facts" of geography. Rather, the arrangement follows what Ernst van den Boogart has recently called a "rough and ready formula": "'the more dress the more civility, the more nudity the more savagery'".[47] The map also suggests that the toponym "Africa" was beginning to be equated in European minds predominantly with the signifiers "black" and "nude", as the quantitative changes indicate: sixteen galleries have been reduced to ten, with only three representing Moorish Africa, and seven depicting black Africa (as opposed to seven and nine galleries respectively on the 1608 wall map). The popularity of Blaeu's 1617 map ensured that its colour paradigm dominated the European cartography of Africa throughout the seventeenth century, with the portraits allocating people to their "proper" spaces, and attaching moral value to those spaces.

A further variant of the African *carte à figures* makes this point even more directly. The 1614 map of Africa by Pieter van den Keere, "the earliest Africa map with decorative borders to be published in folio format",[48] and the continental map included in John Speed's *Prospect of the Most Famous Parts of the World* (1626) – an entirely derivative, English version of the world atlas (fig. 1.5) – both include portraits based almost exclusively on Blaeu's templates in the left and right margins.[49] The sequential arrangement of images in relation to the land is identical to the 1617 example. But in one feature both maps differ significantly from Blaeu's: the pictorial galleries are all populated by single figures. Individuals stand under the arches that on Blaeu's maps framed either crowds or couples; social space is not defined in these examples as a collective experience. On Speed's map, the graphic changes follow a clear pattern: in each of the couple-occupied galleries that he found on Blaeu's 1617 map, he simply left out the second (usually the female) figure.[50] The

---

47   Ernst van den Boogart, "De Bry's Africa", in *Inszenierte Welten / Staging New Worlds*, ed. Susanna Burghartz (Basle: Schwabe, 2004), 95–155 (97).

48   Betz, *The Mapping of Africa*, 221. The map is reproduced on page 220.

49   Speed uses only Blaeu's figure portraits; van den Keere uses Blaeu for five of his eight galleries, relying on Jodocus Hondius' 1598 wall map for the remaining three. On the wall map by Hondius, see Günter Schilder, *Monumenta Cartographica Neerlandica VIII* (Alphen aan den Rijn: Uitgeverij Canaletto, 2007), 231–235; and Betz, *The Mapping of Africa*, 185–186.

50   See Betz, *The Mapping of Africa*, 242. Traub argues that most of Speed's maps, even though they display single figures in the margins, actually portray couples, because "the marital idiom is reasserted, with heterosexual spouses divided from one another by the geography of nation or empire" ("Mapping the Global Body", 73). While this is true for most of the country maps in Speed's atlas, it is not the case on his continental map of Africa, in which only three out of ten portraits display women, and none of the ten figures are socially or geographically linked.

FIGURE 1.5 *Map of Africa by John Speed (1626).*
© THE BRITISH LIBRARY BOARD, SHELF-MARK MAPS C.7.A.2.

remaining individuals are attached to regions or countries via their captions, and thus geographically defined but no longer given a social or any other identity apart from their generic "race". This individualized version of the African *carte à figure* was popular in Britain; the van den Keere map served as the model for two continental maps printed in 1658 and 1668;[51] further derivates were published in several eighteenth-century atlases.

Mapping Blackness

The variations between the different versions and derivatives of the 1608 wall map printed throughout the seventeenth century are prefigured by the

---

51   See Betz, *The Mapping of Africa*, 302–303, for the 1658 map by Robert Walton; and 350–351, for the 1668 map by John Overton. See also the Frederick de Wit variant published in Amsterdam in 1660 and described by Betz on pages 321–323.

changes made to the visual sources in Blaeu's Amsterdam workshop during the original production of this map. The graphic differences between these sources and the nine images of sub-Saharan Africans that appeared first on the wall map, and then with slight alterations on practically all continental maps of Africa over the next century, reveal in detail how these maps performed their cultural work. Eight of these nine images probably came to Blaeu's engraver, Hessel Gerritsz, through the early volumes of the de Bry brothers' *India Orientalis* series (the "lesser voyages" or *Petits Voyages*), though he could have also found seven of them in the books from which the de Brys themselves took their visuals.[52] The image of the inhabitants of Congo ("Magnates in Congo"),

---

52   The nine images I am including in this count are all eight galleries in the left-hand margin, and the bottom one on the right. The sources are the following: for galleries 2 to 4 on the left (counting from the top), either Johan Theodor and Johan Israel de Bry, *Sechster Theil der Orientalischen Indien. Warhafftige Historische Beschreibung deß gewaltigen Goltreichen Königreichs Guinea* (Frankfurt: W. Richtern, 1603) [= volume six of *India Orientalis*], plates 2, 3 and 20, or Pieter de Marees, *Beschryvinghe ende historische verhael vant Gout Koninckrijk van Gunea* (Amsterdam: Cornelisz Claesz, 1602); for galleries 5 and 6, either Johan Theodor and Johan Israel de Bry, *Warhaffte und Eigentliche Beschreibung des Königreichs Congo in Africa* (Frankfurt: J. Saur, 1597) [= volume one of *India Orientalis*], plates 3, 4 and 5, or Filippo Pigafetta, *Relatione del reame di Congo e delle circonvicine contrade* (Rome: Bartolomeo Grassi, 1591); for gallery 7, Johan Theodor and Johan Israel de Bry, *Dritter Theil indiae orientalis* (Frankfurt: Matthaeum Becker, 1599) [= volume three of *India Orientalis*], plate 7 (the image is loosely based on, but not a direct copy of, an image of Cape dwellers in Willem Lodewijcksz, *D' Eerste boeck. Historie van Indien, waer inne verhaelt is de avontueren die de Hollandtsche schepen bejeghent zijn* [Amsterdam: n.p., 1598]); for gallery 8, either volume three of *India Orientalis*, plate 11, or Lodewijcksz, *D' Eerste boeck*; for the bottom gallery on the right, either Johan Theodor and Johan Israel de Bry, *Ander Theil der Orientalischen Indien* (Frankfurt: J. Saur, 1598) [= volume two of *India Orientalis*], plate 3, or Jan Huygen van Linschoten, *Itinerario, Voyage ofte Schipvaert van Jan Huygen van Linschoten naer Oost ofte Portugaels Indien* (Amsterdam: Cornelis Claesz, 1596). The most complete list of the sources of the de Bry engravings is appendix 3, "The origins of the engravings in the De Bry collection", in Michiel van Groesen, *The Representations of the Overseas World in the de Bry Collection of Voyages* (Leiden and Boston: Brill, 2008), 509–522. The source for the image on the top left ("Senagenses") has not yet been identified, though the female on the right of the image may have been taken from the earlier wall map of Africa by Jodocus Hondius (1598), which includes the portrait of a "Fæmina Senege", itself possibly a variation of the image of a "Fille Moresque esclaue en Algier" in Nicolas de Nicolay, *Quatre premiers livres de navigations et de pérégrinations orientales* (Lyon: Guillaume Roville, 1568), following page 19. The sources for the other seven images on the 1608 wall map, not all of which have been identified, include Enea Vico, *Diversarum gentium nostrae aetatis* (Venice, 1558); Ferdinando Bertelli, *Omnium fere gentium nostrae aetatis habitus* (Venice, 1563); Nicolay, *Quatre premiers livres*; Hans

for example, wandered from Filippo Pigafetta's 1591 Italian account based on the Portuguese merchant Duarte Lopez' residency in Congo (1578–83), to volume one of *India Orientalis*, first published in German in 1597.[53] Gerritsz could have used either one of these books, or both, since the illustrations differ little between them. His precise source is less important than the manner in which the image was altered on the map. In both Pigafetta and the de Brys, the Congolese (male and female) have white skin, European faces, and "are neither 'black' nor represented with negroid physiognomies".[54] On Blaeu's map, however, with the images torn from their narrative context, the Congolese have been given black skins and distinctly negroid faces.[55]

The reasons for these changes are not immediately obvious. The original illustrations in Pigafetta are unlikely to have been based on eyewitness observation, which has led van den Boogart to argue that the designer may have followed the textual account,[56] in which the Congolese were distinguished from the Nubians and Guineans as being neither "deformed" nor having "thick lips", resembling instead the Portuguese in appearance with "large, narrow and varied" faces.[57] But Pigafetta also gave the Congolese black or olive-coloured skin and curly hair, which the designer ignored. It is more likely that both Pigafetta's designer and the de Brys were working within a set of received norms and practices that governed the dissemination of images in print,[58] and

   Weigel, *Habitus praecipuorum populorum* (Nuremberg, 1577); and Abraham de Bruyn, *Omnium pene Euopae, Asiae, Aphricae atque Americae gentium habitus* (n.p., 1581). Images were frequently copied between these various works.

53   See also Schilder, *Monumenta Cartographica Neerlandica V*, 146–147.

54   van den Boogart, "De Bry's Africa", 106.

55   See also Schilder, *Monumenta Cartographica Neerlandica V*, 147–148.

56   See van den Boogart, "De Bry's Africa", 96, 106.

57   Pigafetta, 6–7: "Gl'huomini sono negri, & le donne, & alcuni manco tirando più all'Oliuastro, & hanno li capelli crespi neri, & alcuni anco rossi; la statura de gl'huomini è di mezzana grandezza, & leuatone il colore nero sono à Portoghesi somiglianti: le pupille de gl'occhi di varij colori nere, & del color del Mare, & le labra non grosse, como li nubi, & altri negri, & cosi li volti loro sono grossi, & sottili, & varij come in queste contrade, non come li neri di Nubia, & di Guinea, che sono difformi". ["The men are black, and so are the women, though some are verging more towards olive-coloured, and their hair is curly and black, some also have red hair; in stature the men are of medium height, and apart from the black colour they resemble the Portuguese: the pupils of the eyes are variously coloured, and of the colour of the sea, and the lips are not thick, as those of the Nubians and other Negroes, and that way their faces are large, narrow and varied as they are in these parts, not like those of the blacks in Nubia and Guinea, who are deformed" (my translation).]

58   See Stephanie Pratt, "Truth and Artifice in the Visualization of Native Peoples: From the Time of John White to the Beginning of the Eighteenth Century", in *European Visions: American Voices*, ed. Kim Sloan (London: The British Museum, 2009), 33–40.

that neither of them was particularly interested in race and ethnicity as key signifiers of alterity, prioritizing instead cultural and social markers of difference.
The approach of the de Brys was reasonably consistent in this respect across
their published voyage accounts. On their engravings of the John White water-
colours, for example, which they used for their images of the north American
Algonquians published in the *India Occidentalis* (or *America*) series, they deliberately altered the source and "Europeanized" their subject matter. Critics have
accused the de Brys in this instance of "erasing the alterity of native bodies and
making them more familiar, and aesthetically pleasing, to European viewers",[59]
but arguably, the representational templates which the de Brys applied to the
depiction of foreign faces and bodies allowed them to deflect attention away
from race and focus instead on nuances of dress, custom and culture. Maps
of Africa are doing the opposite work: alterity is not erased but created, with
recourse not to eyewitness accounts and images drawn *ad vivum* but to established and racially inflected visual tropes about sub-Saharan Africans.

The kingdom of Congo, whose rulers had converted to christianity at the
end of the fifteenth century, may perhaps be expected to receive preferred
treatment in European representations, which in turn could have led Blaeu
into making these changes in order to ensure overall visual coherence on
his map. But this was not the case: other images were subjected to the same
process of graphic redaction. To cite one more striking example, the image of
the inhabitants of the Cape is based on a plate included in volume three of the
de Brys' *India Orientalis* series (1599; fig. 1.6),[60] in which a coprophagic Cape
dweller is shown in the centre of the image standing next to the carcass of a
dead oxen, being handed raw entrails by one of the Europeans who have ex-
pertly performed the slaughter. In the background on the left, as the caption
explains, four Khoikhoi are warming up the intestines in water on an ox-hide,

---

59   Traub, "Mapping the Global Body", 63.
60   Michiel von Groesen lists this image as an invention of the de Brys in his appendix on
      the origins of the de Bry engravings (*The Representations of the Overseas World*, 517).
      This is correct in terms of the visual statement made in the image, though details of the
      Cape dwellers' appearance are clearly copied from an image in Lodewijcksz, *D' Eerste
      boeck*, as von Groesen shows in his discussion in *ibid.*, 180–181 (the Lodewijcksz image
      is reprinted on page 182). The text of *India Orientalis*, volume 3, is based on Jan Huygen
      van Linschoten's travel accounts in which coprophagy at the Cape is described but not
      illustrated. The image has been reproduced before, e.g. in van Groesen, 183; in Walter
      Hirschberg, *Schwarzafrika*, Monumenta Ethnographica I (Graz: Akademische Druck- und
      Verlagsanstalt, 1962), 47, where it is mistakenly attributed to van Linschoten; and in Major
      R. Raven-Hart, *Before van Riebeeck. Callers at South Africa from 1488 to 1652* (Cape Town:
      Struik, 1976), facing page 84, where it is mistakenly attributed to Willem Lodewijcksz.

FIGURE 1.6 *An early image of the Khoikhoi at the Cape of Good Hope. From Johann Theodor and*
Johann Israel de Bry, India Orientalis, *vol. 3 (1599).*
© THE BRITISH LIBRARY BOARD, SHELF-MARK G.6607.

before consuming them semi-raw. In Blaeu's gallery, the single Khoikhoi in
the centre of the de Brys' image stands next to a mirror image of himself, white
skin has become black, straight hair curly, and European facial features have
turned negroid (fig. 1.7). Similar graphic changes can be identified for all other
galleries (bar one[61]): formulaic European faces become exaggeratedly African,
blackness is introduced through densely criss-crossing lines on the exposed
skin of the African figures (and is further emphasized through the colour added after printing). And even though details of dress, jewelry, and weaponry
are generally retained, these changes clearly serve to strengthen the implied
cultural and civilizational gap between Africa and Europe. On the image of the
Cape dwellers, they are particularly distorting, since the de Brys' caption made

---

61   The one exception is the bottom gallery on the right ("Cafres in Mozambique"), the sources
       for which (see above, n. 51) already depict Africans with negroid facial features and black
       skin.

PROMONTORII BONÆ SPÆI HABITATORES.

FIGURE 1.7   *Inhabitants of the Cape of Good Hope.*
DETAIL FROM THE WALL MAP BY WILLEM JANSZOON BLAEU (1608/1624;
FIG. 1.3 ABOVE).

a point of emphasizing that the skin colour of the "Hottentots" was not black but "reddish-brown".[62]

Significantly, when Aphra Behn described her hero's face in *Oroonoko*, the shift in image went the opposite way, as she took care to erase exactly this negroid image in the minds of her readers: "[Oroonoko's] nose was rising and Roman, instead of African and flat. His mouth, the finest shaped that could be seen, far from those great turned lips, which are so natural to the rest of the Negroes".[63] The point here is not just that a tale based on an African character's

---

62   Johan Theodor and Johan Israel de Bry, *Dritter Theil indiae orientalis*, plate 7. The caption reads: "Dieses Volck ist zimlich kleiner Statur, von Farben rohtbraun, gehet ganz nackend" ["These people are of fairly small stature, reddish-brown in colour, and go completely naked" (my translation)].

63   Behn, *Oroonoko*, ed. Salzman, 12.

inherent nobility required Behn to extract her black hero from the rigid racial categories maps had helped to establish, but also that these facial features only seemed "natural" because visual depictions of sub-Saharan Africans such as those available on seventeenth-century maps had been persistently working to codify these representational conventions. The cartographic portrait that would fit Oroonoko's geographical and social origins most closely (the second gallery on the left of the 1608 wall map depicting a "lord" of Guinea with attendants) was given exactly the "Africanizing" treatment described above. It is important to note in this context that Blaeu's main source for the black African portraits on his maps, the image arsenal of the de Brys, which has proved "a goldmine to scholars seeking visual material for the study of Europe's attitudes toward foreign others",[64] may have actually influenced European attitudes to the non-European world in less significant ways than the work of cartography, which, through its wider dissemination and higher public visibility, had the potential of reaching much larger audiences. While the de Bry visuals of Africa certainly contained plenty of instances of African "savagery", they did not, as a whole, follow a programme of systematic racial stereotyping and were not "geared to a priori negative constructions of alterity".[65] Maps made far more racially biased statements about the alleged lack of civility in black Africa.

Geography and Difference

The argument that I have been working towards in my discussion of African maps is to suggest that there is a conceptual affinity between the uniqueness and clearly defined ethnic and racial identity of Behn's protagonist, and the rigid spatial categories through which maps are beginning to define the nexus between people and land, race and space, ethnicity and geography – exemplified nowhere more clearly than in the individually encased and exhibited figures on maps like van den Keere's and Speed's. The link is speculative to

---

64   Maureen Quilligan, "Theodor De Bry's Voyages to the New and Old Worlds", *Journal of Medieval and Early Modern Studies*, XLI/1 (2011), 1–12 (1).

65   van den Boogart, "De Bry's Africa", 146. Alden T. Vaughan and Virginia Mason Vaughan argue that the situation was different in England, where the notion prevailed "that sub-Saharan Africans were uniquely deficient in color, culture, and character". See Vaughan and Vaughan, "Before Othello: Elizabethan Representations of Sub-Saharan Africans", *William and Mary Quarterly*, LIV/1 (1997), 19–44 (42). The Vaughans draw mainly, though not exclusively, on fictional English descriptions of sub-Saharan Africans. With regard to non-fictional accounts, P.E.H. Hair has argued very differently in "Attitudes to Africans in English Primary Sources on Guinea up to 1650", *History in Africa*, XXVI (1999), 43–68.

some extent, not least because the three examples of African *cartes à figures* I have discussed in this essay (figs. 1.3 to 1.5) do not form a neat chronological sequence but coexist throughout the seventeenth century. All three maps are also presentational items, existing as decorative wall hangings, single folio-sized sheets or pages in glossy scholarly tomes, rather than as practical way-finding tools, and thus reflect assumptions held by the sedentary classes, not necessarily by the voyagers and seafarers involved in first-hand encounters with non-European cultures.

But then the argument presented here depends neither on a linear development nor on the usefulness of these maps to travellers, but on the availability of various representational and visual tools that enabled maps to encode, taxonomize and contain forms of racial and ethnic difference. These tools were not developed exclusively with reference to Africa or non-European spaces more generally: the origin of the visual convention that places people in the margins of maps was the cartography of Europe, developed and refined in the Dutch mapmaking centres of the seventeenth century. But once these representational conventions were extended across the globe and applied to other ethnicities, ways of seeing and processing forms of geographical difference changed as a result. The example of European maps of Africa demonstrates that the amalgamation of topographical map, city view and figure portrait in a single image developed a normative force in seventeenth-century cartography that could break down the unwieldy mass of geographical information about foreign lands to the smallest social and spatial unit – the individual body – and in the process made race an inherent component of the cartographic ordering and rationalizing of the world.

A similar move towards the presentation of geographical knowledge in the form of discrete, isolated entities can be observed elsewhere, for example on the title-page of Edmund Bohun's *Geographical Dictionary* (1688; fig. 1.8),[66] recycled from Peter Heylyn's identical frontispiece adorning his *Cosmographie* of 1652, on which all four continents are represented by single, ethnically and sartorially defined figures. The spatial personifications on the image are no longer traditional geographical allegories but figurative representations of the continents, separated into male and female, and characterized by local costume, insignia of royalty for the women, and (in the lower gallery) the regional warrior dress for the men. In yet another application of Zurara's ethnically motivated north–south split, Africa is represented by a turbaned north African male and a sub-Saharan woman (the latter portrayed with precisely the same facial features

---

66   Edmund Bohun, *A Geographical Dictionary ... of the Whole World* (London: Charles Brome, 1688).

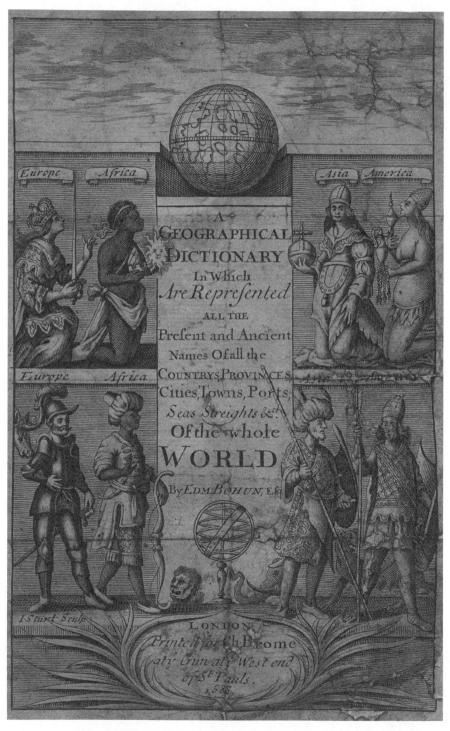

FIGURE 1.8 *Title-page of Edmund Bohun's* Geographical Dictionary ... of the Whole World
(*1688*).

that Behn worked so hard to suppress in her fictional hero). Bohun's work is an alphabetical sequence of all known toponyms around the globe, that strives towards a "more perfect knowledge of each Respective Place",[67] and processes geographical knowledge by listing, classifying and cataloguing. The title-page could work as the illustration of the comment made by another contemporary geographer, Robert Sibbald, who thought that through geography, "all the face of the World is exposed to us", and that the world is "a Theater, whereupon each act their Part, and ... [represent] several Personages".[68] Sibbald was a Scottish physician and geographer who summarized his praise for maps in 1683 when he wrote in the preface to one of his works that "Man ... cannot but find the advantages of *Geography*, by which we see all the parts of this great Machine, even which are most remote from us, and look upon these who are absent, as if they were present with us".[69]

This is the mystery of maps: they make visible what otherwise remains hidden from human eyesight, and they bring together in one image and one unifying representational system the totality of spatial and social diversity on earth. "Machine" implies structure and connectedness, and here has the principal meaning of the "fabric of the world", or the "universe". But the metaphor works differently in the context of Behn's novel, which describes the inhuman, *mechanistic* workings of colonialism and the transatlantic slave trade. In *Oroonoko*, Behn exhibits a trained cartographic gaze right at the beginning of the novel when she divides the inhabitants of Suriname into three distinct groups: first, European settlers; second, the "natives of that place", whom the colonists dare not "command"; and third, those people the Europeans "make use of there",[70] in other words, African slaves. With the same curiosity of the naturalist she offers accounts of Suriname's natural flora and fauna, the local customs, the country's wildlife and many of its animals. For contemporary geographers, the description of peoples and places, both at home and abroad, formed a subgenre of natural history. Sibbald's work focused on Scotland but once exported beyond the British Isles, the parameters and descriptive paradigms of this brand of national geography could easily be put to use in the service of a globally operating colonial "machinery". The system relied on images as much as on words, and it is in this sense that Oroonoko fell victim not only to a modern slave economy in which his nobility and moral virtue mattered little, but also to an uncomfortable alliance between literature and cartography.

---

67   J.A. Bernard, preface to 1693 edition of Bohun's work, n.p.

68   Robert Sibbald, *An Account of the Scottish Atlas, or The Description of Scotland, Ancient and Modern* (Edinburgh: David Lindsay et al., 1683), 3.

69   *Ibid.*

70   Behn, *Oroonoko*, ed. Salzman, 6.

Works Cited

Behn, Aphra. *Oroonoko and Other Writings*, edited by Paul Salzman. Oxford: Oxford University Press, 1994.

Betz, Richard L. *The Mapping of Africa: A Cartobibliography of Printed Maps of the African Continent up to 1700*. Utrecht Studies in the History of Cartography 7. 't Goy-Houten: Hes & de Graaf, 2007.

Blackmore, Josiah. *Moorings: Portuguese Expansion and the Writing of Africa*. Minneapolis: University of Minnesota Press, 2009.

Bohun, Edmund. *A Geographical Dictionary … of the Whole World*. London: Charles Brome, 1688.

Boissard, Jean-Jacques. *Habitus Variarum Orbis Gentium*. Cologne: Caspar Rutz, 1581.

Braun, Georg, and Frans Hogenberg. *Beschreibung und Contrafactur der vornembster Stätt der Welt*. Cologne: Heinrich von Ach, 1574.

Cartelli, Thomas. *Repositioning Shakespeare: National Formations, Postcolonial Appropriations*. London and New York: Routledge, 1999.

Chedgzoy, Kate. *Women's Writing in the British Atlantic World: Memory, Place and History, 1550–1700*. Cambridge: Cambridge University Press, 2007.

Conley, Tom. "Early Modern Literature and Cartography: An Overview". In *The History of Cartography, vol. 3: Cartography in the European Renaissance*, 2 parts, edited by David Woodward. Part 1, 401–411. Chicago: The University of Chicago Press, 2007.

Conley, Tom. *The Self-Made Map: Cartographic Writing in Early Modern France*. Minneapolis: University of Minnesota Press, 1996.

Cosgrove, Denis. "Introduction: Mapping Meaning". In *Mappings*, edited by Denis Cosgrove, 1–23. London: Reaktion, 1999.

De Bry, Johan Theodor, and Johan Israel de Bry. *Warhaffte und Eigentliche Beschreibung des Königreichs Congo in Africa*. Frankfurt: J. Saur, 1597.

De Bry, Johan Theodor, and Johan Israel de Bry. *Ander Theil der Orientalischen Indien*. Frankfurt: J. Saur, 1598.

De Bry, Johan Theodor, and Johan Israel de Bry. *Dritter Theil indiae orientalis*. Frankfurt: Matthaeum Becker, 1599.

De Bry, Johan Theodor, and Johan Israel de Bry. *Sechster Theil der Orientalischen Indien. Warhafftige Historische Beschreibung deß gewaltigen Goltreichen Königreichs Guinea*. Frankfurt: W. Richtern, 1603.

De Certeau, Michel. *The Practice of Everyday Life* [1974], translated by Steven Randall. Berkeley et al: University of California Press, 1988.

De Marees, Pieter. *Beschryvinghe ende historische verhael vant Gout Koninckrijk van Gunea*. Amsterdam: Cornelisz Claesz, 1602.

De Nicolay, Nicolas. *Quatre premiers livres de navigations et de pérégrinations orientales*. Lyon: Guillaume Roville, 1568.

Douglas, Mary. *Purity and Danger: An Analysis of the Concepts of Pollution and Taboo*. London: Routledge, 1966.

Ferguson, Margaret. "Transmuting *Othello*: Aphra Behn's *Oroonoko*". In *Cross-Cultural Performances: Differences in Women's Re-Visions of Shakespeare*, edited by Marianne Novy, 15–49. Champaign: University of Illinois Press, 1993.

Gallagher, Catherine. "Introduction: Cultural and Historical Background". In Aphra Behn, *Oroonoko*, edited by Catherine Gallagher, 3–25. Boston and New York: Bedford/St. Martin's, 2000.

Gillies, John. *Shakespeare and the Geography of Difference*. Cambridge: Cambridge University Press, 1994.

Gordon, Andrew, and Bernhard Klein (eds.). *Literature, Mapping, and the Politics of Space in Early Modern Britain*. Cambridge: Cambridge University Press, 2001.

Hair, P.E.H. "Attitudes to Africans in English Primary Sources on Guinea up to 1650". *History in Africa*, XXVI (1999): 43–68.

Harley, J.B. *The New Nature of Maps: Essays in the History of Cartography*, edited by Paul Laxton. Baltimore: Johns Hopkins University Press, 2001.

Helgerson, Richard. *Forms of Nationhood: The Elizabethan Writing of England*. Chicago: Chicago University Press, 1992.

Hirschberg, Walter. *Schwarzafrika*, Monumenta Ethnographica I. Graz: Akademische Druck- und Verlagsanstalt, 1962.

Jacob, Christian. *The Sovereign Map: Theoretical Approaches in Cartography throughout History*, translated by Tom Conley. Chicago and London: The University of Chicago Press, 2006.

Klein, Bernhard. *Maps and the Writing of Space in Early Modern England and Ireland*. Basingstoke: Palgrave, 2001.

Klein, Bernhard. "Staying Afloat: Literary Shipboard Encounters from Shakespeare to Equiano". In *Sea Changes: Historicizing the Ocean*, edited by Bernhard Klein and Gesa Mackenthun, 91–109. New York: Routledge, 2004.

Klein, Bernhard. "*Tamburlaine*, Sacred Space, and the Heritage of Medieval Cartography". In *Reading the Medieval in Early Modern England*, edited by David Matthews and Gordon McMullan, 143–158. Cambridge: Cambridge University Press, 2007.

Klemp, Egon. *Afrika auf Karten des 12. bis 18. Jahrhundert*. Leipzig: Ed. Leipzig, 1968.

Lefebvre, Henri. *The Production of Space* [1974], translated by Donald Nicolson-Smith. Oxford: Blackwell, 1991.

Lewis, Martin W., and Kären E. Wigen. *The Myth of Continents: A Critique of Metageography*, 21–46. Berkeley and Los Angeles: University of California Press, 1997.

Lodewijcksz, Willem. *D' Eerste boeck. Historie van Indien, waer inne verhaelt is de avontueren die de Hollandtsche schepen bejeghent zijn*. Amsterdam: n.p., 1598.

Marlowe, Christopher. *Tamburlaine*, Part 2. In *The Complete Plays*, edited by J.B. Steane. Harmondsworth: Penguin, 1969.

Norwich, Oscar I. *Maps of Africa: An Illustrated and Annotated Carto-Bibliography*. Johannesburg: Ad. Donker, 1983. [Republished as *Norwich's Maps of Africa*, edited by Jeffrey Stone. Vermont: Terra Nova, 1997].

Pigafetta, Filippo. *Relatione del reame di Congo e delle circonvicine contrade*. Rome: Bartolomeo Grassi, 1591.

Pory, John. "A General Description of all Africa", preface to Leo Africanus, *A Geographical Historie of Africa*, translated by John Pory, 4. London: Georg Bishop, 1600.

Pratt, Stephanie. "Truth and Artifice in the Visualization of Native Peoples: From the Time of John White to the Beginning of the Eighteenth Century". In *European Visions: American Voices*, edited by Kim Sloan, 33–40. London: The British Museum, 2009.

Quilligan, Maureen. "Theodor De Bry's Voyages to the New and Old Worlds". *Journal of Medieval and Early Modern Studies*, XLI/1 (2011), 1–12.

Ralegh, Sir Walter. *Discoverie of the Large, Rich, and Bewtifvl Empire of Guiana*. London: Robert Robinson, 1596.

Raven-Hart, Major R. *Before van Riebeeck. Callers at South Africa from 1488 to 1652*. Cape Town: Struik, 1976.

Schilder, Günter. *Monumenta Cartographica Neerlandica III*. Alphen aan den Rijn: Uitgeverij Canaletto, 1990.

Schilder, Günter. *Monumenta Cartographica Neerlandica V: Tien wandkaarten van Blaeu en Visscher / Ten Wall Maps by Blaeu and Visscher*. Alphen aan den Rijn: Uitgeverij Canaletto, 1996.

Schilder, Günter. *Monumenta Cartographica Neerlandica VII*. Alphen aan den Rijn: Uitgeverij Canaletto, 2000.

Schilder, Günter. *Monumenta Cartographica Neerlandica VIII*. Alphen aan den Rijn: Uitgeverij Canaletto, 2007.

Seaton, Ethel. "Marlowe's Map" [1924]. In *Marlowe: A Collection of Critical Essays*, Twentieth-Century Views, edited by Clifford Leech, 36–56. Eaglewood Cliffs: NJ, Prentice Hall, 1964.

Shakespeare, William. *Othello*, The Arden Shakespeare, edited by E.A.J. Honigmann. Walton-on-Thames, Surrey: Thomas Nelson, 1997.

Sibbald, Robert. *An Account of the Scottish Atlas, or The Description of Scotland, Ancient and Modern*. Edinburgh: David Lindsay et al., 1683.

Smith, Andrew B. "Different Facets of the Crystal: Early European Images of the Khoikhoi at the Cape, South Africa". *Goodwin Series*, VII (1993): 8–20.

Smith, D.K. *The Cartographic Imagination in Early Modern England: Re-writing the World in Marlowe, Spenser, Raleigh and Marvell*. Burlington: Ashgate, 2008.

Speed, John. *The Theatre of the Empire of Great Britain*. London: Iohn Sudbury & George Humble, 1611.

Steinmetz, George. *The Devil's Handwriting: Postcoloniality and the German Colonial State in Qingdao, Samoa, and Southwest Africa*. Chicago: Chicago University Press, 2007.

Tooley, Ronald Vere. *Collector's Guide to Maps of the African Continent and Southern Africa*. London: Carta Press, 1969.

Traub, Valerie. "Mapping the Global Body". In *Early Modern Visual Culture: Representation, Race, and Empire in Renaissance England*, edited by Peter Erickson and Clark Hulse, 44–97. Philadelphia: University of Pennsylvania Press, 2000.

Van den Boogart, Ernst. "De Bry's Africa". In *Inszenierte Welten / Staging New Worlds*, edited by Susanna Burghartz, 95–155. Basle: Schwabe, 2004.

Van Groesen, Michiel. *The Representations of the Overseas World in the de Bry Collection of Voyages*. Leiden and Boston: Brill, 2008.

Van Linschoten, Jan Huygen. *Itinerario, Voyage ofte Schipvaert van Jan Huygen van Linschoten naer Oost ofte Portuqaels Indien*. Amsterdam: Cornelis Claesz, 1596.

Vaughan, Alden T., and Virginia Mason Vaughan. "Before Othello: Elizabethan Representations of Sub-Saharan Africans". *William and Mary Quarterly*, LIV/1 (1997), 19–44.

CHAPTER 2

The Early Modern Couch: Richard Brome's *The Antipodes* as Freudian Material

Miguel Ramalhete Gomes

Abstract

This chapter focuses on Richard Brome's play, *The Antipodes* (1638/1640) as material that Freud could have found stimulating, had he encountered the play, while reinterpreting the confluence, in *The Antipodes*, of psychiatry and travel writing, by focusing on its use of spatial metaphors to explain a mental condition. This chapter then explores the question of whether the fear of anachronism might not be one of the reasons why a play such as *The Antipodes* has gathered so much scholarly effort in regard to theatrical performance and to travel writing, but so little, in comparison, to its representation of psychiatry, which appears to constantly invite anachronistic reflections.

Couching the Case History

New historicism and cultural materialism have by now been the object of numerous case histories. Their shift of the means and ends of historical research as applied to literature and culture, with a special focus on the early modern period, has had profound and wide-ranging consequences, one of which has been the continuing stimulation of a healthy debate about theories of historiography, even beyond the nominal disavowal of both positions as so many ways of doing history. Some of their stylistic traits – such as the opening anecdotes of new historicism – having become too generalised, more discreet ways of doing cultural history have settled in, such as new materialism's ostensible focus on material objects as seen from a supposed "post-theoretical moment".[1] Indeed, David Scott Kastan's self-avowed "greater delight in particularity"[2] has come to epitomise a view of historicism purified of historiographical theorising and overly presentist intrusions into the study of the past.

---

1 David Scott Kastan, *Shakespeare after Theory* (New York: Routledge, 1999), 31.
2 *Ibid.*, 18.

Kastan's form of analysis did not constitute a simple return to older forms of historicism – themselves more complex and with a greater history than they are sometimes represented to be –, but it betrayed some discomfort with the nakedness of intentions to be then found in new historicist and critical materialist work. As John Joughin has put it, "At its height cultural materialism began to resemble an inverse of the work of E.M.W. Tillyard as a critical practice of dismantling his Elizabethan World Picture by reading for slippage, instability, or subversion itself confirmed a new form of orthodoxy".[3]

As one form of historicism thus struggled to rid itself of unconcealed agendas, it cannot, of course, escape one's notice that other, related forms of cultural and literary criticism of a historical bent have, in fact rather unproblematically, kept their agendas up front, offering Marxist, post-colonial, or gendered readings of texts from much earlier times. One might indeed argue that such readings have not been deemed outright anachronistic because some of their methods and insights developed in parallel and became meshed almost inextricably with the new historicist and cultural materialist work being produced during the 1980s, and which, for better or worse, has formed the backbone of historicist developments ever since.

If such approaches are, in a sense, tolerated by a more purified form of historicism and allowed to function in a historicist no man's land where they have gained the respectability accorded to traditional approaches, one can nonetheless verify that they have also sometimes participated in a broader pull towards a more impure form of historicism. Indeed, as Lucy Munro has shown in an excellent 2011 survey of the field, called "Shakespeare and the Uses of the Past: Critical Approaches and Current Debates", the study of Shakespeare and of the early modern period has witnessed an explosion of historical methods and angles that increasingly challenge the idea of purifying historicism of most present concerns. Munro's review of the investment in "queer" temporalities, of the revised relations between the medieval and early modern periods, and of the attention paid to questions of memory and trauma, culminates conceptually in an account of what has come to be called "presentism". In this context, presentism is no longer understood as an obstacle to be removed from proper historical research, or as an anachronistic impurity to be refined away, but rather as the driving impulse and necessarily acknowledgeable angle of any historicist work. Having first appeared in the works of Hugh Grady and the late Terence Hawkes, and being named as such by the mid-1990s, presentism has come to inform a growing number of titles interested in questioning

---

3   John J. Joughin, "Shakespeare Now: An Editorial Statement", *Shakespeare*, 1/1–2 (2005), 1–7 (2).

the by now familiar strains of much historicist research.[4] As Munro neatly encapsulates it, "For such critics, the problem with new historicism is not that it was too 'presentist', ... but that it was not presentist enough".[5] Indeed, rather than simply providing a negative acknowledgement of the inherent limitations of historicism,[6] presentism has considered intervention of and in the present to be a positive factor in historical criticism. As Terence Hawkes puts it, "All history, said Benedetto Croce, is contemporary history. The present ranks, not as an obstacle to be avoided, nor as a prison to be escaped from. Quite the reverse: it's a factor actively to be sought for, grasped and perhaps, as a result, understood".[7]

Rather than dismissing historicist approaches to literary texts and cultural contexts, presentists instead insist on the critic's own contextual placement, while remaining particularly attentive to the risks of rashly positing some sort of universality or progressive development meant to celebrate present concerns and practices, as had been the case with Whig historiography.[8] Aiming

---

4   Some proto-presentist works, in the sense used in Shakespeare studies, initially included Terence Hawkes, *That Shakespeherian Rag: Essays on a Critical Process* (London: Methuen, 1986); the same author's *Meaning by Shakespeare* (London: Routledge, 1992); and Richard Halpern, *Shakespeare among the Moderns* (Ithaca: Cornell UP, 1997). These were followed by monographs and collections more openly announced as presentist, though markedly eclectic: Hugh Grady, *Shakespeare's Universal Wolf: Studies in Early Modern Reification* (Oxford: Clarendon Press, 1996), and *Shakespeare, Machiavelli, and Montaigne: Power and Subjectivity from* Richard II *to* Hamlet (Oxford: Oxford UP, 2002); Terence Hawkes, *Shakespeare in the Present* (London: Routledge, 2002); Ewan Fernie, ed., *Spiritual Shakespeares* (London: Routledge, 2005); Linda Charnes, *Hamlet's Heirs: Shakespeare and the Politics of a New Millenium* (London: Routledge, 2006); Hugh Grady and Terence Hawkes, eds, *Presentist Shakespeares* (London: Routledge, 2007); Gary Taylor. "Historicism, Presentism and Time: Middleton's *The Spanish Gypsy* and *A Game at Chess*", *Sederi*, XVIII (2008): 147–170; Evelyn Gajowski, ed., *Presentism, Gender, and Sexuality in Shakespeare* (London: Palgrave Macmillan, 2009); Lynne Bruckner and Dan Brayton, eds, *Ecocritical Shakespeare* (Farnham and Burlington: Ashgate, 2011); James O'Rourke, *Retheorizing Shakespeare through Presentist Readings* (London: Routledge, 2012); Cary DiPietro and Hugh Grady, eds, *Shakespeare and the Urgency of Now: Criticism and Theory in the 21st Century* (Hampshire: Palgrave Macmillan, 2013).

5   Lucy Munro, "Shakespeare and the Uses of the Past: Critical Approaches and Current Debates", *Shakespeare*, VII/1 (2011), 102–125 (115).

6   Hugh Grady, for instance, refers to an "inevitable 'presentism' of all critical discourse", in "Hamlet and the Present: Notes on the Moving Aesthetic 'Now'", in *Presentist Shakespeares*, ed. Hugh Grady and Terence Hawkes (London: Routledge, 2007), 141–163 (142).

7   Hawkes, *Shakespeare in the Present*, 3.

8   See Herbert Butterfield, *The Whig Interpretation of History* (New York: W.W. Norton & Company, 1965); David Hackett Fischer, *Historians' Fallacies: Toward a Logic of Historical*

to dismantle spurious continuities or, on the contrary, looking for momentary points of contact capable of destabilising present discourses, presentists have done work which partly responds to T.S. Eliot's remark in "Tradition and the Individual Talent": "Whoever has approved this idea of order, of the form of European, of English literature will not find it preposterous that the past should be altered by the present as much as the present is directed by the past".[9] This practice has thus also mirrored recent, as well as not so recent, engagements with the fraught issue of anachronism, now occasionally grasped as an enabling mechanism in approaches to historical subjects.[10] In fact, the adjective "preposterous" is not used accidentally by Eliot. The word means inverting the order of what comes before and after, thus corresponding to the rhetorical device of "hysteron proteron", literally placing the latter before. Mieke Bal comes back to precisely this sense in her expression "preposterous history", which she explains in the introduction to her book on Caravaggio: "This reversal, which puts what came chronologically first ("pre-") as an aftereffect behind ("post-") its later recycling, is what I would like to call a *preposterous history*".[11]

It is in this context and conceptual framework that I would like to bring together an early modern play, Richard Brome's *The Antipodes* (staged in 1638; Quarto printing from 1640), and some aspects of the method and reputation of Sigmund Freud, which, I argue, have been carefully kept apart perhaps because such a juxtaposition might not only complicate historicist readings of early modern psychology, but also invite one to revise the relevance of Freud in a time that seems to want to consider itself post-psychoanalytic. While this is emphatically neither a declaration that Freud's work is transhistorical, nor a plea for the return of Freud to his former place, this essay does, however, want to suggest that such an intervention may help bring out the inescapable situatedness of historicist work in the present, thus stressing the impurities and multiple temporalities at play when doing such work. It is one of my arguments that, rather than being hermetically sealed categories, both the present and the past need to be considered porously open to temporal infiltrations of all sorts.

    Thought (New York: Harper Perennial, 1970); Hayden White, *Metahistory: The Historical Imagination in Nineteenth-Century Europe* (Baltimore: The Johns Hopkins UP, 1975).

9   T.S. Eliot, *Selected Prose of T.S. Eliot*, ed. Frank Kermode (London: Faber and Faber, 1987), 39.

10   See especially Mieke Bal, *Quoting Caravaggio: Contemporary Art, Preposterous History* (Chicago: The U of Chicago P, 1999); Alexander Nagel and Christopher S. Wood, *Anachronic Renaissance* (New York: Zone Books, 2010); Jeremy Tambling, *On Anachronism* (Manchester: Manchester UP, 2010).

11   Bal, 7.

The Strangest Doings

Freud is known to have mined literature from different times and places for examples which might inform, explain or prove his continuously changing theories of psychoanalysis. One of Freud's favourite sources was, of course, Shakespeare. As we also know, the privilege accorded to Shakespeare, by Freud as well as by many others, has kept lesser-known authors, Shakespeare's contemporaries or near contemporaries, hidden by his canonical authority for too long. It is, therefore, no surprise that Brome's *The Antipodes* has been critically neglected until the twentieth century and theatrically so until the twenty-first century. I would like to read some aspects of this play which pertain to what eventually became the domain of psychiatry as material that Freud might have considered valuable, had he come across Brome's play. Because he did not, my philology must be partially derivative, for it can only look at *The Antipodes* through the mediation of existing categories and concepts taken from some of Freud's works.

On the subject of early modern texts, Freud's knowledge and uses of Shakespeare have been widely discussed and are the object of several studies, but Freud also showed an interest in exploring Shakespeare's sources and some of his predecessors and contemporaries, having read Francis Bacon, Holinshed, marginalia by Gabriel Harvey, excerpts from Thomas Nashe's *The Terrors of the Night*, which Freud contemplated having published as "psychological significant anticipations of psychoanalytic studies of dream and nightmare",[12] and Robert Burton's *The Anatomy of Melancholy*, which he acquired very late in his life and seems not to have read extensively. As we know, Freud used Shakespearean examples and allusions very frequently and even devoted some essays to analysing themes or characters from Shakespeare, for instance in "The Theme of the Three Caskets" or "Some Character Types Encountered in Psychoanalytic Work". Beyond these more focused essays, Freud's uses of Shakespeare often turned on intimations of a character's subjectivity or alleged hints towards the author's own biography.[13] But, despite scenes of madness and usually unsuccessful attempts at some form of treatment in plays

---

12   S.S. Prawer, *A Cultural Citizen of the World: Sigmund Freud's Knowledge and Use of British and American Writings* (London: Legenda, 2009), 21–22. This sentence follows Prawer's account of Freud's readings of early modern authors, 21–27.

13   Whomever that biography may have belonged to. Freud's scattered comments on Shakespeare are complicated by his support to the notorious Oxfordian theory of Shakespearean authorship.

such as *Hamlet, King Lear, Macbeth,* or *The Two Noble Kinsmen,* nowhere in Shakespeare could Freud have found a scene of analysis comparable to that of Brome's *The Antipodes.*

According to Matthew Steggle, Brome's play includes "the first practising psychiatrist to appear on the English stage" "after Corax in Ford's *The Lover's Melancholy* (1624)".[14] In a clever variation of the city comedy, Brome's best-known play brings to the stage the alienated Peregrine, who has failed at performing his marital duties due to a serious mental disturbance caused partly by his obsessive interest in travel and travel accounts, namely by Mandeville. As the play begins, one "HUGHBALL, *a doctor of physic*" has already been called.[15] Doctor Hughball's physic, however, is a special one, prompting one character to point out that his cures proceed "not so much by bodily physic (no,/He sends few recipes to th'apothecaries)/As medicine of the mind".[16] In a play so preoccupied with mental "distraction", it is perhaps not surprising *for us* to find that such phenomena as intimately associated with Freud's name as slips of the tongue start appearing in the opening conversation between Joyless, Peregrine's father, and Blaze, who has called for the doctor. As Blaze extols the doctor's feats, he takes conspicuous care not to mention any names – "I name no man", "I name no lady", "but I name no parties".[17] Yet, when arriving at the delicate theme of "horn-mad citizens, my neighbours",[18] who have been cured by the doctor, Blaze adds that "we live/As gently with our wives as rams with ewes"[19] and is caught out:

Joyless	We do, you say – were you one of his patients?
Blaze	[*Aside*] 'Slid, he has almost catched me. – No, sir, no.
	I name no parties, I, but wish you merry.
	I strain to make you so, and could tell forty
	Notable cures of his to pass the time
	Until he comes.

---

14   Matthew Steggle, *Richard Brome: Place and Politics on the Caroline Stage* (Manchester: Manchester University Press, 2004), 115.

15   Richard Brome, *The Antipodes,* in *Three Renaissance Travel Plays* (*The Travels of the Three English Brothers; The Sea Voyage; The Antipodes*), ed. by Anthony Parr (Manchester: Manchester University Press, 2007), 220. All quotations from *The Antipodes* refer to this edition.

16   Brome, 1.1.22–24.

17   *Ibid.,* 1.1.44, 47, 63.

18   *Ibid.,* 1.1.79.

19   *Ibid.,* 1.1. 80–81.

> *Joyless*   But, pray, has he the art
>   To cure a husband's jealousy?
> *Blaze*   Mine, sir, he did – [*Aside*] 'Sfoot, I am catched again.[20]

The doctor then arrives and starts questioning the father as to the son's illness: first, whether it takes him by fits or if it is constant and always the same; and secondly, if it was born with him, if it was natural or accidental, and if either of the parents had ever been affected by such an illness.[21] The father's reference to the son's "travelling thoughts"[22] already betrays the source of Peregrine's "distraction", itself a loaded word in this context, whose Latin origin means to be drawn in different directions. The doctor proceeds to uncover "the ground of his distemper",[23] which he declares is "the next way to the cure",[24] and asks about Peregrine's studies or practises. Joyless then offers the following narrative:

> In tender years he always loved to read
> Reports of travels and of voyages.
> And when young boys like him would tire themselves
> With sports and pastimes and restore their spirits
> Again by meat and sleep, he would whole days
> And nights (sometimes by stealth) be on such books
> As might convey his fancy round the world.
> ...
>   When he grew up towards twenty,
> His mind was all on fire to be abroad.
> Nothing but travel still was all his aim;
> There was no voyage or foreign expedition
> Be said to be in hand, but he made suit
> To be made one in it. His mother and
> Myself opposed him still in all and, strongly
> Against his will, still held him in and won
> Him into marriage, hoping that would call
> In his extravagant thoughts. But all prevailed not,
> Nor stayed him – though at home – from travelling

---

20   *Ibid.*, 1.1.82–89.
21   *Ibid.*, 1.1.105–115.
22   *Ibid.*, 1.1.124.
23   *Ibid.*, 1.1.129.
24   *Ibid.*, 1.1.130.

So far beyond himself that now, too late,
I wish he had gone abroad to meet his fate.[25]

Freud might have been delighted to read this short case history. In fact, although Doctor Hughball proceeds by a method of questions and answers and,
therefore, a progressive uncovering, Brome makes it clear in the very first scene
of the first act where the origin of the problem lies, as opposed to Freud's own
narrative method, which, out of an alleged respect for chronology in the narra-
tion of the treatment, maintains suspense by managing to leave the uncovering of the condition's origin to the very end of the case history. Peregrine's case
history has several elements in common with some of Freud's cases: the origin
of the problem in childhood; the manifestation of a fixed idea in early adult-
hood; and, to be outrageously anachronistic, the outcome of a "neurosis" after a
series of acts of parental repression which frustrate the son's desire. Peregrine's
escape thus takes the form of a fantasy: allegedly he speaks of a "huge tympany
of news – of monsters,/Pygmies and giants, apes and elephants,/Griffins and
crocodiles, men upon women/And women upon men, the strangest doings".[26]

One of Freud's driving themes, sexuality, begins to be glimpsed in these
"men upon women/And women upon men". The play is packed with sexual
references and scenes, which is hardly surprising, but these become interesting as they relate to Doctor Hughball's project of enacting Peregrine's fantasies
in the "anti-London" of the play-within-the-play.[27] He first announces a journey to the Antipodes, said to be the exact opposite of London, drugs Peregrine
and wakes him up in this imaginary world of the play-within-the-play. Interestingly enough, Peregrine often refers to dreams in this context: after he awakes,
he laments having experienced his transportation to the Antipodes as "Mere
shadowy phantasms, or fantastic dreams"[28] and, after his cure, refers to his
condition as a dream, adding that he feels he has been "far transported in a
long/And tedious voyage of sleep".[29] The Antipodes themselves include such
perceived inversions as a Buff Woman[30] and a Man-Scold,[31] who refers to "the
chief [natural member] that man takes pleasure in, /The tongue!"[32] Peregrine

---

25   *Ibid.*, 1.1.131–150.
26   *Ibid.*, 1.1.178–181.
27   *Ibid.*, 2.2.38.
28   *Ibid.*, 2.2.11.
29   *Ibid.*, 5.2.313–314.
30   *Ibid.*, 3.1.160.
31   *Ibid.*, 4.1.131.
32   *Ibid.*, 4.1.150–151.

himself, referring to Mandeville, mentions the people of the Gadlibriens and their husbands' custom of hiring a man to couple with the bride "To clear the dangerous passage of a maidenhead",[33] for "She may be of that serpentine generation/That stings oft-times to the death (as Mandeville writes)",[34] in an allusion to the fear of the *vagina dentata*. Parallel to Peregrine's fantastic world, the spectators of the play-within-the-play and Letoy, the aristocrat who hosts the play, engage themselves in games of deception where betrayal and intimations of incest seem always on the verge of becoming real: Diana, Joyless' wife, confesses that, had not Peregrine been her husband's son, she might have offered herself up as the means of a carnal cure;[35] Diana is herself the object, first of Letoy's fictive sexual advances, and then of Letoy's revelation that she is in fact his daughter, given away in a fit of jealousy, as Letoy believed her to have been fathered by someone else.

Confronted with the onstage representation of his fantasies, Peregrine's cure is finally effected as he begins to exhibit an acceptable standard of normalcy which allows him to perceive the inversions of the Antipodes as mere fantasies: his exclamation "Sure these are dreams,/Nothing but dreams"[36] only seems to confirm the prediction that "He begins to govern/With purpose to reduce the manners of/This country to his own".[37] In fact, as Matthew Steggle has pointed out in *Richard Brome: Place and Politics on the Caroline Stage*, "the Antipodes function as a metaphor for the subconscious".[38] Steggle's preference for an un-freudian term, "subconscious" instead of "unconscious", does not hinder the suggestion of a Freudian reading.[39] Steggle, for instance, argues that Peregrine's problems may derive from the death of his mother, and that the characters' subconscious sexual urges are always on the verge of making a rampant entrance, sometimes even producing "almost physical symptoms".[40] Indeed, by performing Peregrine's fantasies of greatest inversion, the play-within-the-play

---

33   *Ibid.*, 4.1.465.

34   *Ibid.*, 4.1.467–468.

35   *Ibid.*, 4.1.514–524.

36   *Ibid.*, 4.1.158–159.

37   *Ibid.*, 3.1.320–322.

38   Steggle, 111.

39   Freud clearly refused the spatial understanding behind the term "subconscious", while insisting on the quality of absence or negation of consciousness as a defining trait of the unconscious: "what we have within us is not a second consciousness, but psychic acts that are devoid of consciousness. We can also reject the term 'subconsciousness' as incorrect and misleading". Sigmund Freud, *The Unconscious*, trans. Graham Frankland (London: Penguin, 2005), 54.

40   Steggle, 112.

stages a therapeutic journey to Peregrine's repressed and occult world, a world which, in the process, is brought to the light of knowledge and self-knowledge. The cure is a process which does not hinge on Peregrine simply being told of the unreality of his fantasies but demands that he acknowledge and work through his daydreams.

It's *Not* My Mother

To bring up Freud in the context of *The Antipodes* may come close to being an arbitrary choice, governed perhaps by Freud's lasting fame even after the relative demise of psychoanalysis. There is, after all, no causal relation, no direct link, between Brome and Freud. One finds here not only the anachronistic application, to use a blunt term, of Freud to Brome, but also perhaps the unfashionable use of Freud in a historical moment, ours, which has come to favour the much less offensive, and much more hygienic, discipline of psychology (and increasingly even neuroscience), while dropping some of psychoanalysis' still somewhat distasteful insistence on such things as libido and incest fantasies.[41] Even when psychoanalysis is used in an academic context, its practitioners will tend to favour Lacan's more abstract version at the expense of Freud's, which is felt to be too rooted in the culture of turn-of-the-century Vienna.[42] While the academia has duly historicised Freud, like everything else, popular culture, on the other hand, has turned the author of *The Joke and its Relation to the Unconscious* into the butt of the jokes of our superior age, "a reductive dirty joke"[43]

---

41   The theme of anal sexuality is a case in point. Despite the generalization of queer studies in our own time and the attention devoted to the question of sodomy in early modern studies, Jonathan Goldberg could still announce, in the opening note to the essay "The Anus in *Coriolanus*", and not without some amusement, that, when originally presented in 1994, the text of the paper, the manner of delivery and an illustration distributed among the members of the audience proved shocking to some. Jonathan Goldberg, "The Anus in *Coriolanus*", in *Historicism, Psychoanalysis, and Early Modern Culture*, ed. by Carla Mazzio and Douglas Trevor (New York: Routledge, 2000), 260–271.

42   For such a preference, but with a different rationale, see Stephen Greenblatt, *Learning to Curse: Essays in Early Modern Culture* (New York: Routledge, 2007), 191. See also Carla Mazzio and Douglas Trevor, "Dreams of History: An Introduction", in *Historicism, Psychoanalysis, and Early Modern Culture*, ed. by Carla Mazzio and Douglas Trevor (New York: Routledge, 2000), 1–18 (2).

43   Jeri Johnson, "Introduction", in Sigmund Freud, *The Psychology of Love*, trans. by Shaun Whiteside (London: Penguin, 2006), vii–xxvi (viii).

easily available in cartoons and films such as *Shakespeare in Love*.[44] Most of us probably just smile at Freud's cunning opening of the essay on "Negation" ("Die Verneinung"), in which his patient declares: "'You ask who this person in my dream can be. It's *not* my mother'. This we amend: 'So it is your mother'".[45] To engage Freud today as a medium of analysis and not as the object of analysis himself borders already on the untimely, if not on the anachronistic. There is indeed a difference between engaging Freud as an enabler of criticism, which implies suggesting that Freud can still be a relevant voice today, and dismissing him as a result of his historical context and personal quirks. In an obvious parody of Freud's own suspicious hermeneutic, historicist approaches to texts from the past may tend to look for hidden motivations and historical backdrop, while avoiding discussing whatever uses these texts may still hold for us now.

Replicating this very strategy, one might indeed wonder if the fear of anachronism might not be one of the reasons why a play such as *The Antipodes* has gathered so much scholarly effort in regard to its relation to theatrical performance, travel writing, and contemporary politics, but so little, in comparison, to its representation of psychiatry, which appears to constantly invite anachronistic reflections. Indeed, as Alexander Nagel and Christopher S. Wood have put it in *Anachronic Renaissance*, to look at a work of art for what it does as art, as opposed to grasping it "as a witness to its times, or as an inalienable trace of history", is to understand it as *anachronic*, as opposed to a work of art which is deemed anachronistic because, from an acutely historical perspective, it "appears to be out of step with [a stylistic] 'program'".[46] If we look at how *The Antipodes* "anachronises", to use Nagel and Wood's verb, we may perhaps find ways in which it challenges the norm of historical difference by responding particularly well to Freudian categories, for instance. If Freud did subject all manners of texts from the past to his methods, it is also probably true that he produced these methods not only from direct observation of patients but also from an attentive reading of older texts, including literary texts.[47] If we accept

---

44   At the beginning of the film, Will Shakespeare consults one Dr. Moth, announced as a "Seer, Apothecary, Alchemist, Astrologer", as well as "Interpreter of Dreams" and "Priest of Psyche". For a transcription and discussion of the relevant scene from *Shakespeare in Love*, see Philip Armstrong, *Shakespeare in Psychoanalysis* (London: Routledge, 2001), 1–3.

45   Freud, *The Unconscious*, 89.

46   Nagel and Wood, *Anachronic Renaissance*, 14.

47   For a discussion of Shoshana Felman's notion of the *mutual implication* between psychoanalysis and literature, rather than an *application* of psychoanalysis to literature, see Armstrong, 42–45. The following statement, posthumously attributed to Freud, suggests as much: "The poets and philosophers before me discovered the unconscious. What I discovered was the scientific method by which the unconscious can be studied". This famous

this not entirely absurd hypothesis, then we may indeed wonder what Freud would have made of a play such as *The Antipodes*, with its "medicine of the mind", its "travelling thoughts" and its "huge tympany of news – of monsters,/ Pygmies and giants, apes and elephants,/Gryphons and crocodiles, men upon women/And women upon men, the strangest doings".[48]

Upside-down

Bringing Freud to bear on an early modern play that he never knew of produces its own set of problems, as I have already suggested. Both Freud and Brome come into this essay as previously historicised material. What I am acknowledging here is not only the temporal and cultural distance between their texts and the present moment, but also the choice adopted here of analysing one historical text through another equally historical text, none of which might be said to occupy the position of an entirely valid means of analysis in contemporary academy. None of these texts can thus provide an academically dependable way into the other, as theorisations coming from post-colonialism, gender studies, or new historicism still do. Indeed, just as much a product of history as psychoanalysis, post-colonialism, gender studies, or new historicism have simply not yet acquired that historical alterity which marks a once legitimate approach as being well on its way to join Russian formalism or Anglo-American new criticism in the history of past literary theories. Moreover, another reason for the strangeness of the juxtaposition of Freud and Brome is the temporal and cultural distance between the authors themselves. To read *The Tempest* with the help of contemporaneous accounts of shipwrecks is one thing, but

---

quotation initially appeared without a source in Lionel Trilling's *The Liberal Imagination* (Garden City: Anchor Books, 1953), 32. Jeffrey Berman first located the quotation back to a reported conversation in Philip R. Lehrman's "Freud's Contributions to Science", *Harofé Haivri* I (1940), 161–176, and notes that Lerhman dated the statement in question to 1928. See Berman, *The Talking Cure: Literary Representations of Psychoanalysis* (New York: New York University Press, 1987), 304 n. 40. However, Berman does not provide a page number for the exact quotation in Lehrman and all other references are based on either Trilling or Berman, never directly on Lehrman. I too was unable to consult Lehrman's article and cannot therefore verify Berman's finding. The natural appeal of such a statement for literary critics and the fact that an alternative, more quotable version of it also exists, in which Freud allegedly says "Not I, but the poets discovered the unconscious", cannot but arouse suspicion.

48   Brome, 1.1.178–181.

cultural poetics begins to reach its breaking point in the combination of temporally distant texts.

However, to bring Freud into a reading of psychiatry in Brome's *The Antipodes* risks bringing with it more than might be wished for, namely an excess of interpretation. One might, therefore, begin to suspect that my essay's ironical replication of Freud's sometimes abusive hermeneutics of suspicion has itself replicated some of Freud's abuses. We could invoke Freud's *Fragment of an Analysis of Hysteria*, the Dora case which has done so much to undo his reputation and to expose him and his methods. As Jeri Johnson has pointed out,

> No work of Freud has so incited, or enticed, feminists to rage, to defence, or to intrigued elaboration, as this, marked as it is at points by a brisk, if Victorian, patriarchal peremptoriness (as when Freud refuses to believe that a healthy, fifteen-year-old girl would not respond favourably – and in kind – to the pressure on her groin of her father's lover's husband's unsolicited erection).[49]

If we now turn to *The Antipodes*, one can easily see that, apart from Peregrine's initial lack of sexual interest in his wife, his first sexually charged statement only comes up in act IV, when he expresses fear at the myth of the *vagina dentata*, that is, quite some time into Hughball's play within the play.[50] By this time, Hughball's play has already made all sorts of sexual suggestions, in what can be seen as a projection into Peregrine's delirium, much in the same way that Freud looked for sex in every case of mental illness that he found. If Freud found strange, and therefore symptomatic of neurosis, that Dora did not respond positively to the advances of a much older man, one might point out that Peregrine's disinterest in his wife is also interpreted as a sign of illness by Hughball.[51] Peregrine's sexual fear at the *vagina dentata* may thus simply be a response to Hughball's highly charged sexual suggestions.

---

49   Johnson, xx.

50   Another possible sexual fantasy, which I have already made mention of, "men upon women/And women upon men" (1.1.180–181), is significantly only reported by another character, Barbara.

51   Anthony Parr, who, in his edition of *Three Renaissance Travel Plays*, provides an excellent discussion of Brome's play, bearing on the relations between madness, travel, and spatiality, also points out that "Dr Hughball, driven by professional zeal, is determined to see mental disorder everywhere". Anthony Parr, "Introduction", in *Three Renaissance Travel Plays*, 1–54 (38).

Travelling Thoughts

Another way to understand psychology in this play might begin by looking again at Matthew Steggle's use of an unfreudian term, "subconscious" instead of "unconscious", when he argues that "the Antipodes function as a metaphor for the subconscious".[52] Steggle's choice of words can be taken seriously to suggest a spatial perspective: "subconscious" is a much more adequate word than "unconscious" here, because, in the popular misreading of Freud, the subconscious is what is underneath the conscious, much in the same way that the Antipodes are underneath – actually on the opposite side of – London. And *The Antipodes* is certainly rife with metaphors which interpret mental illness spatially.[53] In the first act alone, the contemporaneous moral discourse about man's proper place in the world can be detected in expressions like "such distracted ones", "travelling thoughts", "extravagant thoughts", and "travelling/So far beyond himself".[54] All these words, "distracted", "travelling", and "extravagant", have a spatial dimension which suggests that madness comes from wandering away from one's proper place. This only serves to accentuate the way the Antipodes function as a physical, geographical location of madness, a paradigmatic instance of the *topos* of the *mundus inversus*, or the world upside-down.[55] Because of its inverted location in relation to London, the Antipodes are the proper place for madness, although one of the points of the play-within-the-play will be to show that London itself, not just Anti-London, is also the site of equally unhinged actions and behaviours.

In a historicist account, the mention of the commonplace of the *mundus inversus* might be taken to historically ground in a sufficient manner the play's spatial understanding of mental disturbance. It would contribute to partially dispel the strangeness of Brome's text with the help of a cultural *topos* that was commonly available to him. However, if again one wishes to turn to twentieth-century psychoanalysis, a spatial interpretation similar to this one becomes available not so much in Freud's but in Carl Jung's research into the symbolism of the unconscious.[56] In his account of the hypothesis of the collective

---

52 Steggle, 111.

53 This spatially inflected language eventually crosses over into critical texts about the play, as when Julie Sanders explains that Peregrine has "*descended* into a kind of clinical depression" (my emphasis). Julie Sanders, *Caroline Drama: The Plays of Massinger, Ford, Shirley and Brome* (Plymouth: Northcote House, 1999), 53.

54 Brome, 1.1.21; 1.1.124; 1.1.147; 1.1.148–149.

55 See Sanders, 54, and Parr, 35.

56 This is not to deny the importance of spatial tropes in Freud's texts. The use of topographical vocabulary in Freudian psychoanalysis is well-known, from the notion of a topography

unconscious, Jung describes its relation to the personal unconscious as one of layering: the personal unconscious occupies a "more or less superficial layer", whereas the collective unconscious "rests upon a deeper layer".[57] One of Jung's symbols for the unconscious is that of water, more specifically a dark lake at the bottom of a valley. Jung explains this spatial symbol in the following manner:

> Water is the commonest symbol for the unconscious. The lake in the valley is the unconscious, which lies, as it were, underneath conscious-ness, so that it is often referred to as the "subconscious", usually with the pejorative connotation of an inferior consciousness.[58]

Although Jung systematically uses the term "unconscious", he acknowledges here the symbolic potential of this popularly accepted misreading. The force of spatial symbols even affects some of Jung's archetypes, namely those he calls archetypes of transformation. Differently from many of Jung's other, personalised archetypes, these "are not personalities, but are typical situa-tions, places, ways and means, that symbolise the kind of transformation in question".[59] Jung's interest in and exploration of these symbols of spatial lay-ering are certainly derived from his reading of alchemical and religious texts dating from the early modern period, and again one can only wonder what he might have made of Brome's play.[60]

Ultimately, the choice to read *The Antipodes* in a Freudian or perhaps a Jungian manner may partially hinge upon the play's precise use of words. The expression "travelling thoughts",[61] which appears both in the 1640 Quarto and

---

of the psyche and of depth psychology to Freud's impressive analogy between mental retention and the archaeology of Rome, in *Civilization and Its Discontents*. See Freud, *The Unconscious*, 56–57, 63. See also Sigmund Freud, *Civilization and Its Discontents*, trans. by David McLintock (London: Penguin, 2002), 7–9.

57   Carl G. Jung, *The Archetypes and the Collective Unconscious* (Abingdon, Oxon: Routledge, 1991), 3.

58   *Ibid.*, 18.

59   *Ibid.*, 38.

60   On a side note, one could speculate that Jung would most probably have been interested in Brome's forceful staging of such a political topos as that of the *mundus inversus* only four years before the beginning of the First Civil War, in 1642. In many of his works, Jung discussed what he considered to have been alarming psychological intimations of mo-ments of crisis, usually of a collective and archetypical nature. The most relevant essays dealing with this phenomenon are probably those having to do with the Second World War, which have been collected in Carl G. Jung, *Essays on Contemporary Events* (London: Routledge, 2002). See also Carl G. Jung, *Memories, Dreams, Reflections*, trans. by Richard and Clara Winston (London: Fontana Press, 1995), 199–201.

61   *Ibid.*, 1.1.131.

in Anthony Parr's edition of the play in the volume *Three Renaissance Travel Plays*, is differently edited by David Scott Kastan and Richard Proudfoot for the Globe Quartos collection. Here the expression appears as "travailing thoughts",[62] while the glossarial notes explain that "travailing" means "labouring".[63] This reading most probably finds its justification in the understanding that "travailing" is an early modern homophone of "travelling". The choice of word decisively influences interpretation: "travelling" suggests a spatial interpretation, whereas "travailing" suggests a more sexualised interpretation, in which, by going into labour, thoughts are either given birth to or themselves give birth to further wild notions. This word, "travailing", which is unseen but not left unheard, and which may indeed have been heard in 1638, during the play's performance in Salisbury Court theatre, encapsulates the ambivalence of *The Antipodes'* representations of psychiatry and mental illness. It may or may not have been there. It may have been lying hidden, waiting to be unlocked by David Scott Kastan and Richard Proudfoot, or it may have never existed outside the minds of these two editors. Ultimately, the editors' aural speculation may be historicised out of existence or it may be openly responded to.

Beside the Point

The reason why a psychoanalytic reading might seem pertinent in regard to a text such as Brome's is advanced by Stephen Greenblatt in his essay "Psychoanalysis and Renaissance Culture" (1986):

> An experience recurs in the study of Renaissance literature and culture: an image or text seems to invite, even to demand, a psychoanalytic approach and yet turns out to baffle or elude that approach.... The problem, I suggest, is that psychoanalysis is at once the fulfilment and effacement of specifically Renaissance insights: psychoanalysis is, in more than one sense, the end of the Renaissance.[64]

Rather than advance either one of the two main commonplaces in defence of applying psychoanalysis to early modern literature and culture, namely that this literature was ahead of its time, or that psychoanalytic theories are transhistorical and universal, Greenblatt simply points out that a historical link

---

62   Richard Brome, *The Antipodes*, ed. by David Scott Kastan and Richard Proudfoot, Globe Quartos (London: Nick Hern Books, 2000), 13, 1.1.124.

63   Brome, *The Antipodes*, 124.

64   Greenblatt, 176.

exists between the two, that psychoanalysis finishes what the Renaissance started. Though there is enough common ground between the two to ensure the psychoanalytic temptation, there is also a considerable amount of uncommon ground, which will always guarantee that the invitation to psychoanalyse can never be fully met. As Greenblatt readily admits in his discussion of the case of Martin Guerre,

> [These] latter conclusions, though they are ones with which I myself feel quite comfortable, are not ones drawn either explicitly or implicitly by anyone in the sixteenth century. They are irrelevant to the point of being unthinkable: no one bothers to invoke Martin's biological individuality or even his soul, let alone an infancy that would have seemed almost comically beside the point.[65]

Greenblatt rightly acknowledges the silence of historical records regarding precisely those explanations which we, from our contemporary perspective, would have most welcomed. This story, however, does not produce absolute otherness, but rather "intimations of an obscure link between those distant events and the way we are".[66] It is important that it be taken as a story, one in a series of signifying representations, neither a confirmation of the universalising grasp of psychoanalysis nor its utter rebuttal, or, in Greenblatt's words, "neither a universal myth nor a perfectly unique and autonomous event".[67] Somewhere between total universality and total particularity, Martin Guerre's story responds somewhat favourably, but never in a wholly committed manner, to invitations stemming from both positions.

Although running the danger of effacing the peculiarly Renaissance traits of texts such as Brome's play, psychoanalysis can, nevertheless, provide a point of entry into this text. By focusing on such things as slips of the tongue, fantasies that are taken seriously and the role of infancy – the account made by Peregrine's father indeed begins chronologically with Peregrine's "tender years"[68] – psychoanalysis *does* respond to certain aspects of the text which, according to early modern cultural historians, played no emblematic role in that culture. That these aspects may be "almost comically beside the point", that is, wholly unrepresentative of early modern culture, may well be true.

---

65   *Ibid.*, 182–183.
66   *Ibid.*, 186.
67   *Ibid.*, 187.
68   Brome, 1.1.131.

They are nevertheless to be found in this text. In fact, these elements offer such a striking superficial resemblance to aspects of Freud's psychoanalytic theories that it would be very awkward indeed were one to silence them merely for their embarrassingly anachronic quality. From this perspective, it would be historicism that would be effacing certain traits of a text for their not conforming to our current historical views of Renaissance psychiatry. As my text has also suggested, there are aspects of *The Antipodes* which do conform to our expectations regarding the Renaissance and these must evidently be taken into account. However, an exercise in anachronism such as this one may be a useful reminder that, historical determination notwithstanding, cultures also produce texts that do not represent them entirely and that such historically unrepresentative moments are by no means to be neglected as an object of study.

Works Cited

Armstrong, Philip. *Shakespeare in Psychoanalysis*. London: Routledge, 2001.

Bal, Mieke. *Quoting Caravaggio: Contemporary Art, Preposterous History*. Chicago: The U of Chicago P, 1999.

Berman, Jeffrey. *The Talking Cure: Literary Representations of Psychoanalysis*. New York: New York University Press, 1987.

Brome, Richard. *The Antipodes*, edited by David Scott Kastan and Richard Proudfoot. Globe Quartos. London: Nick Hern Books, 2000.

Brome, Richard. *The Antipodes*, in *Three Renaissance Travel Plays* (*The Travels of the Three English Brothers; The Sea Voyage; The Antipodes*), edited by Anthony Parr. Manchester: Manchester University Press, 2007.

Bruckner, Lynne, and Dan Brayton, eds. *Ecocritical Shakespeare*. Farnham and Burlington: Ashgate, 2011.

Butterfield, Herbert. *The Whig Interpretation of History*. New York: W.W. Norton & Company, 1965.

Charnes, Linda. *Hamlet's Heirs: Shakespeare and the Politics of a New Millenium*. London: Routledge, 2006.

DiPietro, Cary, and Hugh Grady (eds). *Shakespeare and the Urgency of Now: Criticism and Theory in the 21st Century*. Hampshire: Palgrave Macmillan, 2013.

Eliot, T.S. *Selected Prose of T.S. Eliot*, edited by Frank Kermode. London: Faber and Faber, 1987.

Fernie, Ewan, ed. *Spiritual Shakespeares*. London: Routledge, 2005.

Fischer, David Hackett. *Historians' Fallacies: Toward a Logic of Historical Thought*. New York: Harper Perennial, 1970.

Freud, Sigmund. *Civilization and Its Discontents*, translated by David McLintock. London: Penguin, 2002.

Freud, Sigmund. *The Unconscious*, translated by Graham Frankland. London: Penguin, 2005.

Gajowski, Evelyn (ed.). *Presentism, Gender, and Sexuality in Shakespeare*. London: Palgrave Macmillan, 2009.

Goldberg, Jonathan. "The Anus in *Coriolanus*". In *Historicism, Psychoanalysis, and Early Modern Culture*, edited by Carla Mazzio and Douglas Trevor. 260–271. New York: Routledge, 2000.

Grady, Hugh. *Shakespeare's Universal Wolf: Studies in Early Modern Reification*. Oxford: Clarendon Press, 1996.

Grady, Hugh. *Shakespeare, Machiavelli, and Montaigne: Power and Subjectivity from* Richard II *to* Hamlet. Oxford: Oxford UP, 2002.

Grady, Hugh. "Hamlet and the Present: Notes on the Moving Aesthetic 'Now'". In *Presentist Shakespeares*, edited by Hugh Grady and Terence Hawkes, 141–163. London: Routledge, 2007.

Grady, Hugh, and Terence Hawkes (eds). *Presentist Shakespeares*. London: Routledge, 2007.

Greenblatt, Stephen. *Learning to Curse: Essays in Early Modern Culture*. New York: Routledge, 2007.

Halpern, Richard. *Shakespeare among the Moderns*. Ithaca: Cornell UP, 1997.

Hawkes, Terence. *That Shakespeherian Rag: Essays on a Critical Process*. London: Methuen, 1986.

Hawkes, Terence. *Meaning by Shakespeare*. London: Routledge, 1992.

Hawkes, Terence. *Shakespeare in the Present*. London: Routledge, 2002.

Johnson, Jeri. "Introduction", in Sigmund Freud. *The Psychology of Love*, translated by Shaun Whiteside. vii–xxvi. London: Penguin, 2006.

Joughin, John J. "Shakespeare Now: An Editorial Statement". *Shakespeare*, I/1–2 (2005), 1–7.

Jung, Carl G. *The Archetypes and the Collective Unconscious*. Abingdon, Oxon: Routledge, 1991.

Jung, Carl G. *Memories, Dreams, Reflections*, translated by Richard and Clara Winston. London: Fontana Press, 1995.

Jung, Carl G. *Essays on Contemporary Events*. London: Routledge, 2002.

Kastan, David Scott. *Shakespeare after Theory*. New York: Routledge, 1999.

Lehrman, Philip R. "Freud's Contributions to Science". *Harofé Haivri* I (1940): 161–176.

Mazzio, Carla and Douglas Trevor. "Dreams of History: An Introduction", in *Historicism, Psychoanalysis, and Early Modern Culture*, edited by Carla Mazzio and Douglas Trevor. 1–18. New York: Routledge, 2000.

Munro, Lucy, "Shakespeare and the Uses of the Past: Critical Approaches and Current Debates". *Shakespeare*, VII/1 (2011), 102–125.

Nagel, Alexander and Christopher S. Wood. *Anachronic Renaissance*. New York: Zone Books, 2010.

O'Rourke, James. *Retheorizing Shakespeare through Presentist Readings*. London: Routledge, 2012.

Parr, Anthony. "Introduction", in *Three Renaissance Travel Plays* (*The Travels of the Three English Brothers; The Sea Voyage; The Antipodes*), edited by Anthony Parr. 1–54. Manchester: Manchester University Press, 2007.

Prawer, S.S. *A Cultural Citizen of the World: Sigmund Freud's Knowledge and Use of British and American Writings*. London: Legenda, 2009.

Sanders, Julie. *Caroline Drama: The Plays of Massinger, Ford, Shirley and Brome*. Plymouth: Northcote House, 1999.

Steggle, Matthew. *Richard Brome: Place and Politics on the Caroline Stage*. Manchester: Manchester University Press, 2004.

Tambling, Jeremy. *On Anachronism*. Manchester: Manchester UP, 2010.

Taylor, Gary. "Historicism, Presentism and Time: Middleton's *The Spanish Gypsy* and *A Game at Chess*". *Sederi*, XVIII (2008): 147–170.

Trilling, Lionel. *The Liberal Imagination*. Garden City: Anchor Books, 1953.

White, Hayden. *Metahistory: The Historical Imagination in Nineteenth-Century Europe*. Baltimore: The Johns Hopkins UP, 1975.

CHAPTER 3

A World of One's Own: Margaret Cavendish and the Science of Self-fashioning

Kate De Rycker

Abstract

Margaret Cavendish is well-known as a scientific philosopher who was excluded from the Royal Society, despite being the first woman to attend one of their meetings in 1667. Cavendish used this outsider status to question the Society's claims to authority and objectivity, and instead suggested that their experimental methods could be misused to construct scientific proof, by distortion of the senses. By reading Cavendish as addressing the construction of scientific knowledge, this essay will argue that her writing is resonant in the current academic climate, which has become increasingly self-reflective about the role of the researcher in making as well as communicating knowledge.

In 1665 Robert Hooke's bestselling *Micrographia* and the Royal Society's *Philosophical Transactions,* the oldest continuously published scientific journal, were first printed as part of the Society's campaign to garner public support for the "New Science". Two years later, on May 30, 1667, the Duchess of Newcastle, Margaret Cavendish, was to be the first woman invited to observe the experiments being conducted by the Royal Society.[1] An adherent of natural philosophy, Cavendish was however sceptical of this new methodology and its reliance on technology.

The publishing of *Micrographia* and Cavendish's visit occurred during an epistemological battle that was being fought in the early years of the Royal Society. On the one hand its members were trying to share their scientific discoveries with a wider audience, presenting themselves as a collective who were objectively reporting their experimentation with the latest scientific

---

1 She may have been the first to be invited inside the Society's hallowed grounds, but it would not be until 1945 that women were allowed to become Fellows of the Society. Today, women make up only 5 per cent of overall fellowship, a surprisingly low figure, even with the underwhelming caveat that 10 per cent of new fellows within the past ten years have been women.

© KONINKLIJKE BRILL NV, LEIDEN, 2018 | DOI 10.1163/9789004349360_006

technology. On the other, for Cavendish this technological progress meant not so much an opening up of horizons, but instead the closing down of opportunities for women such as herself to participate in the cutting edge of science. While she was living in Paris during the Interregnum, Cavendish had found herself at the centre of a scientific salon which became an "unofficial university of mechanical philosophy", where she met such luminaries as René Descartes, Thomas Hobbes, and Pierre Gassendi.[2] Now, Cavendish's exclusion from male-only membership of the Royal Society meant that she like many others was rendered an observer rather than a contributor to the New Science. Refusing to accept this, Cavendish went on the offensive, publishing her *Observations upon Experimental Philosophy* together with the utopian fiction *The Blazing World* in 1666, in which she attempted to engage with the New Science, while simultaneously undermining the Royal Society's epistemological claims of objectively relating their experiments to the public.

Mad Madge

Unfortunately for Cavendish, many of her contemporaries agreed that she was an eccentric, and ridiculed her for her ambition to be a philosopher and author. In Dorothy Osborne's letters to her future husband, William Temple, she refers to Cavendish's newly published *Poems, and Fancies* (1653) as indicating that "the poor woman is a little distracted, she could never be so ridiculous else as to venture at writing books, and in verse too. If I should not sleep this fortnight I should not come to that". In a later letter, she remarks that "there are soberer people in Bedlam" and that Cavendish's "friends are much to blame

---

2 Cavendish's intellectual connections and philosophy have been dealt with in a number of studies, most fully by Katie Whitaker, *Mad Madge: The Extraordinary Life of Margaret Cavendish, Duchess of Newcastle, The First Woman to Live by her Pen* (New York: Basic Books, 2002) and Anna Battigelli, *Margaret Cavendish and the Exiles of the Mind* (Lexington: The University Press of Kentucky, 1998). Further to this are Lisa T. Sarasohn, *The Natural Philosophy of Margaret Cavendish: Reason and Fancy During the Scientific Revolution* (Baltimore: John Hopkins University Press, 2010); Sarah Hutton, "In Dialogue with Thomas Hobbes: Margaret Cavendish's Natural Philosophy", *Women's Writing*, IV (1997), 421–32; Elizabeth Spiller, "Books written of the wonders of these glasses: Thomas Hobbes, Robert Hooke, and Margaret Cavendish's Theory of Reading", in *Science, Reading, and Renaissance Literature* (Cambridge: Cambridge University Press, 2004), 137–177; Lisa Walters, *Margaret Cavendish: Gender, Science, and Politics* (Cambridge: Cambridge University Press, 2014).

to let her go abroad".[3] Osborne's words echo the contemporary disdain that a woman may wish to have her writing read by the public. The wish to publish was seen as a transgression of the line between private and public sphere, and so Cavendish was judged to be mad. This label stuck with Cavendish long after it became acceptable for women to seek publication, as we can see in Virginia Woolf's description of her in *A Room of One's Own* (1929) as "hare-brained, fantastical Margaret", a woman unable and unwilling to tame her overflowing genius into an acceptable form. "What a waste", thinks Woolf, that Cavendish "frittered her time away scribbling nonsense and plunging ever deeper into obscurity and folly till the people crowded round her coach when she issued out. Evidently, the crazy Duchess became a bogey to frighten clever girls with".[4]

If contemporaries like Dorothy Osborne claimed that the Duchess was "a little distracted", Cavendish certainly lived up to this reputation. In the epistle attached to the end of *The World's Olio* (1655) she informs her reader that:

> I know, my Book is neither wise, witty, nor methodical, but various and extravagant ... for I have not tyed myself to any one Opinion, for sometimes one opinion crosses another and in so doing, I do as most several Writers do; onely they contradict one and another, and I contradict, or rather please my-self, with the varieties of Opinions whatsoever.[5]

There are two main points to highlight from this excerpt. Firstly, an issue which she would return to later in *Observations* is apparent here more than a decade earlier, namely, that her male contemporaries "contradict one another" but crucially do not acknowledge that their disagreement means that there is a plurality of perceptions and opinions. Secondly, she is also foreseeing and disarming any potential criticism that her work is disorganised by levelling the criticism at herself first.

By admitting her own tendency to contradict herself, however, Cavendish made it easy for others to patronise her by declaring her mad and therefore unaccountable for what she wrote. It was this presentation of an untutored mind that Woolf pounced on as an illustration for what happens when naturally gifted women are not properly educated: "As it was, what could bind, tame or civilise for human use that wild, generous, untutored intelligence? It

---

3 Dorothy Osborne, *Dorothy Osborne: Letters to Sir William* Temple, ed. Kenneth Parker (Aldershot: Ashgate, 2002), 89, 94.

4 Virginia Woolf, *A Room of One's Own* (Peterborough: Broadview Press, 2001), 74, 75.

5 Margaret Cavendish, *The World's Olio, written by the Right Honorable, the Lady Margaret Newcastle* (London: Printed for J. Martin and J. Allestrye, 1655), sig.T3r.

poured itself out, higgledy-piggledy, in torrents of rhyme and prose, poetry and philosophy".[6]

We could say, then, that Cavendish's rhetorical strategy created her lacklustre reputation as an author. For the purposes of my argument, however, I want to return to my first point, that whatever the ultimate consequences were, at the time Cavendish was presenting her world view as a viable alternative to those of her male contemporaries. Indeed, her claim is not just that her view is an alternative, but rather a superior option, as she understands the world better than other writers for seeing it holistically rather than myopically. She acknowledges that her mind is changeable, and implies that "other writers" meanwhile are wrong to stay firm in their opinions, as they only end up arguing among themselves. It is here that we see the beginnings of her campaign for a stake in the scientific debate that surrounded her.

A Self-reflective Style

In her attempt to be a participant in the scientific debate of the time, Cavendish constructed a public persona which would not allow for her to be ignored, in either her writing style or her choice of dress. Remarkably self-aware, Cavendish had noticed that the members of the Royal Society were equally culpable of fashioning public personas for themselves, claiming to be purveyors of "truth" and "reason".

Cavendish began her campaign for recognition by claiming that her authority derived not from learning, but from her natural genius. The proto-feminist Bathsua Makin wrote in 1673 that Cavendish, "by her own Genius, rather than any timely Instruction, over-tops many grave Gown-men",[7] while, as we have seen, Woolf wondered what would have happened to Cavendish had she had access to education: "No one checked her. No one taught her".[8] Yet both Makin and Woolf were misled, as Margaret had been lucky to have access to a unique education. In addition to taking part in her husband's scientific salon in Paris, Cavendish, while portraying herself as an unlearned and natural thinker, also wrote that both her husband and her brother-in-law, William and Charles Cavendish, had helped her to read various works, "expounding the hard and obscure passages therein". She acknowledges that had she not met William,

---

6   Woolf, *A Room of One's Own*, 74.

7   Bathsua Makin, *An Essay to Revive the Antient Education of Gentlewomen*, ed. Paula L. Barbour (Los Angeles: University of California, 1980), 10.

8   Woolf, *A Room of One's Own*, 74.

she would have been "inclosed from the world, in some obscure place ... having not the liberty to see the World, nor conversation to hear of it, I should never have writ of so many things".[9]

Once she did begin to write nothing could stop her, as twenty three works, from plays, romances and poetry, to letters, biographies and treaties, poured forth. As Dorothy Osborne's letter implies, this propensity for writing was seen as a form of madness by others. As ever, Cavendish managed to turn this slight to her advantage in the preface to her *Observations*:

> It is probable, some will say, that my much writing is a disease; but what disease they will judge it to be, I cannot tell ... they will take it to be a disease of the brain; but surely they cannot call it an apoplectical or lethargic disease: Perhaps they will say, it is an extravagant, or at least a fantastical disease; but I hope they will rather call it a disease of wit.[10]

She continues that, if it is a disease, then she is in good company, naming such greats as Aristotle, Homer, and St. Augustine in her list of fellow sufferers. Here, she has turned the argument around to align herself with authoritative men, and indeed underlines her own ambitions: "Now, to be infected with the same disease ... is no disgrace; but the greatest honour that can happen to the most ambitious person in the world".[11]

Her contemporaries saw Cavendish's "disease[d] mind" materialised in her unusual dress-sense. The diarist John Evelyn writes of visiting the Cavendish home and being entertained with "the extraordinary fancifull habit, garb, & discourse of the Dutchesse".[12] Much like her pose as a scattered, uneducated genius, Cavendish may have used this eccentric fashion as a barrier between herself and the outside world; rather be mocked for your appearance than your thoughts.[13]

For her visit to the Royal Society in May 1667, Cavendish dressed in a wide cavalier hat and a just-au-corps, a new fashion from France of a knee-length

---

9   Cavendish, *World's Olio*, 47.

10   Margaret Cavendish, "The Preface to the Ensuing Treatise", in *Observations Upon Experimental Philosophy*, ed. Eileen O'Neill (Cambridge: Cambridge University Press, 2001), 7.

11   *Ibid.*

12   John Evelyn, *The Diary of John Evelyn*, vol. 3, ed. E.S. de Beer (Oxford: Clarendon Press, 1955), 478.

13   On Cavendish's public persona, see Mona Narain, "Notorious Celebrity: Margaret Cavendish and the Spectacle of Fame", *The Journal of the Midwest Modern Language Association*, XLII/2 (2009), 69–95.

coat fitted at the waist, usually worn by men. Her transgression of wearing masculine clothes is again documented by Evelyn, who wrote:

> I was half afeared,
> God bless us! When I first did see her:
> She looked so like a Cavalier,
> But That she had no beard[14]

Samuel Pepys, another visitor, meanwhile describes his disappointment at the discrepancy between her appearance ("so antick") and her behaviour ("deportment so ordinary ... [he did not] hear her say anything that was worth hearing, but that she was full of admiration"). In Arundel House, the then meeting place of the Society, Pepys describes how "very much company" had gathered "in expectation of the Duchesse of Newcastle".[15] Having been invited as a spectator, Cavendish was clearly also the main spectacle.

Her cavalier costume can be explained partly as a tribute to her husband, who was a famed general in Charles I's army, but it also shows her allegiance to the former queen, Henrietta Maria, in whose exiled court Margaret had spent the first years of the Interregnum. Henrietta Maria had described herself as a warrior queen, a "she-majesty generalissima", and took on an Amazonian persona in the entertainments of her exiled court as a show of military solidarity with her husband.[16] Echoing this in her play *Bell in Campo* (1662), Cavendish's heroine Lady Victoria leads an army of women to rescue her husband and his men from the enemy.

For both women, their presentation as cavalier wives is a sign of support for their husbands, but Cavendish's costume serves an additional purpose: it is a form of armour within the entirely male space of Arundel House, indicating to them that she is a strong woman, and equal to the men of the Royal Society. Her preface to *The Blazing World* notoriously presents Cavendish in

---

14   John Evelyn, quoted in Emma L.E. Rees, *Margaret Cavendish: Gender, Genre, Exile* (Manchester: Manchester University Press, 2003), 13.

15   Samuel Pepys, *The Diary of Samuel Pepys: A Selection* (London: Penguin, 2003), 780–781.

16   Henrietta Maria describes herself as the "she-majesty generalissima" in a letter to Charles I, on June 27, 1643, when she tells him that she is moving "3000 foot[soldiers], 30 companies of horse and dragoons, 6 pieces of cannon, and two mortars" to Newark. Quoted in Agnes Strickland and Elizabeth Strickland, *Lives of the Queens of England from the Norman Conquest* (Cambridge: Cambridge University Press, 2010), 302. See Karen Britland, *Drama at the Courts of Queen Henrietta Maria* (Cambridge: Cambridge University Press, 2006) for more on Henrietta Maria as Amazonian queen.

military terms, as a female warrior able to create worlds through the powers of her imagination:

> Though I cannot be Henry the Fifth, or Charles the Second, yet I endeavour to be Margaret the First; and although I have neither power, nor time nor occasion to conquer the world as Alexander and Caesar did; yet rather then not to be Mistress of one, since Fortune and the Fates would give me none, I have made a World of my own: for which no body, I hope, will blame me, since it is in every ones power to do the like.[17]

Cavendish's famous visit to the Royal Society took place one year after she had published her *Observations* in which she had criticised (even if she did not specifically name) the Society's methodology. Her work was met with silence from the Society's members. The visit did nothing to alleviate the tension between the two camps, and the next year Cavendish re-published an edited version of her scientific treaty, once again printed alongside *The Blazing World*. Here the men of the Royal Society, who had made a spectacle of her, were represented under her own terms, as subjects of Empress Margaret.

Authority Claims

Through her dress and prefaces to her writing, Cavendish had presented herself as a female cavalier, empowering herself within a man's world. At the same time, her dual publication would attempt to expose her male counterparts as megalomaniacs desirous of scientific dominion. In *Observations,* Cavendish accuses the members of the Royal Society of dismantling the work of ancient philosophers, like "those unconscionable men in civil wars, which endeavour to pull down the hereditary mansions of noblemen and gentlemen, to build a cottage of their own; for, so do they pull down the learning of ancient authors, to render themselves famous in composing books of their own".[18] Her analogy of the disruption wrought by the Civil War is not surprising, coming from a Royalist who had suffered what we would now describe as depression caused by the upheaval of a life in exile.

---

17   Margaret Cavendish, prefatory letter to "The Blazing World", in *The Description of a New World, called the Blazing World and other Writings,* ed. Kate Lilley (London: Pickering and Chatto, 1992), 124.

18   Cavendish, *Observations,* 8.

Although she accuses the adherents of the New Science of being destructive, it is actually she who intentionally levels their work by deconstructing their epistemological concerns with attaining a perfect, objective approach to scientific investigation. Such an approach began with their use of language. Thomas Sprat, the writer of *The History of the Royal Society* (1667), had claimed that the Society was shaping a resolutely plain style for a new epoch of scientific writing, following the precedent of Francis Bacon. This involved the removal of rhetorical tropes, which were considered to be "in open defiance against Reason [and] they give the mind a motion too changeable and bewitching to consist with right practice".[19] One of the Society's leading lights, Robert Boyle, exemplified this use of the new "rational" manner of writing, described his style as a "naked way of writing" which eschewed the more "florid" rhetorical mode, and instead emphasises the functionality of science writing.[20]

Cavendish pointed out, however, that the writing of Royal Society members was not at all "plain", but filled with jargon or "hard words". If old rhetorical tropes had been removed for their lack of clarity, then Sprat and others were simply replacing them with a new form of rhetoric which was just as obscure. By arguing for clarity in scientific writing, Cavendish was much more in tune with the methodology of New Science than she may have cared to admit, as Richard Nate observed.[21] In full "natural genius" mode, Cavendish claims that her work, though it may appear uneducated and whimsical, is written with clarity in mind, "For, what benefit would it be to me, if I should put forth a work which by reason of its obscure and hard notions, could not be understood?"[22]

In searching for similarities, however, Nate elides two separate aspects of "clarity" that the two parties profess. Sprat et al imagine clarity to be the opposite of a highly stylised, metaphorical form of language. When Sprat outlines this in his *History*, he genders clarity as "masculine" and "native", as opposed to "feminine" and "foreign": "as the Feminine Arts of Pleasure and Gallantry have spread some of our neighbouring Languages to such a vast Extent; so the English Tongue may also in Time be more enlarg'd, by being the Instrument of

---

19   Thomas Sprat, *The History of the Royal Society of London, for the Improving of Natural Knowledge* (London: Printed for John Martyn, 1667), 112.

20   Robert Boyle, *Proëmial Essay ... with Some Considerations touching Experimental Essays in General* (1661), quoted in Steven Shapin, "Pump and Circumstance: Robert Boyle's Literary Technology", *Social Studies of Science*, XIV/4 (1984), 481–520 (495).

21   Richard Nate, "'Plain and vulgarly express'd': Margaret Cavendish and the Discourse of the New Science", *Rhetorica*, XIX/4 (2001), 403–417, esp. 408.

22   Cavendish, *Observations*, 11.

conveying to the World the Masculine Arts of Knowledge".[23] I would argue that, in comparison, Cavendish does not contrast "clarity" with "florid language", but instead contrasts it with the jargon-heavy, specialist language that alienates readers such as herself. Sprat is worried about achieving accurate and objective scientific writing, while Cavendish is concerned about making scientific discourse understandable to non-specialists.

Cavendish claims that writers of philosophy intentionally use "hard words" to "obstruct" people like herself from understanding them, creating a shibboleth for readers. "The truth is", she writes,

> if anyone intends to write Philosophy, either in English, or any other language; he ought to consider the propriety of the language as much as the Subject he writes of, or else to what purpose would it be to write? ... if you will write for those that do not understand Latin ... you must explain those hard words, and English them in the easiest manner you can. What are words but marks of things? And what are Philosophical Terms, but to express the Conceptions of one's mind in that Science?[24]

Writing should be clear, but this clarity is not obtained by the followers of the New Science, Cavendish implies. They may claim that the Society's writing is intended to be "plain", but this is purely an authority claim. "Instead of making hard things easy" they intentionally "make easy things hard". She sees no "reason for it, but that they think to make themselves more famous by those that admire all what they do not understand, though it be nonsense".[25]

Cavendish was of course making her own authority claim, and so she continues to argue that, in contrast to these philosophers, she

> shun[s hard words] as much in my writing as is possible for me to do, and all this, that they may be the better understood by all, learned as well as unlearned. [I will not] deceive the World, nor trouble my Conscience by being a Mountebanck in learning, but rather prove naturally wise

---

23   Sprat, 129. Nate does acknowledge this gendered language, but as his argument is that
       Cavendish is influenced by the Royal Society, he places less emphasis on the significance
       of gendered language than Denise Tillery, who differentiates between Cavendish and
       the Royal Society's different intentions behind the use of "plain" language. See Tillery,
       "'English them in the easiest manner you can': Margaret Cavendish on the Discourse and
       Practice of Natural Philosophy", *Rhetoric Review*, XXVI/3 (2007), 268–285.
24   Cavendish, *Observations*, 12.
25   *Ibid.*

then artificially foolish; for at best I should but obscure my opinions, and render them more intricate instead of clearing and explaining them.[26]

It is she, Cavendish suggests, who is the true promoter of natural philosophy, not the members of the Royal Society. The lack of interest in her published work thwarted any hopes of influence she may have had. However, this should not undermine Cavendish's epistemological point, which was that, by claiming to write objectively and unemotionally, members of the Royal Society were themselves using a rhetorical pose.

The Royal Society's insistence on a clear, plain writing style to convey their findings was only one part of a campaign to promote the New Science as the right manner in which to conduct scientific investigation. As Steven Shapin has argued, the Society's publication of their findings was a way not only of publicising the New Science, but also a way of multiplying the amount of "virtual witnesses" necessary to give authority to these findings.

> The technology of virtual witnessing involves the production in a reader's mind of such an image of an experimental scene as obviates the necessity for either its direct witness or its replication. [Publication] was therefore the most powerful technology for constituting matters of fact. The validation of experiments, and the crediting of their outcomes as matters of fact, necessarily entailed their realization in the laboratory of the mind and the mind's eye. What was required was a technology of trust and assurance that the things had been done and done in the way claimed.[27]

The New Science was to be a project of collective endeavour, which acknowledged that no single scientist could claim absolute knowledge. The results of experimentation were instead to speak for themselves, through the author dispassionately relating his experiments to the "virtual witness".

However, while Robert Boyle especially was trying to use publication to open up the proceedings of the Royal Society to people outside of its limited membership, Elizabeth Spiller reminds us that this wider audience of "virtual witnesses" was not meant to include women like Cavendish. Because of her exclusion not only literally from partaking in the experiments, but also figuratively by having her work ignored by the very men that she wished to engage

---

26   *Ibid.*
27   Shapin, "Pump and Circumstance", 491.

in a dialogue, Cavendish's line of defence was to point out that this "virtual witnessing" and sense of inclusion in the experiments was only an illusion.[28]

Together with the reports of experiments written in minute detail in the *Philosophical Transactions* journal, Robert Hooke's *Micrographia* was commissioned by the Royal Society to showcase their new methodology and reassure the public of the accuracy of the experiments being described. In the second dedicatory letter, Hooke emphasises the benefits of the methodology introduced by the New Science: "The Rules YOU have prescrib'd YOUR selves in YOUR Philosophical Progress do seem the best that have ever yet been practis'd. And particularly that of avoiding *Dogmatizing*, and the *espousal* of any *Hypothesis* not sufficiently grounded and confirm'd by *Experiments*".[29]

The *Micrographia* is at the same time a very literary, self-conscious text. Hooke's first "observation" is of the point of a needle, but soon he crosses over to a more literary "point", "the mark of a full stop", and shows how, though to our eyes the punctuation mark looks round, when magnified it "appeared to be rough, jagged, and uneven all about its edges". Handwritten marks "look but like so many furrows and holes; and their printed impressions, but like smutty daubing on a mat, or uneven floor, made with a blunt extinguished brand".[30]

Hooke's observation highlights the fact that, with a changed perspective, our understanding of the construction of something as simple as a punctuation mark can be altered. This is, of course, the entire point of using an instrument like a microscope or a telescope, but Cavendish latched onto this issue of perspective to undermine Hooke's claims to scientific objectivity. For Hooke, the microscope could uncover nature's secrets, and so in truth the punctuation mark is jagged, not smooth. For Cavendish, meanwhile, the microscope does not uncover any hidden truth, but rather provides a warped perspective which creates a new way of seeing things, interpreted primarily through the imagination.

Perception

More than a hundred pages in *Observations* are filled with a discussion of the inability of humans to perceive accurately, whether with the aid of optical instruments or not. This, Cavendish argues, is because sight must

---

28   Spiller, esp. 141, 151.

29   Robert Hooke, "To the Royal Society", in *Micrographia: or some Physiological Descriptions of Minute Bodies Made by Magnifying Glasses with Observations and Inquiries thereupon* (London: for John Martyn, 1667). All further references are to this edition.

30   *Ibid.*, 3.

be interpreted by the mind of the individual, and therefore there is always space for misinterpretation. The subjectivity of the observer that comes with the distance between sense and thought is at the crux of Cavendish's argument against the Royal Society. Art as much as science informs their study: "a Lowse by the help of a Magnifying-glass, appears like a Lobster.... The truth is, the more the figure by Art is magnified, the more it appears mis-shapen from the natural".[31] *The Blazing World* continues Cavendish's argument when she discusses with her own "virtual witnesses", that is, the users of telescopes and microscopes, the "Bear-men" of this alternate dimension, what they believe to be seeing in their "glasses". They tell the Empress that their microscopes "never delude, but rectify and inform their senses".[32] The Bear-men are so enamoured of their technological equipment that when the Empress demands that their telescopes be broken, they beg her "that they might not be broken, for, said they, we take more delight in Artificial delusions, than in natural truths".[33]

Of course, we would say that microscopes and telescopes do not distort reality; we are well aware that a louse is not, in fact, a lobster, even if it appears so under the microscope. What Cavendish does appear to be saying, however, is that optical equipment may give a false sense of security to the observer, so that they fetishise the object, and rely on it so heavily that they remove themselves from the interpretive process. In contrast, Hooke claims in the preface to his *Micrographia* that the microscope *restores* human sight to its pre-Adamite condition:

> in respect of the Senses, [it] is a supplying of their infirmities with *Instruments*, and, as it were, the adding of *artificial Organs* to the *natural*; ... in every *little particle* of its matter, we now behold almost as great a variety of Creatures, as we were able before to reckon up in the whole *Universe* itself.[34]

By using equipment such as telescopes and microscopes, the new scientists were imagining themselves to be finding out the objective truth of their surroundings, which concerned Cavendish because they used this sense of power to make truth-claims about the natural world.[35]

---

31   Cavendish, *Observations*, 50.

32   Cavendish, *The Blazing World*, 143.

33   *Ibid.*, 142.

34   Hooke, *Micrographia*, "Preface", sig.b1r–v.

35   See Eve Keller, "Producing Petty Gods: Margaret Cavendish's Critique of Experimental Science", *English Literary History*, LXIV (1997), 447–471, especially 454, on Cavendish's suspicion that optical glasses distorted the senses.

Ultimately Cavendish suggests that visual evidence, whether it be distorted or accurate, is still being interpreted by a human mind: you cannot remove the role of the imagination.[36] Interestingly, Hooke acknowledges this issue when defending the accuracy of his illustrations. In his preface he claims that "the [en]gravers have pretty well follow'd my directions and draughts", and that his images give a "plain representation" of the "true appearance" of what he saw through his microscope. He admits, however, that "there is much more diffi-culty to discover the true shape, then of those visible to the naked eye, the same Object seeming quite differing in one position to the Light, from what it really is, and may be discover'd in another". After this sentence, however, Hooke begins to use a rhetoric of utter certainty: "And therefore I never began to make any draught before by many examinations in several lights, and in several positions to those lights, I had discovered the *true form*".[37]

Hooke believes that while it is possible to distort an image, it is a trick of the light which can be corrected. For him, the mind's distortions are not an issue. Boyle too argues that "the Study of Physiology is not only Delightful, as it teaches us to Know Nature, but also as it teaches us in many Cases to *Master and Command her ... Dominion ...* is a Power that becomes Man as Man".[38] This gendered description of man's scientific discovering of Nature's secrets is especially disconcerting for Cavendish, who writes that "Man has a great spleen against self-moving corporeal Nature, although himself is part of her, and the reason is his *Ambition*; for he would fain be supreme and above all other Creatures, as more towards a divine Nature: he would be a God".[39]

Cavendish declares that the true desire of men like Hooke and Boyle is to have a godlike authority over nature, claiming that "the bare authority of an Experimental Philosopher is sufficient to them to decide all Controversies, and to pronounce the Truth without any appeal to Reason; as if they onely had the Infallible Truth of Nature, and ingrossed all knowledge to themselves".[40] Cav-endish is arguing what modern critics such as Spiller and Shapin are discussing today, that the production and communication of knowledge are heavily in-terwoven, and that there is no way for the observer to stand outside of nature.

This is backed up in research by Alan Hogarth and Mike Witmore, who, in an as yet unpublished article on the Society's "plain style", used a text-analysis

---

36   For more on this theory of perception, see Spiller, 148–160.

37   Hooke, *Micrographia*, "Preface", sig.f2v.

38   Robert Boyle, *Some Considerations Touching the Usefulnesse of Experimental Naturall Philosophy* (Oxford: printed by Henry Hall, 1663), 19.

39   Cavendish, *Observations*, 209.

40   *Ibid.*, 196.

programme, Docuscope, to examine 1,979 scientific texts of the period. This processing of "big data" unearthed "the covert presence of 'subjective' rhetorical feature". Their finding that, for example, Robert Boyle used much more tentative and contingent language than would have been expected "appears to jar with the prescriptions on style and method explicitly laid out by Boyle and adopted as a mantra of the Royal Society".[41] The question they raise through this discovery is whether the drive to narrate is stronger than the desire to present work as a collective endeavour.

Conclusion

Cavendish should not be understood only as an outsider speaking truth to the power of the Royal Society. She wished to be taken seriously as a philosopher, and was therefore not only trying to undermine the authority of these men, but to grab another form of authority by representing herself as an intuitive, natural genius. What provoked Cavendish was that she was being locked out of a discourse that she so wished to be a part of. With the New Science came new methodologies and a new reliance on equipment and experiments that were inaccessible to her. Worse, she had been paraded around the Royal Society, shown experiments as if they were magic tricks, but was never invited to make use of them herself. To repeat what Virginia Woolf said of Cavendish, "She should have had a microscope put in her hand".[42] By trying to undermine the efficacy of these new instruments, and by emphasising the subjectivity of any evidence they provided, Cavendish was trying to bring herself back into this discourse, as an interpreter of the scientific discussion that was taking place.

For Cavendish, the only power available to her was through writing. If men like Hooke and Boyle could create new worlds beyond the scope of the human eye, then so could she, declaring herself "Margaret the First", creator of new worlds. If they had described their discoveries as a form of dominion over nature, Cavendish would describe her work as a martial conquest over a terrain unblemished by their investigations. She aligns herself with great kings and emperors, differing from them only in gender, not in ambition. Her campaign against the Royal Society may have failed, but along the way she had made a dent in their armour.

---

41   Alan Hogarth, & Mike Witmore, *The Subject as Object: Boyle, the Royal Society and Scientific Style* (2016). Manuscript submitted for publication.

42   Woolf, *A Room of One's Own*, 74.

Cavendish's attempt to engage with the debate was met with silence from the Royal Society and the rest of her contemporaries. In turn, Cavendish symbolically silenced her adversaries by refusing to name them in her *Observations*, instead grouping them together as "experimental philosophers". When she does allow them a voice it is not in the scientific tract, a world and language which they know, but in her own *Blazing World*. While she was only allowed to see, but not participate in their experiments in Arundel House, here Cavendish dramatises their discussion, and her responses to them. By doing so, she creates a space for her voice within the discourse of the New Science, which in truth she was never afforded.

I would also argue that the high level of self-awareness that Cavendish shows in her writing may result from her status as a woman writer, constantly having to justify her ambition to publish her own work in the numerous "letters to the reader" that accompany her various books. By doing so, she is already in a position of having to argue for her right to be included in scientific debates with her male counterparts. She is also used to the idea of being a spectacle, and of the potential for a person to fashion herself in multiple ways. In *The Blazing World* Cavendish creates multiple worlds, and multiple selves by dividing herself into three perspectives, both outside the main narrative as the author, and inside the narrative as the Empress of the Blazing World, and as the Duchess of Newcastle, whom the Empress employs as her secretary after it transpired that Aristotle, Galileo and Descartes are "so self-conceited, that they would scorn to be scribes to a woman".[43] This multiplication of selves suggests that Cavendish is not only highly self-reflective, in contrast to Hooke's attempt to distance himself from what he observes via the microscope, but also that she is fully aware that there is a variety of possible perspectives, even within one person. This, together with her awareness of holding conflicting opinions in *The World's Olio*, adds up to Cavendish being a seventeenth-century example of the self-reflective observer, the importance of which scholars across the humanities are becoming ever more aware of today.

Since his iconoclastic *Metahistory* (1973), Hayden White has identified the use of rhetorical devices by historians in narrating past events, while simultaneously presenting their accounts as being almost scientific in their objectivity. White suggested that by not openly acknowledging that in first selecting their sources, and secondly constructing a narrative from them, academics were not merely reporting history but remaking it in their own image. Since White,

---

43   Cavendish, *The Blazing World*, 181. On Cavendish's multiple selves and subjectivity see Catherine Gallagher, "Embracing the Absolute: The Politics of the Female Subject in Seventeenth-Century England", *Genders*, 1 (1988), 24–39.

scholars have become ever more aware of the determinism of much academic writing, as is the case of Michael Wener and Bénédicte Zimmermann's theory of *histoire croisée*. Amongst the problems that they identified with comparative history, was that the position of the academic or observer was assumed to be external to the historical events or objects being compared. Instead, Werner and Zimmermann suggest that the historian must always acknowledge that they are always within the object that they observe, and that therefore "His or her position is thus off center".[44]

Interestingly, Werner and Zimmermann use similar metaphors to Hooke and Cavendish. In producing the fairest observation, the historian must "see clearly and limit optical illusions", and take "the vantage point ... ideally situated at equal distance from the objects so as to produce a symmetrical view".[45] What they do not make clear, and what Hooke and Cavendish were essentially arguing about, was what actually causes these "optical illusions" in our understanding, and how we can even know. Their suggestion that the observer be placed equidistant to the two cultures that they study is also reflected in Cavendish's explanation of publishing a scientific tract and a utopian prose fiction together, as being "two worlds at the ends of their poles" with herself as the hinge between them.[46] In comparison to Werner and Zimmermann's suggestions, the Royal Society's belief that, to quote George Orwell, "good prose is like a windowpane" is problematic because, although it may make for a clearer writing style, by imagining themselves as outside observers with their personalities effaced from the communication of what they observe, they present their work as an objective truth.

Comparing Cavendish's points to those of twenty-first century historians may seem ahistorical; however, as Frances Dolan and Barbara Shapiro have argued, the seventeenth century saw an intensification of debate over what could be regarded as truth and evidence.[47] Dolan also argues that there are parallels between the seventeenth century and today, when she says that she was interested in the "self-consciousness regarding the contingency of truth claims because it was a defining feature of the period. But I am also interested in the seventeenth century because contemporaries' struggles remind us that

---

44   Michael Werner and Bénédicte Zimmermann, "Beyond Comparison: Histoire Croisée and the Challenge of Reflexivity", *History and Theory*, XLV/1 (2006), 30–50 (34).

45   *Ibid.*, 33.

46   Cavendish, *The Blazing World*, 124.

47   Frances E. Dolan, *True Relations: Reading, Literature, and Evidence in Seventeenth-Century England* (Philadelphia: University of Pennsylvania Press, 2013); Barbara J. Shapiro, *A Culture of Fact: England, 1550–1720* (Ithaca: Cornell University Press, 2003).

our own uncertainty about how to achieve historical understanding is not just a function of postmodern theory or the simple passage of time".[48] Unintentionally, Cavendish's points about the Royal Society may make us rethink our own role as academics, thinking of ourselves not as outside observers, but as historical beings ourselves, complicit in the rewriting of what we observe according to what we expect to see.

Works Cited

Battigelli, Anna. *Margaret Cavendish and the Exiles of the Mind*. Lexington: The University Press of Kentucky, 1998.

Boyle, Robert. *Some Considerations Touching the Usefulnesse of Experimental Naturall Philosophy*. Oxford: printed by Henry Hall, 1663.

Britland, Karen. *Drama at the Courts of Queen Henrietta Maria*. Cambridge: Cambridge University Press, 2006.

Cavendish, Margaret. *The World's Olio, written by the Right Honorable, the Lady Margaret Newcastle*. London: Printed for J. Martin and J. Allestrye, 1655.

Cavendish, Margaret. *The Description of a New World, called the Blazing World and other Writings*, edited by Kate Lilley. London: Pickering and Chatto, 1992.

Cavendish, Margaret. *Observations Upon Experimental Philosophy*, edited by Eileen O'Neill. Cambridge: Cambridge University Press, 2001.

Dolan, Frances E. *True Relations: Reading, Literature, and Evidence in Seventeenth-Century England*. Philadelphia: University of Pennsylvania Press, 2013.

Evelyn, John. *The Diary of John Evelyn*, vol. 3, edited by E.S. de Beer. Oxford: Clarendon Press, 1955.

Gallagher, Catherine. "Embracing the Absolute: The Politics of the Female Subject in Seventeenth-Century England". *Genders*, I (1988), 24–39.

Hogarth, Alan, and Mike Witmore. *The Subject as Object: Boyle, the Royal Society and Scientific Style* (2016). Manuscript submitted for publication.

Hooke, Robert. *Micrographia: or some Physiological Descriptions of Minute Bodies Made by Magnifying Glasses with Observations and Inquiries thereupon*. London: for John Martyn, 1667.

Hutton, Sarah. "In Dialogue with Thomas Hobbes: Margaret Cavendish's Natural Philosophy". *Women's Writing*, IV (1997), 421–432.

Keller, Eve. "Producing Petty Gods: Margaret Cavendish's Critique of Experimental Science". *English Literary History*, LXIV (1997), 447–471.

---

48   Dolan, *True Relations*, 5.

Makin, Bathsua. *An Essay to Revive the Antient Education of Gentlewomen*, edited by Paula L. Barbour. Los Angeles: University of California, 1980.

Narain, Mona. "Notorious Celebrity: Margaret Cavendish and the Spectacle of Fame". *The Journal of the Midwest Modern Language Association*, XLII/2 (2009), 69–95.

Nate, Richard. "'Plain and vulgarly express'd': Margaret Cavendish and the Discourse of the New Science". *Rhetorica*, XIX/4 (2001), 403–417.

Osborne, Dorothy. *Dorothy Osborne: Letters to Sir William* Temple, edited by Kenneth Parker. Aldershot: Ashgate, 2002.

Pepys, Samuel. *The Diary of Samuel Pepys: A Selection*. London: Penguin, 2003.

Rees, Emma L.E. *Margaret Cavendish: Gender, Genre, Exile*. Manchester: Manchester University Press, 2003.

Sarasohn, Lisa T. *The Natural Philosophy of Margaret Cavendish: Reason and Fancy During the Scientific Revolution*. Baltimore: John Hopkins University Press, 2010.

Shapin, Steven. "Pump and Circumstance: Robert Boyle's Literary Technology", *Social Studies of Science*, XIV/4 (1984), 481–520.

Shapiro, Barbara J. *A Culture of Fact: England, 1550–1720*. Ithaca: Cornell University Press, 2003.

Spiller, Elizabeth. "Books written of the wonders of these glasses: Thomas Hobbes, Robert Hooke, and Margaret Cavendish's Theory of Reading". In *Science, Reading, and Renaissance Literature*. 137–177. Cambridge: Cambridge University Press, 2004.

Sprat, Thomas. *The History of the Royal Society of London, for the Improving of Natural Knowledge*. London: Printed for John Martyn, 1667.

Strickland, Agnes and Elizabeth Strickland. *Lives of the Queens of England from the Norman Conquest*. Cambridge: Cambridge University Press, 2010.

Tillery, Denise. "'English them in the easiest manner you can': Margaret Cavendish on the Discourse and Practice of Natural Philosophy". *Rhetoric Review*, XXVI/3 (2007), 268–285.

Walters, Lisa. *Margaret Cavendish: Gender, Science, and Politics*. Cambridge: Cambridge University Press, 2014.

Werner, Michael, and Bénédicte Zimmermann. "Beyond Comparison: Histoire Croisée and the Challenge of Reflexivity". *History and Theory*, XLV/1 (2006), 30–50.

Whitaker, Katie. *Mad Madge: The Extraordinary Life of Margaret Cavendish, Duchess of Newcastle, The First Woman to Live by her Pen*. New York: Basic Books, 2002.

Woolf, Virginia. *A Room of One's Own*. Peterborough: Broadview Press, 2001.

CHAPTER 4

The Arts Meet the Sciences in Exploring the Continent: Some Grand Tour Imagology

Mihaela Irimia

Abstract

The complex cultural experience that the Grand Tour was can be grasped from *imagological* evaluations by male "tourists" faced with *otherness* on the Continent. Their female counterparts enjoyed more "frivolous" activities at home. In both cases an exciting *intertwining of the arts and the sciences* could be seen at work, with painting and music, mechanics and transport, fashion and landscape gardening claiming pride of place in one category or another's preferences. This chapter suggests how the arts and the sciences respectively were deemed essential to the construction of personality in living the good life.

Travels of the physical and – more importantly – of the symbolic nature have long connected the insular and, later on, perfidious Albion with the Continent. From the journey to Rome in the age of Bede to the pilgrimage to Jerusalem on which Chaucer's wife of Bath engaged, on to the epoch-making discoveries of Elizabethan times, England, then Britain and then Great Britain have owed a lot to these identitary connections. Voyages of discovery, already present in the collective unconscious of the Elizabethans, discharged an obvious educational function and were related to the "new culture" syndrome, itself undissociable from technological progress and the practical use to which the sciences, as they had come down in time, could be put. Needless to say, they were unavoidably accompanied by difficult, if not quite dangerous complications, and required of those engaged in the business not simply scientific *savoir*, but also pragmatic steadfastness. *Savoir* and *pouvoir* jointly.

The eighteenth-century Grand Tour was relatively "customary and smooth", involving a "picked class, an aristocratic temper, wealth ... and fascination with Europe's artistic, social, architectural, literary and historical attractions".[1] It was

---

1   William Edward Mead, *The Grand Tour in the Eighteenth Century* (Boston & New York: Houghton Mifflin Company, 1914), 3.

an almost all-male business meant to "compleat the gentleman", as the saying went at the time. Its educational purpose was quite overt, as was the ironic definition of the accompanying tutor as bear-leader. Sterne worked out an astute taxonomy of travellers in his *Sentimental Journey to France and Italy* gravitating round the following general causes: infirmity of body, imbecility of mind, or inevitable necessity. In the third class he included "young gentlemen transported by the cruelty of parents and guardians, and travelling under the direction of governors recommended by Oxford, Aberdeen and Glasgow".[2] Their main aim was "to set foot on classic ground, ... the classical heritage [being] civilization".[3] Their tutors made sure that they would thoroughly study "the history, art, and customs of France and Italy, countries that had once been part of the Roman Empire".[4] Instruction attained by direct exploration in the countries toured was as a rule related to, and bound by, the organization of data and information secured by encyclopaedias, dictionaries and other such publications, all imbued by the persuasion that "the unity of the sciences acquired a special significance in relation to the ideals of the Enlightenment"; while this "opened up the possibility of the universality of knowledge", religion was firmly "responsible for the first limiting condition of the unity of the sciences", the various forms of knowledge being normally deemed *ancillae religionis*,[5] as practised along the centuries before the scientific revolution in Western culture. Print eventually came to play a central role in the "birth of modern science ... and the application of the technology of communication",[6] both of major help to those attempting to shape a persuasive individual identity.

The grand tourist of the 1700s was definitely not what we currently designate by that term today. In some form or other, his peregrinations were directed along pedagogical lines, but a certain differentiation between the ordinary and the better instructed and already somewhat travelled young male remains a fact. In the former category the "tourists" would normally let themselves be attracted by subjectively pleasurable objects and places, the *picturesque* playing an important role in their organized circuits. Travelling to the south of the Continent was of necessity more of an *arts*-geared business, archaeological sites, findings and museums featuring as points of utmost interest. Those more widely-read and showing erudite inclinations did not stay content with these

---

2 *Ibid.*, 34.

3 Roger Hudson (ed.), *The Grand Tour 1592–1796* (London: The Folio Society, 1993), 13.

4 William K. Ritchie, *The Eighteenth-Century Grand Tour* (London: Longman, 1972), 4.

5 Robert McRae, "The Unity of the Sciences: Bacon, Descartes, and Leibniz", *Journal of the History of Ideas*, XVIII/1 (1957), 27–48 (27, 29).

6 Jack Goody, *The Theft of History* (Cambridge: Cambridge University Press, 2012), 18.

sine qua non attractions. Rather they searched actual access to instruments of knowledge available in the various places visited. Theirs was more of a scientific attraction.

The Grand Tour secured a fairly elevated degree of cultural information of what we would now call the artistic and the scientific order jointly, at a time of pre-disciplinary separation of knowledge, before, that is, knowledge was eventually understood as a set of well established disciplines. What those benefiting from its cultural effects were exposed to was differentiated and specialized according to the local traditions and experience accumulated in the respective context. A taxonomy of visited countries/cultures operated with the following destinations and targets: Italy, the zero point of ancient Roman grandeur, offering the sights of amphitheatres, monuments and aqueducts, as well as baroque churches and contemporaneous artistic festivities like opera performances (known as "dramas for music") and concerts; France, with its charming Versailles complex, amazing Paris façades, astoundingly elegant shops, as well as with its latest fashion in clothing, footwear and hair styles – a display of what the Aristocratic Age could offer (the term designating French and Frenchified tastes *per se*); Holland, the country of pragmatic and mercantile jobs, of engineering pride and technological precision in the service of free trade; Germany, equally efficient, yet perceived by the English aristocratic tourists as a place of bad inns and boring amusements, though offering fine music and ballroom elegance; Switzerland, with the cantons preserving the fame of Voltaire and Rousseau and showing no little desire to assert their distinction. In all these countries the arts and sciences went hand in hand in equipping the young aristocrats with chic and useful knowledge.

"Serious" travellers were *per force* males from wealthy families brought up in the spirit of Protestant rigour, fed "serious" readings, of which a good deal in learned Latin, less in Greek. They were certainly taught the discipline of reading and grasping the deep meaning of the Bible and grew up disliking, if not loathing, novels as light and immoral. They would be sent to Paris and Rome to consolidate their classical background and be empirically confirmed in their imperial and Christian identity: "Transmission of neoclassicism northward was furthered by travelers returning from Grand Tour trips to Italy".[7] Dislike of Catholic values and rituals went pale in the face of personal modelling according to traditional norms. Their female counterparts were denied such rights. Barred from reading classical Latin, they could read their Shakespeare only after "correction", i.e. pruned of "unserious" vocabulary, in order that their

---

7   Jules David Prown, "A Course of Antiquities at Rome, 1764", *Eighteenth-Century Studies*, XXXI/1 (1997), 90–100 (90).

taste be "cultivated, without offence to the delicate and the religious feelings".[8] They found an escape in novels, of which no little amount of sentimental ones. As Dr Johnson remarks in *The Rambler*, "The works of fiction with which the present generation seems more particularly delighted, are such as exhibit life in its true state".[9] They lived in an age of gallantry, beauty and humour – prerequisites of *salon* life – and one in which "etiquette was the visible representation of power".[10] A time curiously close in spirit to our own age, the 1700s made a remarkable contribution to educating its youth in the spirit of modern art, respectful of the inherited tradition, and desirous of always better and more technologically fit forms of comfort and leisure. In art galleries such as the Uffizi in Florence gatherings of *dilettanti* and amateurs of the arts in general would display their "connoisseurship of the fine arts as one of the highest forms of educated pastime",[11] while the academies whose threshold some of them crossed could persuade them of the beauty of idealized bodies or flawless architecture, as well as of the sense of order instilled by scientific theories and experiments conducted in this spirit. The very artful ordering of nature following classic rules more and more supplanted by landscape gardening principles betrays a sense in which beauty and elegance were conceived of as applied scientific rigour, albeit hiding the direct presence of science in their visible aspect.

While ladies breathed in the emotional reality of life from the fashionable business of novel-reading, their generational male companions looked for sexual maturity in France, before refining their classical taste in Italy. *A Sentimental Journey* seems to suggest as much. Stories pleasing the heart were becoming more potent than the inherited chivalrous exploits of their lovers, to say nothing of the growing desire to shake out of English ways and escape to Paris. Indoor scenes like the one in which an enamoured gentleman is feeling an enchanting lady's pulse or climbing his bookshop ladder to get a much expected and much desired love-story novel for his female customer reveal significant sartorial and bodily details: the male tricorne and walking stick are put to rest, the huge female coiffure is not there, an air of not mere domesticity,

8   Georgiana Ziegler, Frances Dolan & Addison Roberts, *Shakespeare's Unruly Women* (Washington, D.C.: The Folger Shakespeare Library, 1997), 13.

9   Elizabeth Bergen Brophy, *Women's Lives and the Eighteenth-Century English Novel*, (Tampa: University of South Florida Press, 1991), 1.

10   Olivier Bernier, *The Eighteenth-Century Woman* (New York: Doubleday & Co. Inc., Garden City, 1982), 15.

11   Stephen Jones, *The Eighteenth Century* (Cambridge & London: Cambridge University Press, 1985), 7.

but downright intimacy hovers above these scenes. The heart receives its treatment in gentle isolation from the public sphere. There is an *ars amatoria*
articulated to the requirements of modern gallantry. The rational *savoir* of the
day's medical science kneels to the *pouvoir* of the heart's effluvia.

Not only the soul, the spirit too claimed its rights and found them observed.
Sophisticated ladies of the Bluestocking Club, "the first female club ever
known", as Horace Walpole is reported to have remarked in 1769 (the very year
in which the club was founded)[12] aimed very high and were vocal indeed.
Most of them were also accomplished Grand Tour travellers with an acclaimed
cultural agenda. Angelica Kauffman, the celebrated Swiss-Austrian painter
acquainted with Italy since her girlhood, conversant in French, Italian and
English, a personal friend of Goethe's in Italy, of Winckelmann's, Reynolds' and
Canova's, has left us defining images of the Bluestocking spirit: loud reading
and intellectual debates during aristocratic salon afternoon tea parties, social-
izing and philanthropic activities, fostering domestic affections and satisfying
a culture of subjectivity, all of which transpires in her Neoclassic painting. She
could fancy Sappho inspired by Eros inhabiting the self-same landscape as the
one in which an allegory of herself was seen vacillating between Music and
Painting. She deftly couples the Classical tradition with genre painting and
thus provided the clue to Lady Scarlett as the Muse of Literature, or to a lady
resembling Penelope by her loom through a full-fledged inventory of gestures
and sartorial details.

Leading among these were: Lady Elizabeth Montagu, who, like the lady in
Pietro Longhi's *Geography Lesson*, was a passionate student of science, while it
was her conviction that the great object of travelling was to get well acquainted
with the French character, hence her disposition for whatever French values
she could cultivate, from choice readings to her personal demeanour and sartorial identity; Lady Mary Wortley Montagu, author of the *Embassy Letters* written in Istanbul, with due attention to Western arts, while curious about Eastern
institutions; Frances Boscawen, an ardent member of the Bluestocking Club's
artistic activities, from orchestrating literary disputations to supporting com-
positional techniques with a view to promoting an intellectually convincing
feminine profile in society; Elizabeth Vesey, a constant traveller between her
birthplace in Ireland and London, as well as supporter of a *salon* meant as the
locus of cultivated adages, repartees and debates, instead of mere tea, coffee
or cocoa taking, card playing and sexual flirtation; Lady Mary Coke, a devoted
traveller to Europe, in particular to Vienna, where she had a special intellectual

---

12   Horace Walpole, *Memoirs of the Reign of King George the Third*, Vol. I (Philadelphia: Lea &
      Blanchard, 1845), 208.

friend in the person of Maria Theresa, the imperial promoter of educational reform and commercial mobility; Hester Thrale Piozzi, the Welsh-born and eventually Italian-married friend of Dr Johnson and his friend Boswell, who has come down to us as an exciting diarist and patron of the arts, with special attention to music during her second marriage (to a music teacher). They all played an important "public role in the life of the mind",[13] while they called for "improvement in education and intellectual status" and opposed a "double standard in sexual morality".[14] No picture of the said club, from highly serious classic allegories to caricatures of the late eighteenth and early nineteenth century can avoid the presence of the arts and/or the sciences in places destined for this purpose, whether as a temple, a library or a drawing room. Italian cities of undeniable reputation saw in "women of talent and learning ... civic monuments, organic expressions of the qualities that made each city individually great".[15]

Other travellers completed the ranks of the bear-like bad-mannered or monkey-like mimicking youths forced into studying the foundationalist sources of onetime Rome. Among them were writers and arbiters of fashion, *philosophes* and *salonières* cultivating a life of the mind. Gentlemen of learning and ladies of letters embarked on the Grand Tour to enjoy the inspirational force of travelling. To them Italy was the place couching historic-mythological scenes which they knew from their Homer, France a place of emancipation and libertinage "in a Paris-loving age",[16] Switzerland the haven of natural sublimity, the German lands the centre of solid trades and skills. The rough and rather silly young Grand Tourists in the former category were the object of ironic assessments pointing to their artistic and scientific paucity (see figure 4.1). Caricatures of the time raise zoomorphic appearance to symbolic height and capitalize on the *imagological* expansion of literal animal looks and behaviour. England as a bear, heavy, unrefined, stuffing himself with stodgy food and strong beer and appearing downright naked, sits at the other end of the imagological table from France in the guise of a liveried monkey enjoying fine liqueur and dining on mushrooms. A denial of artistic refinement, let

13   Sylvia Harcstark Meyers, *The Bluestocking Circle: Women, Friendship, and the Life of the Mind in Eighteenth-Century England* (Oxford: Clarendon Press, 1990), 244.

14   Alice Browne, *The Eighteenth-Century Feminist Mind* (Brighton: The Harvester Press, 1987), 1.

15   Paula Findlen, Wendy Roworth & Catherine M. Sama, *Italy's Eighteenth Century: Gender and Culture in the Age of the Grand Tour* (Stanford, Calif.: Stanford University Press, 2009), 21.

16   Jeremy Black, *The Grand Tour in the Eighteenth Century* (Bridgend: Alan Sutton and Sutton, 1992), xii.

FIGURE 4.1   *M. Darly, England, Roast Beef and Plumb Pudding, France, Toad Stools and*
Garlick (1775).
COURTESY OF THE LEWIS WALPOLE LIBRARY, YALE UNIVERSITY.

alone scientific advancement, this imagological bestiary illustration transpires
in the image of the bear-leader holding a monkey child's hand on their exemplary way to education.

Perceived as a gentlemen's club, Britain was sensed as refraining from, if not
utterly rejecting foreign languages as inducive of unpatriotic, cosmopolitan
ideas. Europe as a shelter against such pressures was very much an "imaginary
geography",[17] in which cultivated English ladies could commit their feelings
to paper in the guise of letters and eventually have these private matters published, an enterprise that could be called "writing the world" in their "ventur[ing]
to begin their education abroad".[18] France instead was the land of liberty and
libertinage and *Francophilia* in England rivalled *Anglophilia* on the Continent,
much promoted by Voltaire's enthusiastic appraisal of things British. In a
nutshell, these two crazes came down to an appraisal of "the dominant French

17   Brian Dolan, *Ladies of the Grand Tour* (Hammersmith, London: Harper Collins Publishers,
        2001), 17.
18   *Ibid.*, 22.

taste [versus] the simpler English taste".[19] Afternoon tea parties, visits to the theatre and the folly of macaroni fashion made the day. *Italophilia* played a far from lateral role in rituals of appropriation and acculturation (in the first place in the arts). To the best of our knowledge, insufficient attention has been given to the conjunction of *Francophilia and Italophilia*, as favoured by the British Grand Tour. We intend to focus on the macaroni fashion, coiffures and gardening as a means to illustrate this.

•••

In 1772 John Williams started printing and selling the *Macaroni and Theatrical Magazine, or Monthly Register, of the Fashions and Diversions of the Times*. The newly established publication aimed at including portraits and brief memoirs as the printed record of visits to Italy by British youths fostering cultural and intellectual distinction. London saw the grouping of recently repatriated young gentlemen desirous to advertise a freshly adopted culinary and cultural topos: the macaroni dish, a rarity in England, and the *Macaroni Club*. Based in Pall Mall, where gaming and gambling abounded, this growing society of debauched aristocrats set the fashion after Italian and French manners in unrestrained exaggeration of clothing, hairstyle and bodily attitude. The Macaronis were also fond of mincing their words and prattling endlessly in highlife ambiances. The prototype called Macaroni became a "figure ..., [a] catalyst for debate over how Britons could heed the siren call of luxurious consumption, individualism and cultural sophistication".[20] What was rare and hard to find was *chic* and asked for adopting and adapting: it was a *sui generis* way of being artistic.

There was artistry in their astounding hairdos, a conspicuously visible and recognisable sign which percolated into the female world and brought supplementary exacerbation to the public figure of the protagonist. The male macaroni wore a huge knot of artificial hair at the back of his neck and sometimes a minuscule tricorne on top of a tuft of hair raised very high above his forehead. The female exemplar made extensive use of horse hair, cages and glue to display an amazingly high and spacious coiffure which could be embellished with a head dress, hat, feathers, flowers or ribbons. Caricatures of the 1770s show gentlemen offering nosegays to ladies, the latter often bearing flowery names, as suggested in figure 4.2, in which the ridiculous gives

---

19   Jennifer Ruby, *Costume in Context: The Eighteenth Century* (London: Batsford Ltd., 1988), 5.

20   Amelia Rauser, "Hair, Authenticity, and the Self-Made Macaroni", *Eighteenth-Century Studies*, XXXVIII/1 (2004), 101–117 (101).

FIGURE 4.2   *The Polite Maccaroni presenting a Nosegay to Miss Blossom* (1772).
              COURTESY OF THE LEWIS WALPOLE LIBRARY, YALE UNIVERSITY.

way to tenderness. The trio on display make up an elegant *ergon* with Miss
Blossom appositely occupying the very centre of the image. As a metonym
of her delicate person, the basket full of flowers is the source of explicit or implicit compliments paid by her wooer and servant maid, who has

silver-buckled shoes on her feet, like the gentleman. Instead, Miss Blossom wears white satin shoes in accord with her fancy dress, as well as with the dramatic clouds in the background, where nature vibrates to the rhythms of culture.

Deliberate distortion of artistic effects – the very logic of caricature – is the rule at work in prints and drawings of the day showing details of the crazy macaroni fashion. The early 1770s bring together *The French Lady in London* (see figure 4.3) and *The English Lady in Paris* (see figure 4.4), both perfect victims of the latest folly in coiffures. In the former, the fashionable lady from across the Channel brings onto English soil the lunacy of a gigantic hairdo embellished with an elaborate hair-dress and covered in ribbons and beads. This "improvement" on nature is of the order of hideousness, with every sense of Vitruvian proportion violated in her strangely elongated figure halved at the waist. She can only step into a cosy drawing-room by bending her head while holding its impressive weight with unconcealed pain. Such is the French salon invasion into English indoor life that the English gentleman, like his pet dog, cat and bird, are scared out of balance. By the same token, the English lady in Paris defies the psychic and physical difficulties of old age while she is given a special treatment by a specialist. This is the artful protocol of powder puffing, deftly replicated in a picture hanging on the back wall which shows a pair of monkeys only too expectedly aping the whole procedure. The masculine mobilization in the service of feminine beauty was certainly professional and a *sui generis* combination of the arts and sciences in our present-day understanding of the terms (see figure 4.5). The elegant Parisian hair-dresser spreading powder on the English lady's hair had a contemporaneous English equivalent. Here he is, the "hair-engineer" fixing ostrich feathers in the lady's towering coiffure, while, seated at her toilet table, she is assisted by a maid holding a tray of exotic fruits. A more extensive system of travels lies behind this scene, with telling colonial tinges (see figure 4.6). The combined Franco-Italian craze has assumed such proportions that the sea-faring English nation metonymically present in a gentlemanly navigator takes the latitude of the female macaroni coiffure making use of a sextant, while a hair-engineer, no longer on a stool but on nothing less than a ladder, handles a pair of curlers as an extension of his sword. This also makes for macaroni as a mix of threads impossible to really disentangle, just like macaroni verse.

Such artful contrivances caught the eye and set the mind thinking in a peculiar coupling of the aesthetic with the comfortable, of the arts meant as delight and the sciences placed at the disposal of leisure and the good life. Gracious sedan chairs which had undergone mechanical adaptations were advertised with ladies proudly holding their lofty coiffures upright owing to the skilful raising of the vehicle ceiling. It was a technical improvement illustrating a

La Françoise á Londres

The FRENCH LADY in LONDON;

OR, the HEAD-DRESS, for the Year, 1771.

Printed for S. Hooper N.º 25, Ludgate Hill, & Published as the Act Directs, 20.ᵗʰ Nov.ʳ 1770.

FIGURE 4.3   *The French Lady in London* (1771).
COURTESY OF THE LEWIS WALPOLE LIBRARY, YALE UNIVERSITY.

FIGURE 4.4   *The English Lady in Paris* (1771).
COURTESY OF THE LEWIS WALPOLE LIBRARY, YALE UNIVERSITY.

THE PREPOSTEROUS HEAD DRESS,
Or the FEATHERD LADY.

FIGURE 4.5   *The Preposterous Head Dress Or the Featherd Lady* (1777).
COURTESY OF THE LEWIS WALPOLE LIBRARY, YALE UNIVERSITY.

RIDICULOUS TASTE OR THE LADIES ABSURDITY.

Pub.^d accord.^g to Act of Parll.^t July 15.th 1771 by Hedly N.º 139 Strand. & R. Sayer at the Golden Buck Fleet Street.

FIGURE 4.6   *The Ridiculous Taste Or the Ladies Absurdity* (1771).
             COURTESY OF THE LEWIS WALPOLE LIBRARY, YALE UNIVERSITY.

"capital conceit", one gravitating round a spectacular head and one conceived of with obvious dexterity. "Extravaganzas" became *chic* show pieces for public thrill. They were often displayed as head dresses falling out of size and harmony, exceeding mechanical and chromatic limits and violating commonsensical perception, basic in objective scientific evaluations. Heart-shaped hairdos circulated down the social scale from highlife ladies to their maids. A cook imitating her mistress could put up the paraphernalia of her skill in a weird enmeshing of hair, broom, duster and range proper, with fruit and vegetables as a minor addition. Here too the technology superseded art, if only for social promotion in the name of beauty.

This is where the English meets the French-cum-Italian *cultural topos* of the garden and gardening. Open-air landscapes, landscape gardening, garden architecture and the subjacent text of nature as the garden of God put *the cosmic* in logical etymological tandem with *the cosmetic*, the latter seen as a fashionable improvement on the former. Like the art of God, so the art of man. Hairdos supplanting the Eden of the orchard and vegetable garden were regarded as at once the pride of British opulence, the victory of the metropolis over the colonies, and the guarantee of daily comfort. They were big enough and solid enough to literally uphold various forms of socialization, from the May Day festival to rural masquerades. Correlatives of the country proper, they could be perceived as, by extension, metonyms of the country and of the world, of England and Britain, as well as of the one conspicuous colony called America. So much for real political conflicts and ensuing wars, for which technology was badly needed.

But there was at least one salon serving as substitute of bellicose feats: the much enjoyed clash known as "the war of the sexes". Instead of actual coups, a fashionable "coup de bouton" could do. This was the elegant display of technologically efficient silver buttons and buckles thought indispensable in male attire and equipment. For the fun of the occasion, an encounter between an artfully dressed-up lady and her stylish wooer could be portrayed as a confrontation involving an attack with the arms of polite society, with beams sent by the gentleman's buttons on the upper side of his coat and waistcoat blinding the lady and the lowest one suggesting an impending sexual assault, as can be seen in William Humphrey's *Coup de Bouton*, produced in 1777 and now featuring as a holding of the Lewis-Walpole Library. The picture shows the overwhelming effect of steel buttons, a distinct sign of *chic* identity, by the side of silver buckles on male shoes (see figure 4.7).

Flower gardens and floral patterns served the cause of the arts marvellously. They could themselves function as objective correlatives of the skilled

FIGURE 4.7   *William Humphrey, Coup de Bouton* (1777).
COURTESY OF THE LEWIS WALPOLE LIBRARY, YALE UNIVERSITY.

sagacity of highlife exposure. For a female hairdo to stand for grand culture itself was quite a show of dexterity and grace. Technology based on scientific *savoir faire* transpired in the elaborate artistry of the "capital" decoration (see figure 4.8). What would have been a natural background with a female

FIGURE 4.8   *M. Darly, The Flower Garden* (1777).
COURTESY OF THE LEWIS WALPOLE LIBRARY, YALE UNIVERSITY.

portrait in the foreground could be agglutinated to the lady's coiffure as the support of a neatly French-style pruned garden. The arts took precedence over the sciences, the lady over the gentleman, beauty over efficiency. The text of the garden as the text of the world hints at the punning nature of *text* and *texture* as fundamental lexemes. Both become overt in James Stewart's *Plocacosmos: Or the Whole Art of Hair Dressing* (1782), which combines the cosmic and the cosmetic with refined mechanical and artistic skills. Here is the art of hair-plaiting (πλοκή) applied to the world of order and to the ordered world (κόσμος). The Grand Tour did mean a re-writing of individual and collective identity in texts of crucial cultural relevance – topographic as well as identitary narratives with a special contribution of the arts and the sciences.

Cultural texts written in Industrial Revolution vocabulary feature images of male and female success in life: how to make good. God as *modus in rebus* appears measurable with scientific instruments: whatever is is right, if kept within its right bounds. A couple of illustrations by Robert Dighton in 1785 display the perfectly successful model in the masculine, and the feminine version, respectively. With a labour ethos reminding us of Hogarth's allegorical images, he pictures the industrious gentleman standing by a sack bursting out with coins, while scenes of vicious behaviour surrounding the emblematic central portrait show gentlemanly degradation by loss of measure, whether as a life of dissolute gambling, of drinking, or of womanizing (see figure 4.9). The doggerel attached at the bottom of these pictures drives the case home, as in some Classic Modern emblem book: "By honest and industrious means / You'll live a life of ease" is the moral subsumed to the overall urge "Fear God!" kept within measure by a pair of precise compasses.

By the same token, the lady leading a life of prudence should and will expect esteem, while all those exceptions to this rule of morality and common sense point to decay (see figure 4.10). The exemplary lady in the centre holds a book in her hand, whose title reads *The Pleasures of Imagination realized*, but she stands by a box on whose side we can read *The Reward of Virtue*, a phrasing reminding one of Richardson's moralising novels. This is Classic Modernity's instruction book in the service of betterment. And, while she may not be denied the frivolous pleasures of the salon, among which the consumption of cordial and care for her body, she is urged not to defy the borders of decency, or else folly, gambling and downright prostitution can be the next step. Male and female protagonists are therefore, as a clever combination of the arts and sciences, able to secure the harmony of things in this world. They feature in collections of the time as "aristocratic displays ... harnessing wonder as a political

FIGURE 4.10   *R. Dighton, Keeping within Compass: Prudence produces Esteem (1785).*
COURTESY OF THE LEWIS WALPOLE LIBRARY, YALE UNIVERSITY.

and social asset",[21] as they do justice to the growing "emancipatory drive of the century".[22]

A time of artifacts becoming more and more sophisticated and more and more widely enjoyed, the eighteenth century witnessed an impressive expansion of material consumption, an actual "consumer revolution" in which retailers "raised shopping to an art form".[23] As a mid-century gentleman of taste noticed, "Taste is at present the darling of the polite world, and the world of letters; and, indeed, seems to be considered as the quintessence of all the arts and sciences".[24]

Works Cited

Bernier, Olivier. *The Eighteenth-Century Woman*. New York: Doubleday & Co. Inc., Garden City, 1982.

Brophy, Elizabeth Bergen. *Women's Lives and the Eighteenth-Century English Novel*. Tampa: University of South Florida Press, 1991.

Black, Jeremy. *Natural and Necessary Enemies: Anglo-French Relations in the Eighteenth Century*. London: Duckworth, 1986.

Black, Jeremy. *The Grand Tour in the Eighteenth Century*, Bridgend: Alan Sutton and Sutton, 1992.

Browne, Alice. *The Eighteenth-Century Feminist Mind*. Brighton: The Harvester Press, 1987.

Coleman, George. *The Connoisseur, By Mr. Town, Critic and Censor-General*, 3rd ed., 4 vols, London, 1757–1760.

Dolan, Brian. *Ladies of the Grand Tour*. Hammersmith, London: Harper Collins, 2001.

Eger, Elizabeth. *Bluestocking Feminism: Writings of the Bluestocking Circle 1738–1785*. London: Pickering & Chatto, 1999.

Findlen, Paula, Wendy Roworth & Catherine M. Sama. *Italy's Eighteenth Century: Gender and Culture in the Age of the Great Tour*, Stanford, Calif.: Stanford University Press, 2009.

---

21 Marjorie Swann, *Curiosities and Texts: The Culture of Collecting in Early Modern England* (Philadelphia: University of Pennsylvania Press, 2001), 26.

22 Jeremy Black, *Natural and Necessary Enemies: Anglo-French Relations in the Eighteenth Century* (London: Duckworth, 1986), 211.

23 John Styles & Amanda Vickery (eds), *Gender, Taste and Material Culture in Britain and North America, 1700–1830* (London & New York: Yale University Press, 2006), 3.

24 George Coleman, *The Connoisseur, By Mr. Town, Critic and Censor-General*, 3rd ed., 4 vols. (London, 1757–1760), 121.

Goody, Jack. *The Theft of History*, Cambridge: Cambridge University Press, 2012.

Habermas, Jürgen. *The Structural Transformation of the Public Sphere: An Inquiry into a Category of Bourgeois Society*. Cambridge, Mass: MIT Press, 1989.

Hudson, Roger, ed. *The Grand Tour 1592–1796*. London: The Folio Society, 1993.

Jones, Stephen. *The Eighteenth Century*. Cambridge & London: Cambridge University Press, 1985.

McRae, Robert. "The Unity of the Sciences: Bacon, Descartes, and Leibniz". *Journal of the History of Ideas*, XVIII/1 (1957), 27–48.

Mead, William Edward. *The Grand Tour in the Eighteenth Century*. Boston & New York: Houghton Mifflin, 1914.

Meyers, Sylvia Harcstark. *The Bluestocking Circle: Women, Friendship, and the Life of the Mind in Eighteenth-Century England*. Oxford: Clarendon Press, 1990.

Nugent, Thomas. *The Grand Tour, or, A Journey through the Netherlands, Germany, Italy, and France*, 4 vols, London: 1749.

Prown, Jules David. "A Course of Antiquities at Rome, 1764". *Eighteenth-Century Studies*, XXXI/1 (1997), 90–100.

Rauser, Amelia. "Hair, Authenticity, and the Self-Made Macaroni". *Eighteenth-Century Studies*, XXXVIII/1 (2004), 101–117.

Ritchie, William K. *The Eighteenth-Century Grand Tour*. London: Longman, 1972.

Rogers, Katherine M. *Feminism in Eighteenth-Century England*. Brighton: The Harvester Press, 1982.

Ruby, Jennifer. *Costume in Context: The Eighteenth Century*. London: Batsford, 1988.

Sterne, Laurence. *A Sentimental Journey through France and Italy*, edited by Graham Petrie. Harmondsworth: Penguin, 1967.

Styles, George & Amanda Vickery, eds. *Gender, Taste and Material Culture in Britain and North America, 1700–1830*. London and New Haven: Yale University Press, 2006.

Swann, Marjorie. *Curiosities and Texts: The Culture of Collecting in Early Modern England*. Philadelphia: University of Pennsylvania Press, 2001.

Ziegler, Georgiana, Frances Dolan and Addison Roberts. *Shakespeare's Unruly Women*. Washington, D.C.: The Folger Shakespeare Library, 1997.

PART 2

Forms of Discourse and Sociability

∵

CHAPTER 5

From *Inventio* to Invention: John Wilkins' *Mathematical Magick*

Maria Avxentevskaya

Abstract

John Wilkins' *Mathematical Magick, or the Wonders that may be performed by Mechanical Geometry* (1648) elaborated on the techniques of dialectical persuasion, combining the elements of logic and rhetoric. Undermining the opposition between the strategies of text-commenting and observation, Wilkins induced the reader to follow the path of an articulated experience in mechanical wonders. This chapter explores the origins of his dialectical techniques, his scheme for legitimating mechanics as a rational art, and elaboration on scientific methods. I argue that humanist historicising and literary experiential testimonies were employed by Wilkins to solve methodological problems within the contemporary art of mechanics.

∙∙∙

A noble subject which the mind will lift
To easie use of that peculiar gift,
Which poets in their rapture hold most deare,
When actions by the lively sound appeare.
>   JOHN BEAUMONT *To His Late Majesty, Concerning the True Form of English Poetry* (1629)

∙∙
∙

John Wilkins (1614–1672) was a British virtuoso, one of the founding members of the Royal Society of London, an author of popular science narratives, a prominent theologian, and the inventor of an elaborate project of artificial philosophical language. Wilkins' *Mathematical Magick, or the Wonders that may be performed by Mechanical Geometry* (1648) combined the elements of logic and persuasion, rigid geometric proofs and vivid historical accounts, elaborating on the techniques of visualization in scientific rhetoric. Undermining the opposition between the strategies of observation and text-commenting, Wilkins' discourse sought to bring out the domain of individual scientific experience and induce the reader to participate in experimental studies.

In my analysis of John Wilkins' *Mathematical Magick*, I will argue that he employed humanist historicizing and experiential testimonies to solve methodological issues within the art of mechanics. Wilkins' narrative sustained the pulls of the figural and the literal, aiming to compensate for the lack of mathematical and mechanical expertise among his readers. Below, I will explore the origins of his dialectical and rhetorical techniques, his scheme for legitimating mechanics as a liberal art, and his resulting input into the elaboration of scientific methods.

The Rhetorical Background of *Mathematical Magick*

Similarly to many other early modern scientific writers, Wilkins employed verbal and visual figurative forms as performative aids in the procedures of both rhetorical *inventio* and technical invention.[1] He alternated historical and literary sketches of legendary mechanical devices with diagrams and drawings of existing mechanisms, imparting the experience of presence at the scene of his endeavours. Albeit positioned in the past, his historical commentaries were intended as a utopian scenario laying out the perspective of possibilities for the future pursuits of mechanics. Such early modern performative accounts were frequently termed as discoveries but were technically based on the procedures of dialectical invention.[2] Whereas a discovery presumes finding out what really is, the term "invention" pinpoints the contingent character of natural learning.

The discussions of natural philosophy observed the principles of *copia* understood as the effective richness of discourse. Quintilian was the first to distinguish copiousness from a mere emulation of ancient authors: "imitation alone is not sufficient", because in that case "nothing would ever have been discovered".[3] Later, Agricola's version of *copia* emphasised the delight yielded

---

1   On the role of *inventio* in the rhetoric of science, see among others Alan G. Gross, *A Rhetoric of Science* (Cambridge, MA: Harvard University Press, 1996).

2   For a recent study on the early modern phenomenology of discovery, see J. D. Fleming, ed., *The Invention of Discovery, 1500–1700* (Farnham: Ashgate, 2013).

3   Quintilian, *Institutio oratoria*, trans. Harold Edgeworth Butler (Cambridge, MA: Harvard University Press, 1922), Book X, 2: 4.

by the profuseness of details.[4] The existing instructions on producing *enar-geia* stressed the necessity to bring the subject before the eyes of the audience through a detailed description. Agricola employed a direct comparison between the language of words and visual arts, which was intended to persuade the students that both clear, beautiful lines and clear, beautiful speech may not spring solely from *mimesis veterum* but must result from industrious exercises in the art of invention. As Peter Mack notes, for Agricola, dialectic was also "not about what to say but about how to think about what to say".[5] He turned the practice of processing the subject matter through the topics into an instrument for triggering thoughts about all possible kinds of arguments, and recommended processing the key concepts of an argument through a list of topics, such as genus & species, whole & parts, etc. The rhetorician should place each concept into the space between the antithetical *topoi* and see how it might relate to the relevant categories. This treatment created a fresh experiential context and planted the seeds of new argumentation.

Following Agricola, Ramus elaborated on rhetoric as the dialectical practice of bridging various details and narratives into a coherent general scheme. Ramus formalised rhetorical doctrine, reducing the number of parameters considered in rhetorical analysis, which allowed for more combinatorial freedom in composition. The Ramist *loci communes* generated novel combinations, as the language of argumentative resources could be partitioned with "sites of discovery" or the scenes of potentially copious discourse.[6] Later, Erasmus' prescription on how to enhance the originality and copiousness of speech suggested the further reducing of theory in favour of *experientia*, which "fills out the whole case and reinforces it with close-packed convincing details, and ... they fight on their own".[7] In the England of the early seventeenth century, Bacon also made use of the techniques of dialectical rhetoric, even if repudiating the Ciceronian stylistic domination of the Renaissance. For Bacon, rhetoric is a legitimate pool of discursive resources, "a preparatory store for the furniture

---

4   Rudolf Agricola, *De inventione dialectica libri tres*, ed. Lothar Mund (Tübingen: Max Niemeyer Verlag, 1992), L. III, Cap. XV, 135.

5   Peter Mack, *Renaissance Argument: Valla and Agricola in the Traditions of Rhetoric and Dialectic* (Leiden: E.J. Brill, 1993), 120. See also Peter Mack, *A History of Renaissance Rhetoric, 1380–1620* (Oxford: Oxford University Press, 2011).

6   Carolyn R. Miller, "The Aristotelian Topos: Hunting for Novelty", in *Re-Reading Aristotle's Rhetoric*, ed. Alan G. Gross and Alan E. Walzer (Carbondale, IL: Southern Illinois University, 2000), 130–148, 141.

7   Desiderius Erasmus, "De copia", in *Collected works of Erasmus*, ed. Craig R. Thomson (Toronto: University of Toronto Press, 1978), 592.

of speech and readiness of invention",[8] the power of which consists in that the "force of eloquence and persuasion hath made things future and remote appear as present".[9] The figural language "brings nature to speak", and the procedures of *inventio* attract our attention to certain marks or "places" that may excite the mind and direct the inquiry.[10]

In this paper, I will show that John Wilkins employed the early modern rhetorical and dialectical patterns of composition to create a copious and persuasive account of a subject-matter that would only later become commonly viewed as substantially verifiable. The communicative intention of the author of *Mathematical Magic* was to produce wonder and delight, but his discourse was not projected as a mere literary simulacrum of mechanical reality. Wilkins' performative enactment of mechanical operations imparted the experience of discovering the new properties of mechanical "things themselves".

Wilkins' Mechanics as a Liberal Art

In spite of some enthusiastic disclaimers, mid-seventeenth-century British persuasive communities benefited from employing rhetorical *ornamentum* both in the sense of "embellishment" and "apparatus" in the practices of making knowledge.[11] Rhetorical figures often correlated with the visual figures of Ramist and Lullist origin, which allowed for translating new data into a comprehensible representation. Wilkins' *Mathematical Magick* features a number of examples where such figures as *antithesis*, *incrementum*, and *gradatio* were applied in their verbal and visual forms.

The rhetorical figure of *antithesis* usually works as a conceptual tool for inventing an argument by shaping the language to deliver a contrast, which serves for the framing of premises built on opposed concepts. The generation of premises leads to the formulation of claims, which structures the whole program of inquiry, prompting the search for confirming data. Then the data may be presented in the form of a text or an image, such as a table of observations

---

8   Francis Bacon, *The Advancement of Learning* (London: Printed for Henrie Tomes, 1605), XVIII, 7.

9   *Ibid.*, XVIII, 4.

10   *Ibid.*, XVIII, 2.

11   Jeanne Fahnestock, *Rhetorical Figures in Science* (New York: Oxford University Press, 1999), 18. See also Tina Skouen, Ryan J. Stark, eds., *Rhetoric and the Early Royal Society: A Sourcebook* (Leiden: E.J. Brill, 2014). The controversy between John Wallis and Thomas Hobbes on squaring the circle is also illustrative in terms of the use of rhetoric in early modern mathematical discussions.

or an illustration, to explicate the relationship between the antithetical terms. The polarised terms could be mediated with a new third term or a category, which made this new element imprinted on the public mind as an exciting paradoxical wonder and part of a familiar intellectual framework.

For instance, Wilkins' title *Mathematical Magick* pursues a rhetorical goal, as his readers tended to perceive "mathematical magic" as an oxymoron. The reputation of mechanics suffered from "vulgar opinion, which doth commonly attribute all such strange operations unto the power of Magick".[12] The figure of *antithesis* in the title juxtaposes the magical view of the art, discredited as vulgar opinion, with the mathematical interpretation of mechanics, which through the power of antithetical framing becomes showcased as the opposite of vulgar, i.e. profound and genteel.[13] The positioning of mechanics among the *artes ingenuae* allowed for augmenting mechanical practices with the techniques of other liberal arts, such as geometrical demonstrations, computations, and the amplifying patterns of copious discourse.

Wilkins dedicated *Mathematical Magick* to Charles Louis (Karl Ludwig), Elector Palatine,[14] thereby regretting the condition, "under which the Common-wealth of learning does now suffer".[15] This meant not only grieving the losses sustained in the English Civil Wars but also mourning the fate of the Hortus Palatinus. Before its destruction in the Siege of Heidelberg in 1618, the famous pleasure park built by Inigo Jones and Salomon de Caus was labelled as one of the world's wonders. Famed for its exotic plants, the garden also hosted ingenious water-works, such as water organs, recreations of ancient "speaking

---

12   John Wilkins, *Mathematical Magick* (London: Printed by M.F., 1648), "To the Reader". Wilkins relates mechanics to *Mirandorum Effectrix* or "miraculous effect or performance", but he also cites an earlier Greek term, Θαυματοποιητική, which more specifically indicates not only the skill of "orators to strain after the marvellous" but also "building up understanding for thereby creating new things". See Wilhelm Pape, *Handwörterbuch der griechischen Sprache* (Braunschweig, 1914).

13   John Wallis, Wilkins' close collaborator, claimed that in England before the 1650s "Mathematicks were scarce looked upon as Academical studies, but rather Mechanical; as the business of Traders, Merchants, Seamen". However, recent studies show that among University lecturers of mathematics there were several Cambridge Platonists and also Seth Ward, another collaborator of Wilkins. See Mordechai Feingold, "Parallel Lives: The Mathematical Careers of John Pell and John Wallis", *Huntington Library Quarterly*, LXIX/3 (2006), 451–468.

14   Wilkins rendered Karl I Ludwig the services of a private chaplain in London, and in 1648 accompanied him on the route to Heidelberg, visiting on the way back a number of European destinations.

15   John Wilkins, *Mathematical Magick*, "Epistle".

statues", and clock-works with birds singing as nightingales and cuckoos.[16] The Hortus Palatinus could also be viewed as an implementation of the Rosicrucian allegory of botanical cosmos, to which Salomon de Caus might have a secret sympathy.[17]

Wilkins was familiar with these engineering masterpieces, also because the skills of the de Caus brothers were duly acknowledged in England.[18] In 1644, Isaac de Caus published *Nouvelle invention de lever l'eau* containing numerous plates from his brother's book on spectacular hydraulic mechanisms producing musical sounds.[19] Wilkins' *Mathematical Magick* depicts similar mechanisms that could "give several sounds, whether of birds, as Larks, Cuckoes, &c. or beasts, as Hares, Foxes". Wilkins insists that the voices of all these creatures were "rendered as clearly and distinctly ... as they are by those naturall living bodies".[20] However, it is difficult to say whether he is referring to someone's experiential evidence, or his own reading of Hero of Alexandria's *Pneumatica* that had been translated into Latin in 1582 and served as guideline for creating the Hortus Palatinus.[21] In any case, Wilkins' connection to the prince-elector of the Palatinate prompted him to publish his treatise on mechanics.[22]

Mathematical Magick praises the Prince Elector as "a Judge in all kind of ingenuous arts and literature", which on the one hand sought patronage, and on the other hand attempted to place the treatise under the disciplinary

---

16   Salomon de Caus, *Hortvs Palatinvs: A Friderico Rege Boemiae Electore Palatino Heidelbergae Exstructus* (Franckfurt: Theodor de Bry, 1620).

17   Natalia Kaoukji, "Machines and Mathematical Magic" (presentation at symposium "John Wilkins and His Legacy", Wadham College, Oxford, September 15, 2014).

18   In 1615, in Frankfurt, Salomon de Caus published his work on automata *Les Raisons des Forces Mouvantes avec diverses machines tant utiles que plaisantes*. In 1620, there also appeared his *Hortvs Palatinvs*. Isaac de Caus was commissioned to London in 1612 to complete some of his brother's projects. In 1645, *Wilton Garden* was published, a baroque portfolio of Isaac de Caus' garden designs.

19   Isaac de Caus, *New and Rare Inventions of Water-Works* (London, 1659), 26–27, Plate XIV.

20   John Wilkins, *Mathematical Magick*, 176.

21   For an account of the appropriations of Hero of Alexandria's descriptions, see Matteo Valleriani, "The Ancient Pneumatics Transformed during the Early Modern Period", *Nuncius*, XXIX/1 (2014), 127–173.

22   Maarten Van Dyck and Koen Vermeir note that, judging from the references Wilkins made to literature published during his university years, e.g. to Mersenne, Gassendi, and Kircher, his *Mathematical Magick* had been written in several stages for different audiences, adapting previous notes and ideas. This would also fall in line with the appearance of Wilkins' editing in *Of the Principles and Duties of Natural Religion*. See Maarten Van Dyck and Koen Vermeir, "Varieties of Wonder: John Wilkins' *Mathematical Magic* and the Perpetuity of Invention", *Historia Mathematica*, XLI/4 (2014), 463–489.

cover of *artes ingenuae* or the noble liberal arts. Wilkins presents mechanics as an art of pleasure rather than one of practicality, emphasising that "mixed Mathematicks" is a powerful τέχνη of prevalence over nature, which is appropriate and genteel.[23] The association of technical ingenuity with humanist *ingenuousness* as "gentleman-like" became the starting point for his legitimation of mechanics.

Wilkins first secures the ontological status of his art as an important branch of practical studies of "the frame of this great Universe, or the usual course of providence in the government of these created things".[24] The statement correlates with his ideas on the "wise contrivance" of divine dispensations, stated in the *Discourse Concerning the Beauty of Providence* (1649). Mechanics may be instrumental for providence, as, apart from the "plastic nature" of the soul, divine grace can also operate through the plastic nature of the human hand, whose power grows wondrously with practicing the arts.[25] Wilkins' reflections on the plasticity of the hand are reminiscent of the neo-Platonic "plastic principle" as a substance intermediating between matter and spirit.[26]

Mechanical invention is providential, since the properties of weight and power find themselves in such a relation to each other that the overcoming of weight necessitates the power of human ingenuity. The balance between weight and power in nature ensures that men "are not encouraged ... to such bold designes as would not become a created being",[27] but at the same time their ingenuity is stimulated. Mechanics encompasses "all those inventions, whereby nature in any way quickned or advanced in her defects".[28] In moral terms, it may restore humanity from "the first generall curse" and therefore should be celebrated as a liberal art, as *"Que liberum faciunt hominem, quibus curae virtus est"*. Apart from the improvement of individuals, Wilkins also notes the social benefits and the ideological significance of science. He mentions a figurative expression "according to the shekel of the Sanctuary" that can be construed as referring to some "weight or coin, distinct from, and more

---

23   Τέχνῃ κρατμενῶ ὧν φύςει νικώμεθα. John Wilkins, *Mathematical Magick*, Epigraph.

24   *Ibid.*, 2.

25   *Ibid.*, 30.

26   In 1659–1660, while briefly employed in Cambridge, Wilkins supported the Platonists, for instance, by arranging Benjamin Whichcote's appointment as his own successor in the vicarage of St. Lawrence Jewry. There is a remarkable similarity between Whichcote's and Wilkins' specific use of the term "ingenuity". See Robert A. Green, "Whichcote, Wilkins, 'Ingenuity', and the Reasonableness of Christianity", *Journal of the History of Ideas*, XLII/2 (1981), 227–252.

27   John Wilkins, *Mathematical Magick*, 104.

28   *Ibid.*

than the vulgar",[29] i.e. as if the Sanctuary disposed of the power to issue the norms of measure. Wilkins' own etymological investigation suggests that the standards of measurement yield a certain political power that is capable of rectifying an imperfect social order.[30]

Wilkins reproduces the contemporary distinction between the rational part of mechanics and its "cheirurgicall or manuall" part. Rational mechanics "may properly be styled liberall, as justly deserving the pursuit of an ingenious mind" liberated from lusts and passions.[31] Comparing mechanics to the other liberal arts, such as the art of speaking, Wilkins concludes that those "doe not more protect and adorn the mind, then these Mechanicall powers doe the body".[32] What equates rational mechanics with rhetoric is their analogous aesthetic capacity to adorn, resulting from the ingenuity of pointed figures introducing coherence into the abundance of parts and details.

Wilkins' narrative offers an attractive practical scenario "particularly for such Gentlemen as employ their estates", as well as for such common artificers "who may be much advantaged by the right understanding".[33] Presenting mechanics as a liberal art operating with physical force, Wilkins seeks to relate it to the notion of social power and explores the motives of religion, policy, and ambition in supporting mechanical endeavours.[34] The accessibility of the experience of mechanical ingenuity promotes the will for practicing the art, and Wilkins quotes Peter Ramus, who says that the eminence of mechanical industry in Germany was due to the extensive organization of public lectures conducted in the vernacular. Mechanics needs to follow the example of other liberal arts and employ the live language of experiments, which is partly why Wilkins desires to see the "fruit of his leasure" published.[35]

Wilkins' adherence to the use of ordinary language in scientific discourse originates from the linguistics of Reformed theology, where practical divinity should have been augmented through the perusal of Scripture in the native tongue. For Wilkins, the language of an art predetermines the pattern of its

---

29   *Ibid.*, 18.

30   John Wilkins' *Essay towards a Real Character and a Philosophical Language* (London: Printer to the Royal Society, 1668) suggested the use of a decimal system of measurements.

31   John Wilkins, *Mathematical Magick*, 9.

32   *Ibid.*, 10.

33   *Ibid.*

34   *Ibid.*, 79.

35   *Mathematical Magick* (1648) was one of the pioneering English-language publications on mechanics. Wilkins chose to promote innovative subjects several times. Apart from supporting Copernican views in *The Discovery of a World in the Moone* (1638), his *Mercury* (1641) became the first publication on cryptography in English.

development, and the language of "abstracted speculations" causes stagnation, since "once the learned men did forbid the reducing of them to particular use, and vulgar experiment, others thereupon refuse these studies themselves, as being but empty and useless speculations".[36] In other words, as soon as the art stops generating the figures of abundance, it loses the aesthetic appeal and deteriorates. At the same time, Wilkins shows himself concerned about the aptitude of any natural language to expedite the knowledge of things themselves. From his subsequent contribution to supervising the production of the *History of the Royal Society*, we can see that he repudiated the outdated fables but welcomed the new rhetoric of artistry. In his view, artificial languages could neutralise the flaws of natural tongues in the same way as the artificial instruments of mechanics might compensate for the weaknesses of the human body.[37] Wilkins' attitude to mechanical inventions is reminiscent of Joseph Addison's quote on poetic ingenuity which "makes additions to nature, giving greater variety to God's works".[38]

Wilkins' mechanics does not always comply with the abstract laws of motion, also because these laws were not yet formulated in a coherent representation.[39] However, early modern science tended to claim a higher probability rather than the truth of a certain statement. Experimental philosophy assessed propositions not in terms of "truth-value" but of "probability-value".[40] For instance, Thomas Sprat's *History* directly advised that *virtuosi* should use the formula "'tis probable that" for stating their claims.[41] Discussions on probability were also a standard element of literary theory.[42] Aristotle set the requirements for probability within a dramatic composition: empirically impossible elements could be assimilated, if altogether they formed a coherent narrative. Early modern British aesthetics adopted the Aristotelian attitude to probability in poetic inventions: "Beyond the actual works of nature a Poet may now

36 John Wilkins, *Mathematical Magick*, 5.

37 *Ibid.*, 95.

38 Joseph Addison, *The Spectator*, ed. Donald F. Bond (Oxford: Clarendon Press, 1965), Vol. 3, N 421 (Thursday 3 July 1712): 509.

39 A comprehensive scheme of the laws of motion was suggested within the "rational mechanics" of Newton's *Philosophiae Naturalis Principia Mathematica* (London, 1687).

40 For scholarship on Wilkins' use of the concept of probability, see Barbara Shapiro, *Probability and Certainty in Seventeenth-Century England* (Princeton: Princeton University Press, 1983).

41 Thomas Sprat, *The History of the Royal Society* (London: Printed by T.R. for J. Martyn, 1667), 107–109.

42 Meyer H. Abrams, *The Mirror and the Lamp: Romantic Theory and the Critical Tradition* (Oxford: Oxford University Press, 1953), 267.

go; but beyond the conceived possibility of nature, never".[43] Similarly, Wilkins' guidelines for mechanical design recommended to "never so much exceed that force, which the power is naturally endowed with".[44]

Before uncovering the truth, one needs to invent an instrument to do it with, also in the form of a linguistic protocol. Wilkins notes that acquaintance with mechanics is relatively rare outside the circle of "unlettered Artificers",[45] and therefore the special language of the art was yet underdeveloped. Wilkins industriously expounds on the vocabulary of mechanical engineering, and plans not only to popularise mechanical learning but also to standardise its professional vernacular lexicon, by disseminating it among the educated gentry. For instance, he explores the *know-how* of bodily operations, depicting "the *manner* whereby the power is impresst upon it [an object]".[46] Out of the scattered knowing of what pertains to a practical bodily art, he crafts a copious and legitimate philosophical description, as befits a noble liberal art. *Mathematical Magick* brings the "fair lady" of mechanics into the respectable society of educated communication, by giving her a tongue to speak.

Wilkins' Rationalization of Mechanics

The explication of the rational part of mechanics starts from "understanding the true difference betwixt the *weight* and the *power*".[47] In Wilkins' time, weight was commonly viewed as a quality that makes bodies "tend downwards". The Schools regarded the category of quality to be an incalculable parameter, and therefore weight as such could be deemed incalculable. But mathematics, as a liberal art, was entitled to account not only for qualities but also for calculable quantities. To legitimise the calculation of weight, Wilkins argues that Aristotle considered it to be a discrete quantity, meaning that weight could be measured, which reaffirmed the status of mechanics as a mathematical discipline. Wilkins also suggests defining weight as "affection" or the condition of being affected upon by a certain force or power, which shifted the emphasis in formulating the task of mechanics from the overcoming of weight to the acquisition of power.

---

43   Thomas Hobbes, "Answer to Davenant's Preface to *Gondibert*" (1650), in *Critical Essays of the Seventeenth Century*, ed. J. E. Spingarn, Vol. II (1650–1685) (Oxford: Clarendon Press, 1908), 62.

44   John Wilkins, *Mathematical Magick*, 11.

45   *Ibid.*, 10.

46   *Ibid.*, 55.

47   *Ibid.*, 11.

After clarifying the "subject and nature" of mechanics, Wilkins enumerates the basic appliances, such as the balance and the lever, "of which, the force of all Mechanicall inventions must necessarily be reduced".[48] Wilkins' mechanical expertise relied on the literature available on the continent, and his visualizations of mechanical devices derive from the *Mechanicorum Liber* (1577) of Guidobaldo del Monte, who similarly construed mechanics as a mathematical discipline. Some of the mathematical apparatus and the diagrams of engines with "toothed wheels" were borrowed from Marin Mersenne's *Cogitata physico-mathematica* (1644). However, Wilkins and Mersenne pursued different pedagogical targets: whereas Mersenne was more interested in building geometrical models, Wilkins sought to approximate these models to a whole range of experiences associated with mechanical art.[49]

Wilkins' guidelines employ various elements of visual rhetoric, such as depictions of bodily acts and the gestures of the hand. Illustrating his basic explanations with geometrical diagrams, he portrays more complicated mechanisms as if operated by a remarkable hand possessing a certain social status, precision of grasp, and conspicuousness of gesture (see Figure 5.1).

In classical rhetoric, gesture formed an integral part of the *actio* of a speech, which did not only visualise the subject-matter but also marked the boundary between the verbal and the experiential, as the speaker was supposed to translate speech into bodily action when his feelings were presumably beating his verbal resourcefulness. Gesture could be exhibited not only as a conventional expression of emotion but also as an indicator of the permanent character of depicted personality.[50] Apart from being an expression of *pathos*, gesture also represented an outward sign of *ethos*, enhancing the perlocutionary effect by emphasising the moral certainty of the portrayal. In scientific depictions, the gesture was employed for delivering the *historia* of an object.

The hand that governs the operation of machines in Wilkins' mechanics belongs to a gentleman-experimentalist, as we can judge from the fashionable cut of the cloud, out of which the masterful limb emerges.[51] In contrast with a similar illustration of Mersenne's, Wilkins shows not only the hand but also

---

48   *Ibid.*, 13.

49   For an account of Mersenne's views on the relationship between mathematical modelling and scientific experience, see Peter Dear, *Discipline and Experience: The Mathematical Way in the Scientific Revolution* (Chicago: University of Chicago, 1995), 133–136.

50   Caroline van Eck, *Classical Rhetoric and the Visual Arts in Early Modern Europe* (Cambridge: Cambridge University Press, 2007), 19.

51   Cf. John Wilkins' portrait by Mary Beale, painted after he became Bishop of Chester in 1668. http://prints.royalsociety.org/art/579683/portrait-of-john-wilkins-1614-1672

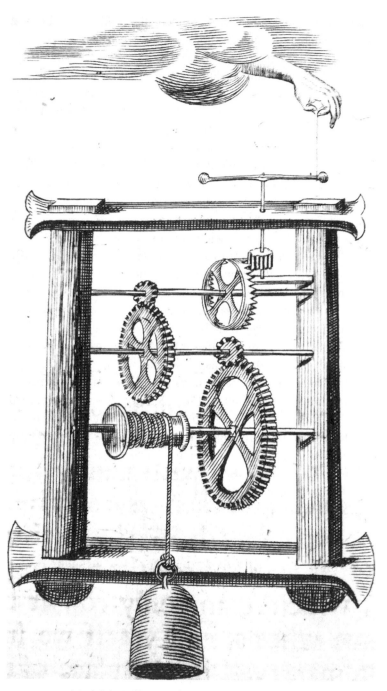

FIGURE 5.1   *A jack. John Wilkins,* Mathematical Magick (*London: Printed by M.F., 1648*), 88.
REPRODUCED BY KIND PERMISSION OF THE PRESIDENT AND FELLOWS OF
QUEENS' COLLEGE, CAMBRIDGE.

a thin hair that connects the living hand with the mechanical device.[52] This magical hand seems to communicate the will for motion to the machine and mediates between the realms of spirit and things, which invites parallels with preaching, and indeed the gesture is reminiscent of the recommendations from popular manuals on homiletics, such as the one Wilkins would craft himself a few years afterwards.[53]

Displaying a human hand in action, Wilkins also sets up a scale for the approximate force that is required to empower his devices. At that time, neither mechanical measurements for that force nor a proper mathematical apparatus to process such measurements was part of common knowledge. The visualization of experience substituted for geometrical demonstrations, and the sketched hand also performed a perlocutionary function. The pictured gesture is conspicuous but not forceful, and the shape of the posed hand is relaxed, which implies that the machine is easy to operate due to the almost magical power of a mechanical contrivance.

Wilkins continues employing rhetorical figures throughout the discourse and again uses *antithesis* to impart the experience of beholding the legendary Colossus of Rhodes.[54] First, the size of the statue is indicated by saying that its thumb could not be grasped by a man with both arms. Interestingly, *Vindiciae Academiarum*, a pamphlet that Wilkins would help to compose later, mentions that "it was heretofore accounted an instance of Mathematical skill, to give the dimensions of Hercules from the measure of his foot".[55] Wilkins might have it in mind to induce his readers not only to visualise the Colossus but also to gauge its approximate dimensions. Second, Wilkins claims that when the statue collapsed, "the brasse of it did load 900 camels".[56] An antithetical pair is composed out of the notions of "a thumb not to be grasped by man with both arms" and the "load [of] 900 camels". The size of a thumb and the load of nearly a thousand camels do not form a natural opposition, also because they refer to different categories of dimension and weight, but Wilkins pairs them into an *antithesis* that juxtaposes the capacities of humans and draught animals. Within this *antithesis*, "one thumb" and "900 camels" are turned into the

52   Cf. Marin Mersenne, "De mechanicis", *Cogitata physico-mathematica* (Parisiis, 1644), 40.

53   See John Wilkins, *A Discourse Concerning the Gift of Prayer: shewing what it is, wherein it consists and how far it is attainable by industry* (London, 1651).

54   *Mathematical Magick* also cites John Greaves on the purposes of building and dimensions of the Egyptian pyramids. See John Greaves, *Pyramidographia* (London, 1646), 68–77.

55   Seth Ward, *Vindiciae Academiarum* (Oxford, 1654), 27.

56   John Wilkins, *Mathematical Magick*, 64.

end points on the scale of physical aptitude. Then the *antithesis* is mediated through the concept of force, which is ultimately intended to communicate the appreciation for the intellectual power of ingenuity. Later in his career Wilkins would attempt to calculate the exact size of Noah's Ark, but in *Mathematical Magick* Wilkins does not disclose the dimensions of legendary monuments, leaving them in the domain of marvellous infinity. However, he does not aim to just superficially amuse the reader, as he ruminates over various conjectures on how the ancients could erect such outstanding structures. With sarcasm, he cites a legend on how a Greek architect proposed to carve the mountain Athos into a human statue, and how the erecting of this "microcosm" was rejected on political and economic grounds. He advises the engineering imagination to go "beyond the actual works of nature" but not "beyond the conceived possibility of nature".

Wilkins' Imaginary Mechanisms

However, at times it seems that the laws of poetic imagination are more imperative for Wilkins than the laws of nature, which would accord with his own maxim that nature ought to be commanded against her own laws.[57] Wilkins uses the "plastic power" of poetical and mechanical ingenuity to create paradoxical designs, which were meant to attest that "it is possible by the multiplication of these [forces] to perform the greatest labour with the least power".[58] The antithetical motto *Datum pondus cum datâ potentiâ*, "the greatest weight with the least power", represented one of the primary values in both rhetorical and mechanical artistry.[59]

Wilkins acknowledges that many of the fabled experiments of the past employed the rhetorical strategies of creating belief. In a famous thought experiment, Archimedes claimed that he could move the globe of the earth, if only he would "know where to stand and fasten his instrument". This posed a mechanical problem, but a social authority came to the rescue, as "the King of *Sirakuse* did enact a law whereby every man was bound to beleeve, whatever *Archimedes* would affirm".[60] Wilkins neither claims to have implemented his own paradoxical trials, nor does he appeal for support from the King of England, which in the year 1648 might not have been helpful. Precisely at that

---

57   *Ibid.*, 10.
58   *Ibid.*, 92.
59   *Ibid.*, 79.
60   *Ibid.*, 80.

point, the British intellectual community received evidence that the state
institutions could not provide a warranty for truth-claims, and had to focus
their attention on studying forces more fundamental than the sacred power
of sovereigns.

Wilkins' first imaginary experiment again employs the figure of *antithesis*
and repeats Archimedes' endeavour. Wilkins states that the globe of the earth
weighs about 2 400 000 000 000 000 000 000 000 pounds, a barely comprehensible numeral that takes up a whole line on the printed page and mathematically almost vanishes into infinity. Then he claims that a single man
could move the globe, if only the right lever were available. As before, the
weight of 2400 sextillion pounds and the power of "one man" do not oppose
each other naturally. But turning them into the end points on the scale of mechanical capacity creates the desired effect of wonder. Wilkins maintains that
his "magical" mechanics does not contradict any laws of nature, since "every
ordinary instrument doth include all these parts *really*, though not sensibly
distinguished".[61]

Various combinations of *antithesis*, *incrementum*, and *gradatio* help Wilkins
create other sophisticated machines that may challenge the laws of nature but
contradict no laws of rhetorical composition. The figure of *incrementum* was
often used to mediate the notions opposing each other within an *antithesis*.
Since the main point of using *antithesis* consisted in its mediation, *incrementum*
was given much attention in early modern rhetorical manuals. Henry Peacham
in *The Garden of Eloquence* (1593) defines it as a form of speech "contrarie to
the naturall order of thinges" that is "apt to bewtifie the speech and to amplifie
the matter" with an effect similar "in force to comparison, and it as it were the
Orators scaling ladder, by which he climeth to the top of high comparison".[62]
A version of *incrementum,* the figure of *gradatio* represents a conceptual series
where the elements are melded into an ascending continuum, overlapping and
distributing each other's properties. The ancients saw *gradatio* as an exceed-
ingly powerful tool, so that Quintilian recommended a sparing use of it, since
otherwise it makes the style look "affected". Interestingly, rhetorical tradition
itself suggested the metaphorical association between rhetorical figures and
the mechanical concepts of force, power, and weight.

Being products of the liberal art of mechanics, Wilkins' imaginary mechanisms represented models composed of basic mechanical and figurative devices. In another thought experiment, he claims that if forcing up an oak by the

---

61   *Ibid.*, 82.

62   Henry Peacham, *Garden of Eloquence* [1593] (Gainesville, FL: Scholars' Facsimiles and
      Reprints, 1954), 169.

roots is equivalent to lifting up the weight of 4 000 000 000 pounds, an engine consisting of two double pulleys, twelve wheels, and a sail should be able to do the job (see Figure 5.2).[63]

In the supplied illustration, we see an imaginary construct where a breath of air turns a cross-shaped sail, which transfers the momentum through a system of toothed wheels, which supposedly amplifies it so as to generate enough force to pull up an oak-tree by the roots. Wilkins' design bears traces of the initial rhetorical figures that led him to shape his creation as a mediated *antithesis*. The concepts of "air" and "oak-tree" are not intrinsically antithetical, but Wilkins juxtaposes the physical power that can be linked to moving these objects and turns these amounts of power into the end-points of the scale of mechanical capacity. Thus the *antithesis* is mediated through the notion of power, which also infers the appreciation of human inventiveness.

In the actual mechanisms with toothed wheels, the momentum generated by a certain force can be slowly accumulated and distributed through the system, making the whole mechanism more potent. However, the difference between Wilkins' imaginary and the real mechanics lies in the fact that a real design also accounts for the loss of momentum, which depends on the various properties of components. Wilkins' imagination does not take into account the materiality of things, also because the necessary computations were not deemed accessible, and the problems of mechanics were routinely solved through hands-on experimentation. Wilkins' experimental imagination moves "contrarie to the naturall order of thinges", only taking into account the amplification of power, just as it happens with the figure of *incrementum*. Thinking along the lines of this figure, Wilkins suggests a pattern for amplifying the force through the system of toothed wheels that are also connected like the overlapping elements of *gradatio*. Although Wilkins admits that this particular design is not feasible, his machine nevertheless succeeds in producing wonder. Similarly to the fabled Archimedes Lever, Wilkins' root-puller essentially remains a figurative but at the same time mechanical model. Upon dealing with the oak, Wilkins tests his device on Archimedes' assignment of lifting up the globe of the earth, and, as we might expect, the imaginary machine elevates the imaginary globe in no time.

Describing more complicated mechanisms, Wilkins continues to develop his argument along the lines of *antithesis*; for instance, he is visibly fascinated with extremely swift and extremely slow motion. He approvingly cites anecdotes about John Dee, such as how he once purchased a vastly expensive instrument that had a wheel not finishing one revolution around its axis in

---

63   John Wilkins, *Mathematical Magick*, 97–99.

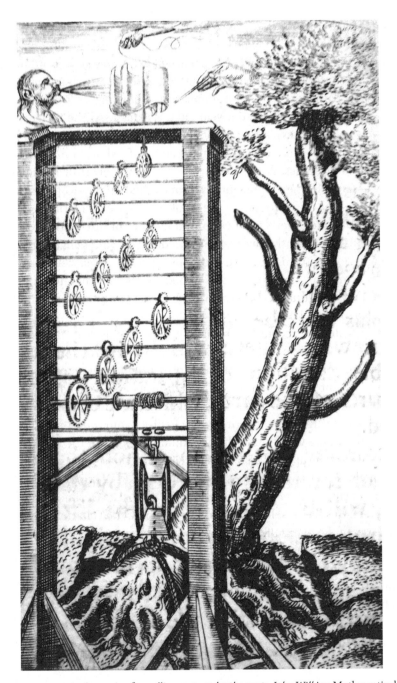

FIGURE 5.2 *An engine for pulling up trees by the roots. John Wilkins,* Mathematical Magick
(*London: Printed by M.F., 1648*), *98.*
REPRODUCED BY KIND PERMISSION OF THE PRESIDENT AND FELLOWS OF
QUEENS' COLLEGE, CAMBRIDGE.

seven thousand years.[64] For Wilkins, extreme slow motion is "no less admirable" than extreme swift motion, since both are barely accessible for observation. Theoretically, one cannot doubt the existence of extremely slow motion, but one also cannot observe it accurately with the naked eye, which makes it into an ideal object for figurative and mathematical modelling. In *Discourse on the Beauty of Providence*, published a year later, Wilkins used the imagery of extremely slow motion to explain how the works of providence may sometimes appear sluggish, if perceived from the perspective of a short human lifespan. In relation to mechanics, Wilkins compares the extremely slow motion to other barely observable phenomena, noting that the human physical senses are "disproportioned for comprehending the whole compasse and latitude of things".[65] Around the mid-seventeenth century, a number of discoveries was made due to the use of recently invented optical devices, which challenged the Baconian criterion of truth based on sensuous perception. Mathematical verification was commonly underdeveloped in mechanics, and therefore the perlocutionary force of figurative patterns worked as the conceptual rails for advancing the experimental practices.

By alternating historical accounts, utopian scenarios, imaginary designs, and poetic pieces, Wilkins demonstrates the heuristic power of rhetorical and mechanical combinatorics. Whenever the rigor of mathematical demonstration appears insufficient, he compensates it by crafting a persuasive narrative. Wilkins' design of a sailing chariot offers ample material for demonstrating his linguistic protocol of bringing the imaginary mechanisms into the world. The sailing chariot represents a variation of the windmill: "The force of the wind in the motion of sails may be applied also to the driving of a Chariot, by which a man may sail on the land as well as by a ship on the water".[66] Wilkins disposes of neither a working model nor a geometrical scheme of this device, and therefore he first enumerates the travelogues according to which such chariots were in widespread use on the plains of China, Spain, and Holland. Then he quotes an eye-witnessing account of travelling by a sailing chariot that can move "with an equal swiftness to the wind it selfe. Men that ran before it seeming to goe backwards, things which seeme at a great distance being presently overtaken and left behind".[67] Wilkins also reproduces Hugo Grotius' "copious and elegant" Latin epigrams from *Grotii Poemata* (1639),[68] praising an invention by

---

64   *Ibid.*, 112.
65   *Ibid.*, 116.
66   *Ibid.*, 154.
67   *Ibid.*, 156.
68   *Ibid.*, 157.

Simon Stevin, who collaborated with Johan de Groote, Hugo Grotius' father. Around 1600, Stevin constructed two wind driven carriages that could move along the beaches in the Netherlands.[69] Wilkins adds that Grotius' account could make one feel distrustful, but upon further enquiry was "attested from the particular eye-sight & experience of such eminent persons, whose names I dare not cite in a business of this nature". Stevin's chariots were well-known to serve for the amusement of Prince Maurice of Orange, but as in the case with the Egyptian Pyramids, Wilkins prefers to position the authority of his witness beyond the reach of documentation.

Emulating further his design of the sailing chariot, Wilkins provides a sketchy version of Simon Stevin's *Zeilwagen*, wind chariot, depicted in an engraving by Jacques de Gheyn. That realistic scene of fashionable entertainment displays two chariots of different sizes, supplied with sails but not shaped like boats, moving along the coastline, with several conventional boats placed in the marine background for comparison. In Wilkins' simpler illustration, several people are traveling on a wheeled boat, shaped like a vessel with a rudder. Then he describes a modification of the boat, where the wheels are replaced with sledges, whose main function seems to be to endow the imaginary design with additional details, as it was recommended by the doctrine of *copia*. Finally, Wilkins introduces his own stylish design of a sailing chariot, providing an elaborate illustration (see Figure 5.3).

Wilkins admits the questionable functionality of his inventions but at the same time regrets that none of the gentry have even attempted to construct anything similar: "The experiments of this kind being very pleasant and not costly: what could be more delightful or better husbandry, then to make use of the wind (which costs nothing, and eats nothing) instead of horses?"[70] In the eighteenth century, the playful reception of endeavours of the previous generation would also mention Stevin's "celebrated sailing chariot", which belonged to Prince Maurice and could "carry half a dozen people thirty German miles, in I don't know how few minutes".[71] Thereby it was likewise questioned why none of the gentry attempts "to make use of the winds, which cost nothing, and which eat nothing".[72] The ironic answer argues that precisely because

---

69   For a study on Simon Steven's biography and engineering achievements, see among others E.J. Dijksterhuis, *Simon Stevin: Science in the Netherlands around 1600* (The Hague: Springer Netherlands, 1970).

70   *Ibid.*, 161.

71   Laurence Sterne, *The Life and Opinions of Tristram Shandy, Gentleman* (London: Printed for R. and J. Dodsley, 1760), 87.

72   *Ibid.*, 90.

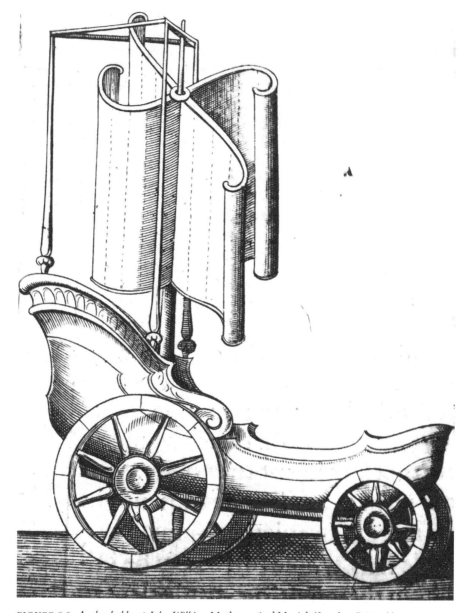

FIGURE 5.3 *A wheeled boat. John Wilkins,* Mathematical Magick (*London: Printed by
M.F., 1648*), *158.*
REPRODUCED BY KIND PERMISSION OF THE PRESIDENT AND FELLOWS OF
QUEENS' COLLEGE, CAMBRIDGE.

such chariots cost nothing, "the scheme is bad", since it is the circulation of trade that "brings in money",[73] and although scientific heads should be recompensed for such inventions, the use of them should be suppressed.

Sailing chariots were never to become a means of transportation on European roads, but later a similar rhetoric was proposed for the spread of wind turbines. In 1648, from the initial grapevine claim that "such Chariots are commonly used in the Champion plains of China" to the graceful landau full of social appeal, Wilkins' chariot is sailing smoothly over all the roughness of technical background.

Liberal Mechanics and the Perspective of New Science

Wilkins pays a lot of attention to the performativity of "fixed automata", i.e. the machines that "move only according to their several parts, and not according to their whole frame".[74] He comments excitedly on various musical and astronomical clocks, as well as other implementations of the principle of *mimesis naturae*. However, his real captivation lies with such complexity of mechanical design that makes a mere machine appear animated, whereby mechanical artistry overcomes nature through imitation.

Among the many fixed automata that Wilkins describes, including the spectacular moving statues and singing birds, he seems particularly captivated by a subtle astronomical instrument supposedly invented by Archimedes, showing the diurnal and annual courses of the sun, the changes and aspects of the Moon, etc. This prime possession in Wilkins' imaginary cabinet of curiosities is first announced with a quote from an epigram of Claudian, in Latin with an English translation:

> Jove saw the heavens framed in a little glasse,
> And laughing, to the gods these words did passe;
> Comes then the power of mortall cares so far?
> In brittle orbs my labours acted are.[75]

Further in the epigram, Jove acknowledges that Archimedes "brings hither the laws of God by art", and that "a poor hand is nature's rival grown". Wilkins analyzes this specimen of ancient poetry with earnest interest, as his very first

---

73   *Ibid.*, 91.
74   John Wilkins, *Mathematical Magick*, 162.
75   *Ibid.*, 165 ff.

remark after finishing its last line sounds "But that this engine should be made of glasse, is scarce credible", as if the rest of the epigram, including the scene with a laughing Jove, were beyond doubt as a historical fact. Wilkins' criticism about the materiality of the "brittle orbs" could be related to his life-long loyalty to Copernican cosmology and the repudiation of Ptolemaic crystal spheres.[76] However, he oversees the dissimilarity between poetical composition and mechanical modelling, because in his own argument they both derive from the *topos* of liberal arts. Wilkins' narrative depicts the possible, and transferring the possible into the condition of reality, uses the refined Archimedes machine as a model for formulating the values of mechanical ingenuity.

"The particular circumstances for which the Automata of this kind, are most eminent" include: "the lastingesse of their motion without needing any other supply", "the easiness and simplicity of their composition", "the multitude and variety of those services for which they may be usefull", and "the littleness of their frame".[77] Wilkins fills two pages clarifying the apparently antithetical criterion of "the art and simplicity of mechanical composition", which is almost four times longer than the rest of his comments on any other criterion for mechanical sophistication. His formula for the perfect ingenuity consists in the notion that "the addition of any such unnecessary parts, as may be supplied some other way, is a sure sign of unskillfulnesse and ignorance", and "the more easie and compendious such inventions are, the more artificial should they be esteemed".[78] In other words, liberal mechanics appreciates the pointed copiousness of design. Similarly to the Erasmian guidelines on rhetorical composition, which praised fresh, pointed similitudes and repudiated cumbersome allegories, Wilkins' mechanical device of style applies the principle of composition common to all liberal arts. The liberalization of mechanics can also be interpreted as a search for the symbolic forms for construing nature:

> Those antiquated engines that did consist of such a needlesse multitude of wheels, and springs, and screws, (like the old *hypothesis* of the heavens) may be compared to the notions of confused knowledge, which are always full of perplexity and complications, and seldome in order, whereas the inventions of art are more regular, simple, and perspicuous, like the apprehensions of a distinct and thoroughly informed judgement.[79]

---

76   For a study on Wilkins' defence of Copernicanism, see John L. Russell, "The Copernican System in Great Britain", in *The Reception of Copernicus' Heliocentric Theory*, ed. J. Dobrzycki (New York: Springer, 1972), 189–240.

77   John Wilkins, *Mathematical Magick*, 168.

78   *Ibid.*, 169 ff.

79   *Ibid.*, 169.

In this context, Thomas Sprat's subsequent explicit target of prevailing over the "false worlds and fables of ancient superstition" means that the excessive ornaments of speech should be removed from scientific discourse for the same reason that excessive screws need to be removed from a mechanism, i.e. since both appear to be "in open defiance against Reason".[80] On the contrary, the pointed copiousness of ingenious inventions could make the meaning of things themselves visible through the facilitating optic of the transparent coherence of discourse.

Wilkins describes various legendary and existing "fixed" automata imitating the singing of birds and human speech, as well as a diverse range of flying chariots. Possibly due to his family history, he is also attentive to the problem of *perpetuum mobile* which he mentions at the end of *Mathematical Magick* as the ultimate wonder.[81] The book appeared in print in the same year as Wilkins was appointed Warden of Wadham College, which hosted the experimental club in Oxford. Later, the practice of mechanics became part of the agenda of the Royal Society of London. The minutes of the Society's initial meetings already depict an experiment on air compression, conducted by Dr Wilkins. Blowing into the pipe "the Trumpet fashion", he made "rise up a platform with a fat boy of about 16 or 17 y.o." sitting on it.[82] Wilkins pledged the establishment of the Society's Mechanical Committee whose first assembly on July 16, 1664, proposed "to make an instrument by which may be found a ship's motion through the water".[83] At times, it was apparently challenging for the Committee to arrive at certain conclusions, as its second gathering on August 6 left an entry according to which, upon inquiry "what any of the Committee had thought upon the method, formerly mentioned, and it being found, that it had not *yet* [inserted] been considered by any, the Company was desired to take it into consideration by the next meeting".[84] The crossed and inserted marks in the minutes are indicative of the lively debates during the Society's meetings, where a few years earlier the Second Duke of Buckingham had promised

---

80 Thomas Sprat, *The History of the Royal Society*, 43, 112.

81 Wilkins' father reportedly attempted to build a *perpetuum mobile*. See John Aubrie, *Brief Lives*, "John Wilkins". For scholarship on various aspects of Wilkins' theological legacy, see Barbara Shapiro, *John Wilkins 1614–1672: An Intellectual Biography* (Berkeley: University of California Press, 1969).

82 "Experiments concerning the force of blowing". Royal Society Archives RBC/1/17, 19 August 1661: 63–64.

83 "Transactions of the Mechanical Committee". Royal Society Archives DM/5/66, 16 July 1664.

84 *Ibid.*, 6 August 1664.

to present the company with a piece of unicorn's horn.[85] The entry for October 17 of the same year mentions that "the mechanicall Authors, formerly brought in, were recommended to the perusal of the members of the Society", including the treatises by Girolamo Cardano, Tycho Brahe, Athanasius Kircher, as well as Guidobaldo del Monte and Marin Mersenne.[86] Wilkins chose *The Jewell House of Art and Nature* (1594) by Hugh Plat, devoted to household recipes, and his own *Mathematical Magick*,[87] whereby his responsibilities within the Society encompassed a wide range of natural and artificial objects of curiosity.

Wilkins' narrative of mechanics represented not a fictional endeavour but an exercise in the modelling of probable knowledge, which was appreciated by posterity. Daniel Defoe in *An Essay upon Projects* (1697) values Wilkins' *Mathematical Magick* for providing "as much of the theory ... as writing a book could do" for the public fascination with scientific experimenting.[88] Samuel Johnson's *The Prince of Abissinia*, better known today as *Rasselas*, venerates the art of building sailing chariots and flying gears, both featured in *Mathematical Magick*, by placing them in the utopian Happy Valley.[89] Finally, Jonathan Swift's *The Battle of the Books* commemorates Wilkins' contribution: "The engineers were commanded by Regiomontanus and Wilkins", whereas "Euclid was chief engineer" of the Ancients.[90] Wilkins employed the techniques of figurative thinking, developed within the aesthetics of rhetorical and poetic composition, as symbolic forms for the designing of the new paradigmatic features of science. Partly due to the specific conditions of the post-war discourse, he was disposed to seek epistemological solutions through the promotion of motoric intelligence in the practices of mechanical artistry.

When learning is viewed as a practice, a different set of epistemological values begins to prevail. Doctrinal argumentation disowns the vividness of

---

85 "Journal Books of the Royal Society". Royal Society Archives JBC/1, 5 June 1660: 24. The translators of the King James Version of the Bible (1611) erroneously followed the Greek and Latin source texts, and employed "unicorn" to translate "re'em", an aurochs bull. Marco Polo also had claimed to have seen a unicorn to be identified as a Javanese rhinoceros. In 1660, the gift promised to the Society could arouse considerable interest in relation to plant and animal classifications, which later became the primary pursuit of John Ray and Francis Willughby, who collaborated with Wilkins on his language project.

86 "Transactions of the Mechanical Committee", Royal Society Archives DM/5/66, 17 October 1664.

87 *Ibid.*, 14 November 1664.

88 Daniel Defoe, *An Essay upon Projects* (London: Printed by R.R. for Tho. Cockerill, 1697), 25.

89 Samuel Johnson, *The Prince of Abissinia* (London: Printed for R. and J. Dodsley, 1760), Vol. I, 35, 37.

90 Jonathan Swift, *A Tale of a Tub: Written for the Universal Improvement of Mankind* (Dublin: re-printed, 1705), 141.

expression, but experimental discourse appreciates the clearness of performance and does not marginalise the sensuous. In this context, the early modern requirement for "speaking plainly" meant the adequate delivery of performative illocutionary intentions. Dialectical and rhetorical techniques may facilitate such plain speaking, even though rhetoric does not employ plain language. Mechanical inventions could be started with the procedures of dialectical *inventio* and hypothetical designing that liberalise engineering practices and extend the horizon of the possible.

Wilkins was among the chief ideologists of the language reformation within the Royal Society, which aimed to turn the language of science into a more pointed instrument of invention and discovery. Wilkins' contribution to the advancement of learning consisted in elaborating on the methods of raising the precision of scientific narratives. The Royal Society's efforts were part of a broader movement from *inventio* as a framework for producing probable knowledge to technical invention as a means of achieving the certainty of knowing through verifiable demonstration. Late seventeenth-century science turned away from learning as *mimesis naturae* to the method of reproducing nature through mathematical modelling. Using Nietzsche's words, nowadays "an imitation is no longer felt to be an imitation", but the techniques of dialectical rhetoric may have continued to play a part in knowledge-making. The programme of natural studies keeps developing along the lines of piercing surfaces, and the experimental access to objects is often obtained through the virtual surface as a notional space where perlocutionary effects may precondition scientific modelling.

Works Cited

Abrams, Meyer H. *The Mirror and the Lamp: Romantic Theory and the Critical Tradition.* Oxford: Oxford University Press, 1953.

Addison, Joseph. *The Spectator*, edited by Donald F. Bond (Oxford: Clarendon Press, 1965), Vol. 3, N 421 (Thursday 3 July 1712): 509–510.

Agricola, Rudolf. *De inventione dialectica libri tres*, edited by Lothar Mund. Tübingen: Max Niemeyer Verlag, 1992.

Bacon, Francis. *The Advancement of Learning.* London: Printed for Henrie Tomes, 1605.

De Caus, Isaac. *New and Rare Inventions of Water-Works.* London: Printed by Joseph Moxon, 1659.

De Caus, Salomon. *Hortvs Palatinvs: A Friderico Rege Boemiae Electore Palatino Heidelbergae Exstructus.* Franckfurt: Theodor de Bry, 1620.

Dear, Peter. *Discipline and Experience: The Mathematical Way in the Scientific Revolution.* Chicago: University of Chicago, 1995.

Dijksterhuis, E.J., *Simon Stevin: Science in the Netherlands around 1600*. The Hague: Springer Netherlands, 1970.

Erasmus, Desiderius. *Collected Works of Erasmus*, edited by Craig R. Thomson. Toronto: University of Toronto Press, 1978.

"Experiments concerning the force of blowing". Royal Society Archives RBC/1/17.

Fahnestock, Jeanne. *Rhetorical Figures in Science*. New York: Oxford University Press, 1999.

Feingold, Mordechai. "Parallel Lives: The Mathematical Careers of John Pell and John Wallis". *Huntington Library Quarterly*, LXIX/3 (2006), 451–468.

Fleming, J.D., ed. *The Invention of Discovery, 1500–1700*. Farnham: Ashgate, 2013.

Greaves, John. *Pyramidographia*. London: George Badger, 1646.

Green, Robert A. "Whichcote, Wilkins, 'Ingenuity', and the Reasonableness of Christianity". *Journal of the History of Ideas*, XLII/2 (1981), 227–252.

Gross, Alan G. *A Rhetoric of Science*. Cambridge, MA: Harvard University Press, 1996.

Hobbes, Thomas. "Answer to Davenant's Preface to *Gondibert*" [1650]. In *Critical Essays of the Seventeenth Century*, edited by J.E. Spingarn, Vol. II (1650–1685), 45–55. Oxford: Clarendon Press, 1908.

"Journal Books of the Royal Society", Royal Society Archives JBC/1.

Johnson, Samuel. *The Prince of Abissinia*. London: printed for R. and J. Dodsley; and W. Johnston, 1760.

Kaoukji, Natalia. "Machines and Mathematical Magic". Presentation at symposium "John Wilkins and His Legacy", Wadham College, Oxford, September 15, 2014.

Mack, Peter. *Renaissance Argument: Valla and Agricola in the Traditions of Rhetoric and Dialectic*. Leiden: E.J. Brill, 1993.

Mack, Peter. *A History of Renaissance Rhetoric, 1380–1620*. Oxford: Oxford University Press, 2011.

Mersenne, Marin. *Cogitata physico-mathematica*. Parisiis, 1644.

Miller, Carolyn R. "The Aristotelian Topos: Hunting for Novelty". In *Re-Reading Aristotle's Rhetoric*, edited by Alan G. Gross and Alan E. Walzer. 130–148. Carbondale, IL: Southern Illinois University, 2000.

Newton, Isaac. *Philosophiae Naturalis Principia Mathematica*. London, 1687.

Pape, Wilhelm. *Handwörterbuch der griechischen Sprache*. Braunschweig, 1914.

Peacham, Henry. *Garden of Eloquence* [1593]. Gainesville, FL: Scholars' Facsimiles and Reprints, 1954.

Quintilian. *Institutio oratoria*, translated by Harold Edgeworth Butler. Cambridge, MA: Harvard University Press, 1922.

Russell, John L. "The Copernican System in Great Britain". In *The Reception of Copernicus' Heliocentric Theory*, edited by J. Dobrzycki. 189–240. New York: Springer, 1972.

Shapiro, Barbara. *John Wilkins 1614–1672: An Intellectual Biography*. Berkeley: University of California Press, 1969.

Shapiro, Barbara. *Probability and Certainty in Seventeenth-Century England*. Princeton: Princeton University Press, 1983.

Skouen, Tina, and Ryan J. Stark, eds., *Rhetoric and the Early Royal Society: A Sourcebook*. Leiden: E.J. Brill, 2014.

Sprat, Thomas. *The History of the Royal Society*. London: Printed by T.R. for J. Martyn, 1667.

Sterne, Laurence. *The Life and Opinions of Tristram Shandy, Gentleman*. London: Printed for R. and J. Dodsley, 1760.

Swift, Jonathan. *A Tale of a Tub: Written for the Universal Improvement of Mankind*. Dublin: re-printed; and are to be sold only at Dick's and Lloyd's Coffee houses, 1705.

"Transactions of the Mechanical Committee". Royal Society Archives DM/5/66.

Valleriani, Matteo. "The Ancient Pneumatics Transformed during the Early Modern Period". *Nuncius*, XXIX/1 (2014), 127–173.

Van Dyck, Maarten, and Koen Vermeir. "Varieties of Wonder: John Wilkins' *Mathematical Magic* and the Perpetuity of Invention". *Historia Mathematica*, XLI/4 (2014), 463–489.

Van Eck, Caroline. *Classical Rhetoric and the Visual Arts in Early Modern Europe*. Cambridge: Cambridge University Press, 2007.

Ward, Seth. *Vindiciae Academiarum*. Oxford: Thomas Robinson, 1654.

Wilkins, John. *Mathematical Magick*. London: Printed by M.F., 1648.

Wilkins, John. *Essay towards a Real Character and a Philosophical Language*. London: Printer to the Royal Society, 1668.

Wilkins, John. *A Discourse Concerning the Gift of Prayer: Shewing what it is, wherein it consists and how far it is attainable by industry*. London, 1651.

CHAPTER 6

"Quitting Now the Flowers of Rhetoric": Anti-rhetorical Continuities in English Science and Literature

Richard Nate

Abstract

This essay traces the impact which anti-rhetorical gestures emerging during the Scientific Revolution had on later writers. Although defenders of the seventeenth-century plain style argued against "rhetorical flourishes", it is obvious that their endeavours led to a new rhetorical decorum rather than to an abolition of rhetorical strategies. A century later, anti-rhetorical postures had become so commonplace that they could be adopted for a number of different purposes. While, in the "War of Pamphlets", authors employed them to defend their political positions, Romantic poets used them to articulate their literary and cultural criticism.

The emergence of the plain-style ideal in early modern England is a well-documented fact. In the wake of Richard Foster Jones' early studies of the late 1920s and early 1930s, a number of scholars have commented on the shift in stylistic attitudes which occurred during the seventeenth century, especially within the context of the Royal Society.[1] It was scientists, in particular, who called for a stylistic reform which they regarded as a vital factor in the "advancement of learning". Still, the "plain-style debate"[2] represented just one aspect of a general concern with problems of verbal communication. The

---

1   See the essays in Richard Foster Jones et al., *The Seventeenth Century: Studies in the History of English Thought and Literature from Bacon to Pope* (Stanford, Cal.: Stanford University Press / London: Oxford University Press, 1969). Later studies include Peter Dear, "*Totius in verba*: The Rhetorical Constitution of Authority in the Early Royal Society", *Isis*, LXXVI (1985), 145–161; and Brian Vickers, "The Royal Society and English Prose Style: A Reassessment", in *Rhetoric and the Pursuit of Truth: Language Change in the Seventeenth and Eighteenth Centuries*, Brian Vickers and Nancy S. Struever (Los Angeles: William Andrews Clark Memorial Library, 1985).

2   Werner Hüllen, "The Royal Society and the Plain Style Debate", in *Fachsprachen / Languages for Special Purposes*, ed. Lothar Hoffmann et al., vol. 2 (Berlin / New York: de Gruyter, 1999), 2465–2472.

interest of scientists in language is discernible in a number of works by authors associated with the new learning, ranging from John Wallis' *Grammatica
linguae anglicanae* (1654), in which the specific character of the English syn-
tax was acknowledged for the first time, to various works by John Wilkins, including his early *Mercury, or the Secret and Swift Messenger* (1641), which listed
and explained various ways of storing and conveying information. Wilkins' *Essay Concerning a Real Character and a Philosophical Language* (1668) shows
to what extreme the scientists' concern with language could lead. In it, the
author suggested an artificial language consisting of a hierarchical classification of terms, supplemented by some rudimentary syntactic devices to make
possible statements of fact.[3] In his introduction, Wilkins even went so far as to
advocate his scientifically based sign system as a universal language and, thus,
as a remedy for the curse of Babel.

In order to understand the vigour with which members of the Royal Society were engaged in the debates on communication, it should be remembered
that the new style was not propagated for its own sake but set against a prevalent form of discourse, which had been inherited from Renaissance humanism
and in which the presentation of rhetorical skills had played a dominant role.[4]
Thus, when writers such as Robert Boyle, Joseph Glanvill, Robert Hooke and
Thomas Sprat reflected on adequate ways of conveying scientific information,
they also demarcated themselves from what they perceived as a hindrance
to their cause. One source to which they could refer was Francis Bacon's *The
Advancement of Learning* (1605). Writing about so-called "distempers of learning", Bacon had complained about a contemporary form of rhetorical "excess",
namely that

> men began to hunt more after words than matter; and more after the
> choiceness of the phrase, and the round and clean composition of the
> sentence, and the sweet falling of the clauses, and the varying and il-
> lustration of their works with tropes and figures, than after the weight

---

3   Wilkins' views on language have received much attention in recent decades, cf. for instance
    the articles collected in *John Wilkins and 17th-Century British Linguistics*, ed. Joseph L. Sub-
    biondo, (Amsterdam & Philadelphia: Benjamins, 1992). On some contradictions inherent in
    Wilkins' undertaking cf. my discussions in "The Interjection as a Grammatical Category in
    John Wilkins' Philosophical Language", *Historiographia Linguistica*, XXIII (1996), 89–109, and
    in *Wissenschaft, Rhetorik und Literatur: Historische Perspektiven* (Würzburg: Königshausen &
    Neumann, 2009), 188–200.

4   For the rhetorical culture of the Renaissance, see the essays in *Renaissance-Rhetorik / Renais-
    sance Rhetoric*, ed. Heinrich F. Plett (Berlin / New York: de Gruyter, 1993).

of matter, worth of subject, soundness of argument, life of invention, or depth of judgment.[5]

While Bacon had still had something positive to say about the art of rhetoric, later authors would often reject it altogether. In such cases, it seems feasible to speak of an anti-rhetorical attitude. Ultimately dating back to Plato's critique of the Sophists, anti-rhetoric can be defined as a way of writing which uses rhetoric as a weapon against the use of rhetoric and which, almost by necessity, relies on strategies of dissimulation and *celare artem*.[6]

In order to understand the scientists' hostility towards rhetoric, it is also worth remembering a shift that had occurred in the wake of sixteenth-century Ramism. While the classical rhetorical system had comprised a whole set of communicative factors ranging from methods of acquiring information (*inventio*), the structuring of this information into coherent discourse (*dispositio*), stylistic expression (*elocutio*), safekeeping in the memory (*memoria*), and various forms of delivery (*actio*), Petrus Ramus had transferred the first two of these categories to the domain of dialectics. As a consequence, the *ars rhetorica* became more and more identified with a storehouse of tropes and figures.[7] No longer representing a highly esteemed art, with the *homo rhetoricus* as its celebrated hero, it became possible to see in rhetoric something superfluous. In its reduced form, rhetoric was perceived as an artificial ingredient "added" to a normal, seemingly natural way of speaking. Since the plain style was defined by the very absence of these additions, it could be considered by its defenders as "non-rhetorical". Such a claim seems hardly justified, if one takes into account the fact that an unembellished *genus humile* had formed a part of the classical rhetorical canon already, but under the impact of Ramism, it assumed an aura of plausibility.

The claim to dispense with all kinds of rhetoric did not mean, of course, that texts were indeed marked by an absence of rhetorical elements. On the contrary, in order to promote a new way of writing scientists took recourse

---

5   Bacon, *The Works of Francis Bacon*, ed. James Spedding, Robert L. Ellis, and Douglas D. Heath.,
     14 vols., Vol. 3 (London: Longman; rpt. Stuttgart, Bad Cannstatt: Frommann-Holzboog,
     1961–1963 [1858–1874]), 284.

6   I have stressed this point and given it a thorough discussion elsewhere, cf. Richard Nate,
     "Rhetoric in the Early Royal Society", in *Rhetorica Movet: Studies in Historical and Modern
     Rhetoric. In Honour of Heinrich F. Plett*, ed. Peter L. Oesterreich and Thomas O. Sloane (Leiden:
     Brill, 1999), 215–231 (215 ff.); rpt. in *Rhetoric and the Early Royal Society: A Sourcebook*, ed. Tina
     Skouen and Ryan J. Stark (Leiden: Brill, 2014).

7   Manfred Hinz, "Systemgeschichte: Frühe Neuzeit", in *Rhetorik: Begriff, Geschichte, Internationalität*, ed. Gert Ueding (Tübingen: Niemeyer, 2005), 118–131 (125).

to a number of persuasive techniques which had already been known in the traditional *ars rhetorica*. Rather than demonstrating a "non-rhetorical" quality, writings which defended the plain style often abounded with metaphors and similes, employed to illustrate the advantages of a seemingly "non-rhetorical style".

During the second half of the seventeenth century, this way of writing became so habitual that writers such as Jonathan Swift could already turn it into an object of ridicule. While several studies have been devoted to this phenomenon,[8] less attention has been paid to the fact that the influence of seventeenth-century anti-rhetoric extended well into the late eighteenth century. By this time, the anti-rhetorical tradition had become so influential that it could be adopted for many different purposes. As the following pages will show, anti-rhetorical strategies were used by political writers such as Thomas Paine and Mary Wollstonecraft as well as by the romantic poet William Wordsworth who is known to have viewed the achievements of the Scientific Revolution in a rather critical light. By pointing out how the scientifically inspired anti-rhetoric of the seventeenth century recurred in non-scientific discourses of the late eighteenth century, I hope to draw attention to some hitherto neglected shifts and continuities between the early modern period and the period which is commonly referred to as romanticism.

Some Aspects of the Early Modern Plain Style

The observation made above, namely that assaults upon the art of rhetoric often relied on strategies of dissimulation, also holds true for the *locus classicus* of seventeenth-century plain-style theory: Thomas Sprat's *History of the Royal Society* (1667). Although Sprat demanded from scientists that they should refrain from a "glorious pomp of words"[9] and instead strive for the "silent, effectual, and unanswerable Arguments of real Productions",[10] his characterizations of the plain style reveal some obvious rhetorical manoeuvres. If one takes a closer look at the way in which Sprat outlined his stylistic program, it is easy to see that it showed some of the very vices which the author criticized. When

---

8   Cf. the references in my *Wissenschaft und Literatur im England der frühen Neuzeit* (München: Fink, 2001), 201 ff., 263 ff.

9   Thomas Sprat, *The History of The Royal-Society of London For the Improving of Natural Knowledge* (London: J. Martyn; rpt. ed. Jackson I. Cope and Harold W. Jones. St. Louis, Mo.: Washington University Press / London: Routledge and Kegan Paul, 1958 [1667]), 62.

10   *Ibid.*

Sprat stated that the members of the Royal Society had agreed on "a constant
Resolution, to reject all the amplifications, digressions, and swellings of style:
to return back to the primitive purity, and shortness, when men deliver'd so
many things, almost in an equal number of words",[11] his phrases revealed not
only his delight in alliterations ("swellings of style", "primitive purity") but also
his love for redundant enumerations ("amplifications, digressions, and swellings of style"). It is clear that such a way of writing went far beyond the author's
aim to deliver all things in an "equal number of words". In addition, it also revealed an underlying historical narrative. When Sprat wrote about "primitive
purity", for instance, he alluded to the religious idea that human language had
once been perfect. According to contemporary interpretations of the Bible, it
was only with Adam's fall that linguistic corruption had set in. Therefore, when
Sprat explained that the Royal Society sought to return to a "pure" linguistic
state, he located its endeavours within the framework of providential history.[12]

It is obvious that Sprat's demand for "a close, naked, natural way of speaking" profited from the tropes it professed to attack.[13] The idea of "nakedness",
for instance, had its roots in the traditional notion that style functioned like
a garment.[14] "Nakedness" was produced, if the garments were taken away. An
impression of nakedness could be achieved by making them transparent. The
idea of transparency was connected to yet another traditional concept, namely
that of *perspicuitas* which in classical rhetoric had been opposed to the principle of *obscuritas*. Thus it turns out that while the images of nakedness or
transparency were employed to illustrate the principle of minimizing rhetorical figures, this did not mean that the texts which described such procedures
necessarily employed a non-figurative style.

One conclusion which could be drawn from such an observation is that Spat
obviously contradicted himself by employing those rhetorical devices he openly rejected. However, one should not ignore the fact that seventeenth-century
views on decorum were more complex than has sometimes been suggested. To
argue that Sprat demanded the abolition of rhetoric altogether would certainly
be misleading since there are passages in his book which point in the opposite

---

11   *Ibid.*, 113.

12   For images of innocence and purity in seventeenth-century scientific discourse, see Jo-
     anna Picciotto, *Labors of Innocence in Early Modern England* (Cambridge, Mass.: Harvard
     University Press, 2010). For an early account of the influence of millenarian views on
     seventeenth-century science see Charles Webster, *The Great Instauration: Science, Medi-
     cine and Reform 1626–1660* (London: Duckworth, 1975), 1 ff.

13   Sprat, *The History of The Royal-Society*, 113.

14   Wolfgang G. Müller, *Topik des Stilbegriffs: Zur Geschichte des Stilverständnisses von der An-
     tike bis zur Gegenwart* (Darmstadt: Wissenschaftliche Buchgesellschaft, 1981), 52 ff.

direction. In one chapter, for instance, he argued for cooperative scientific research on the ground that the "Art of speaking" was much more effective in
public than in private spheres.[15] On another occasion, he reminded his readers
that eloquence was "a Weapon, which may be as easily procur'd by bad man,
as good".[16] The problem was not that this weapon existed but that it had often
been misused by the "wicked".

In this context, it is worth recalling that even Francis Bacon, whose writings influenced the Royal Society's views on language in many respects, had
never regarded the linguistic precision which he demanded in the sciences as
an all-embracing linguistic norm. A study of Bacon's major writings reveals
that the author was keenly aware of the fact that different social occasions
also required different forms of communication. Thus, in *De Augmentis Sci-
entiarum* (1626), he took recourse to the rhetorical idea of *decorum* when he
wrote that although "the proofs and demonstrations of logic [were] the same
to all men ... the proofs and persuasions of rhetoric ought to differ according to
the auditors".[17] Rather than advocating a one-to-one relationship between *res*
and *verba*, which John Wilkins would later strive for in his above-mentioned
Essay, Bacon concluded: "If a man should speak of the same thing to several
persons, he should nevertheless use different words to each of them".

Equally, when members of the Royal Society spoke out for a plain style, this
did not mean that they would also deny the principle of stylistic diversity.[18]
As Maria Avxentevskaya has argued in the preceding essay, even John Wilkins
was an author who made ample use of the established techniques of dialectical rhetoric to win over readers for his subject of *Mathematicall Magick* (1648).
Thomas Sprat also proved that he was aware of the effectiveness of rhetorical persuasion when he reflected on the apologetic character of his *History*.
The style in which it was written, he confessed, was perhaps "larger and more
contentious that becomes that purity and shortness which are the chief beauties of Historical Writings".[19] Indeed, most parts of his *History* were written in
defence of science rather than to provide readers with samples of scientific
discourse. Far from rejecting the art of eloquence altogether, Sprat made use
of it whenever he deemed it appropriate. What is more, he even suggested that
a "Court of Eloquence" should be established "according to whose Censure,

15   Sprat, *The History of The Royal-Society*, 98.
16   *Ibid.*, 111.
17   Bacon, *The Works of Francis Bacon*, IV, 457 f.
18   For a more thorough discussion see Nate, "Rhetoric in the Early Royal Society".
19   Sprat, *The History of The Royal-Society*, "An Advertisement to the Reader", n.p.

all Books, or Authors should either stand or fall".[20] This is not to say that the author of the *History* promoted an *ars rhetorica* of the kind that had been celebrated among the Elizabethans, but it shows that Sprat was ready to grant rhetoric its due place and promote its cause when it seemed necessary. In a recent article, Tina Skouen has aptly concluded that "Sprat emerges, not as a condemner, but as a rescuer of rhetoric".[21] It may be added that in this respect Sprat resembled contemporary philosophers such as Francis Bacon, Thomas Hobbes and John Locke who would reject rhetorical ornaments in scientific discourse but were ready to accept stylistic plurality in other spheres.[22]

Still, it is not without irony that despite Sprat's ambition to achieve a kind of "mathematical plainness" in which "things" were expressed "in an equal number of words", the new stylistic norm would also produce amplifications of a fairly unexpected kind. Despite the claim to concentrate on "things" instead of "words", some scientific writers developed a habit of commenting on their own way of writing at great length. This resulted in meta-communicative passages which were primarily intended to demonstrate that a writer was doing science and which may therefore be characterized as hyper-transparent. Robert Boyle's introduction to his *Certain Physiological Essays* (1661) is a case in point. Instead of going *in medias res*, Boyle deemed it necessary to contrast his own way of writing with the "needless rhetorical ornaments" of other authors. Elaborating on the metaphor of transparency, he compared his own stylistic ideal to the polished glass of a telescope which would guarantee an undistorted view on the world:

> And certainly in these discourses, where our design is only to inform readers, not to delight or persuade them, perspicuity ought to be esteemed at least one of the best qualifications of a style; and to affect needless rhetorical ornaments in setting down an experiment, or explicating something abstruse in nature, were little less improper, than it were (for him that designs not to look directly upon the sun itself) to paint the

---

20   *Ibid.*, 43.

21   Tina Skouen, "Science vs. Rhetoric? Sprat's *History of the Royal Society* Reconsidered", *Rhetorica*, XXIX (2011), 23–52 (23, 30).

22   With reference to linguistic usage Bacon had distinguished between "philosophical matters" and "civil occasions" (Bacon, *The Works of Francis Bacon*, III, 284); Hobbes acknowledged four different uses of language in his *Leviathan* (Thomas Hobbes, *The English Works of Thomas Hobbes*, ed. W. Molesworth, 13 vols. (London: John Bohn; rpt. Aalen: Scientia, 1966 [1839–45]), III, 20), and Locke distinguished between a "philosophical" and a "civil" discourse (John Locke, *The Works of John Locke*, 10 vols. (London: Thomas Tegg et al.; rpt. Aalen: Scientia, 1963 [1823]), II, 251 f.).

eyeglasses of a telescope, whose clearness is their commendation, and in which even the most delightful colours cannot so much please the eye, as they would hinder the sight.[23]

Similarly, when in his *Micrographia* (1665) Robert Hooke wrote that the Royal Society was carrying on the work of natural philosophers such as Copernicus, Galileo, Gilbert and Harvey, he was also eager to point out that this was not done for the sake of self-adulation but merely in order to inform his readers. "I am confident, what I have here said", he wrote in a typical meta-communicative manner, "will not be look'd upon, by any ingenious Reader, as a *Panegyrick*, but only as a *real testimony*".[24]

With respect to the early modern plain style, Michael McKeon has rightly stated that one of its distinguishing marks was "the self-reflexive insistence on its own documentary candor", and even called this a "fundamental trope".[25] It goes without saying that such meta-communicative moves did little to contribute to the "advancement of learning", which Bacon had demanded – let alone a "benefit of mankind". Instead, they fulfilled a performative function: they were meant to demonstrate that a writer paid allegiance to the new stylistic norm. It is obvious, however, that such professions of loyalty were not necessarily scientific in character. On the contrary, the statements made were often so general that they could easily be adapted to other fields of discourse, including those in which the claims of scientists to contribute to the "benefit of mankind" were not even believed.

One writer who used the new anti-rhetorical standards as a means of ridiculing the self-proclaimed followers of the new scientific discourse was Jonathan Swift. Despite the fantastic nature of his *Gulliver's Travels* (1726), Swift's protagonist is eager to present himself as a typical "scientific sailor". Not only does he draw from contemporary travel accounts, but he also refers to geographers of his day and corroborates or refutes their statements as if he belonged to their profession.[26] The book's original title – "Travels into Several Remote

23   Robert Boyle, *New Experiments Physico-Mechanical, Touching the Spring of the Air*, in *The Works*, vol. 1 (London: J. & F. Rivington; rpt. Hildesheim: Olms, 1965 [1772]), 304.

24   Robert Hooke, *Micrographia: Or Some Physiological Descriptions of Minute Bodies Made By Magnifying Glasses With Observations and Enquiries Thereupon* (London: Jo. Martyn and Jo. Allestry, 1665; rpt. Bruxelles: Culture et Civilisation, 1966), "Preface".

25   Michael McKeon, *The Origins of the English Novel 1600–1740* (Baltimore / London: Johns Hopkins University Press, 1987), 105.

26   On *Gulliver's Travels* within the context of early modern travel writing, see Dirk Friedrich Paßmann, *"Full of Improbable Lies": Gulliver's Travels und die Reiseliteratur vor 1726* (Frankfurt a.M.: Lang, 1987).

Nations of the World" – equally creates the impression of a factual account, its supposed author being not Jonathan Swift but "Lemuel Gulliver, first a Surgeon, and then a Captain of several Ships". Significantly, Gulliver characterizes his way of writing as "plain". The crucial point consists in the fact, however, that he also makes use of the meta-communicative strategies described above. Thus, in a typical fashion, he lets the reader know that he has always preferred "truth" before "ornament".[27] Obviously choosing writers such as Robert Hooke and Robert Boyle as his models, Gulliver also violates the cherished principle of factuality by inserting a self-referential remark like the following: "I rather chose to relate plain matter of fact in the simplest manner and style, because my principal design was to inform, and not to amuse thee".[28]

Anti-rhetorical Postures in the "War of Pamphlets"

Despite such satirical attacks, the seventeenth-century plain style, together with its anti-rhetorical polemics and its hyper-transparent quality, would prove to have a long-lasting influence. By the end of the eighteenth century, the anti-rhetorical postures, which Swift had ridiculed in *Gulliver's Travels*, had become so commonplace that their intellectual roots were not always remembered.[29] The dissimulative act of distancing oneself from the art of rhetoric became fashionable especially among the supporters of the French Revolution. While it would go beyond the scope of this essay to recapitulate the intellectual climate from which these writers drew their inspiration, it seems worthwhile to show their indebtedness to a rhetorical tradition of which they were probably not always aware.

In order to explain why the anti-rhetorical postures of the seventeenth century could so easily be adopted by political commentators of later periods, it is worth recalling that the plain style also had carried political connotations. Thus, in stating that the members of the Royal Society preferred "the language of Artizans, Countrymen, and Merchants, before that, of Wits, or Scholars",[30] Thomas Sprat had identified the new style with the rising middle class and had

---

27   Jonathan Swift, *Gulliver's Travels*, ed. Peter Dixon and John Chalker (Harmondsworth: Penguin, 1967), 340.

28   *Ibid.*

29   The following account partly draws from an earlier publication, cf. Nate, *Wissenschaft, Rhetorik und Literatur: Historische Perspektiven* (Würzburg: Königshausen & Neumann, 2009), 92 ff.

30   Sprat, *The History of The Royal-Society*, 113.

set it off against two contemporary privileged groups: the so-called "court wits" and the academic establishment. With social allocations such as these, Sprat had paved the way for a stylistic orientation, which in the changed climate of the late eighteenth century could become associated with the language of the "common man".[31]

A continuation of the anti-rhetorical strategies described in the last section is clearly discernible, for instance, in the "war of pamphlets" carried out among British intellectuals in the wake of the French Revolution. A closer look at the respective tracts soon reveals that the controversy was not only one about politics but also one about decorum. On the one hand, there was Edmund Burke, who had started as a political liberal but had changed sides after reports about atrocities committed by French revolutionaries had reached England; on the other hand there were Thomas Paine and Mary Wollstonecraft, who defended the Revolution.[32] In his *Reflections on the Revolution in France* (1790), Burke minutely depicted the plight of the French royal couple. In doing so, he superficially adhered to a "circumstantial method" advocated by seventeenth-century scientists such as Robert Boyle; his principal aim, however, was to arouse sympathy among his readers. As is known, Burke was a supporter of the relatively stable course which Britain had taken after the Glorious Revolution of 1688. As far as social matters were concerned, he advocated gradual changes rather than revolutionary upheaval. When he complained that the "age of chivalry" had given way to one of "oeconomists, and calculators", he betrayed a nostalgic view of the past which in some respect anticipated the cultural criticism of later writers such as Thomas Carlyle.[33] Interestingly, Burke regretted that "sophisters" had begun to dominate public discourse, an observation which brought him to the conclusion that the "Glory of Europe" was "extinguished forever".[34]

---

31   One author, who pointed to similar continuities quite early, is Rosemund Tuve. Writing as early as 1939, Tuve stressed the importance of a Saxonist myth which she saw at work not only behind Sprat's remarks on the plain style but also behind the romantic search for a "natural" language, cf. Tuve, "Ancients, Moderns, and Saxons", *A Journal of English Literary History*, VI (1939), 165–190 (188–189).

32   Cf. Jane Hodson, *Language and Revolution in Burke, Wollstonecraft, Paine, and Godwin* (Aldershot: Ashgate, 2007). Paine and Wollstonecraft belonged to a group of intellectuals associated with the publisher Joseph Johnson. This included, among others, poet and painter William Blake and philosopher William Godwin, cf. Harold Nicolson, *The Age of Reason (1700–1789)* (London: Constable & Co, 1961), 349 ff.

33   See especially Thomas Carlyle, *Past and Present*, ed. Richard D. Altick (New York: New York University Press, 1965), published in 1843.

34   Edmund Burke, *Reflections on the Revolution in France and on the Proceedings in Certain Societies in London*, 12th ed. (London: Dodsley, 1793), 113.

It is significant that, in his *Rights of Man* (1791/92), Thomas Paine characterized Burke's depiction of the royal couple's fate as insincere.[35] According to
Paine's analysis, Burke had not offered a factual account but created "tragic
paintings ... well calculated for theatrical representation". With his dramatizing account he had "manufactured" facts "for the sake of show". Paine concluded: "Mr. Burke should recollect that he is writing History, and not *Plays*;
and that his readers will expect truth, and not the spouting rant of high-toned
exclamation".[36]

Like Paine, Mary Wollstonecraft criticized Burke not only for his political attitudes but also for his style. As she explained in her *Vindication of the Rights of
Men* (1790), Burke had sacrificed truth for the sake of rhetorical persuasion.[37]
Thereby he had aligned himself with those "sophisters" he openly attacked. In
defending her own way of writing, Wollstonecraft took recourse to the early
anti-rhetorical commonplaces. Her arguments, she stated, owed nothing to
rhetorical instruction. They were as clear as they were authentic. "I have not
yet learned to twist my periods, nor, in the equivocal idiom of politeness, to
disguise my sentiments, and imply what I should be afraid to utter",[38] she explained. As a consequence, she expected her readers to cope with her straight-
forwardness, even if it violated the traditional decorum. Despite such a claim
to transparency, however, it is observable that Wollstonecraft did not refrain
from alluding to Burke's writings in a way that only the educated reader would
have been able to grasp. Given the fact that Burke had started his writing career with *A Philosophical Enquiry into the Sublime and the Beautiful* (1757), her
remark that "truth, in morals has ever appeared to me the essence of the sublime; and, in taste, simplicity the only criterion of the beautiful",[39] was allusive
rather than straightforward. In addition to its literal meaning, it amounted to
saying that, in straying from truth and simplicity, Burke had violated his own
creed.

If Wollstonecraft's pleas for an unembellished style recall the seventeenth-
century plain style ideal, her explicit reference to John Locke's critique of

---

35   On Paine's style and its contemporary impact, see Olivia Smith, *The Politics of Language,
      1791–1819* (Oxford: Clarendon, 1984), as well as Hodson, *Language and Revolution*.

36   Thomas Paine, *Rights of Man, Being an Answer to Mr. Burke's Attack on the French Revolu-
      tion* (London: Watson, 1836), 12.

37   Mary Wollstonecraft, *A Vindication of the Rights of Men*, 2nd ed. (London: J. Johnson; rpt.
      ed. Eleanor Louise Nicholes, Delmar, NY: Scholars' Facsimiles & Reprints, 1960 [1790]), 65
      f. Hodson, *Language and Revolution*, 46 ff., shows that other commentators held similar
      opinions on Burke's style.

38   Wollstonecraft, *A Vindication of the Rights of Men*, 1.

39   *Ibid.*, 2.

rhetoric also proves that she was well aware of this tradition.[40] Furthermore, Wollstonecraft agreed with the principles of scientific rationalism in yet another respect. When she observed that one of Burke's problems lay in the fact that his reason had become the "dupe" of his "imagination",[41] this betrayed her indebtedness to a long-standing tradition in which "fancy", "imagination" and "wit" had been subordinated to "reason" and "judgment".[42] Wollstonecraft's negative use of the adjective "romantic" points in the same direction. In her *Vindication of the Rights of Men* she associated a romantic attitude not only with "false, or rather artificial feelings", but also with the use of artificial expressions. A "romantic spirit" and "empty rhetorical flourishes", she argued, often went hand in hand.[43]

Similar to the early modern writers discussed above, Wollstonecraft's critique on "rhetorical flourishes" did not mean that she would abstain from those flourishes herself. The tension which in seventeenth-century tracts resulted from claims to simplicity on the one hand and extensive meta-communicative statements on the other is observable also in her writings. Curiously enough, it was her announcement to dispense with any rhetoric whatsoever which introduced a passage loaded with metaphors and analogies. "Quitting now the flowers of rhetoric let us, Sir, reason together", she addressed her opponent Edmund Burke and then went on to explain:

I should not have meddled with these troubled waters, in order to point out your inconsistencies, if your wit had not burnished up some rusty, baneful opinions, and swelled the shallow current of ridicule till it resembled the flow of reason, and presumed to be the test of truth.[44]

Even if a passage like this may have been the result of spontaneous writing – a principle that Wollstonecraft conceded to when she characterized her book as

---

40   *Ibid.*, 106. In his *Essay Concerning Human Understanding* (1690), Locke had disparagingly called rhetoric a "perfect cheat". He had asked himself how this "powerful instrument of error and deceit" had its "established professors, [was] publicly taught" (Locke, *The Works of John Locke*, II, 288).

41   Wollstonecraft, *A Vindication of the Rights of Men*, 154.

42   Thus, Thomas Hobbes had stated that "fancy, without the help of judgment, is not commended as a virtue: but ... judgment is commended for itself, without the help of fancy" (Hobbes, *The English Works of Thomas Hobbes*, III, 57). On seventeenth-century juxtapositions of this kind, see Nate, *Wissenschaft und Literatur*, 143 ff.; 183 ff.

43   Wollstonecraft, *A Vindication of the Rights of Men*, 65 ff.

44   *Ibid.*, 6 f.

a "hasty answer"[45] – this does not alter the fact that the way she presented her argument violated the very principle expressed at the beginning of the passage. Instead of "quitting the flowers of rhetoric", Wollstonecraft introduced some far-fetched metaphors ("troubled waters", "shallow current") in order to denounce Burke's reasoning as mere sophistry. That she wrote this passage with a pinch of irony in order to demonstrate the extremes to which "rhetorical flourishes" could lead cannot be ruled out, but it cannot be proven either. What can be said, however, is that her style represented an extreme case of the anti-rhetorical postures discussed earlier.

Such an attitude is also discernible in Wollstonecraft's *Vindication of the Rights of Woman* (1792). This time she rightfully criticised the art of rhetoric as an instrument of power employed to keep up forms of social injustice of which the suppression of women represented a major case. Again, linguistic simplicity was presented as an antidote against the morally dubious arts of persuasion. In a typical meta-communicative fashion, Wollstonecraft promised her readers:

> I shall disdain to cull my phrases or polish my style ...; – I aim at being useful, and sincerity will render me unaffected; for, wishing rather to persuade by the force of my arguments, than dazzle by the elegance of my language, I shall not waste my time in rounding periods, or in fabricating the turgid bombast of artificial feelings, which, coming from the head, never reach the heart. – I shall be employed about things, not words![46]

Almost all elements of the early modern rhetoric of science are included in this remark. The rejection of an embellished style ("culled phrases", "polished style", "elegance of language", "rounding periods") is complemented by appeals to usefulness, sincerity and factuality. *Res* are favoured before *verba*. What sets the argument apart from seventeenth-century predecessors, however, is the fact that in this case emotions ("heart") are valued higher than reason ("head"). In view of the fact that early-modern scientists had often debated what they referred to as "philosophical enthusiasm",[47] this is not without significance.

45   Cf. Hodson's remarks on observations concerning Wollstonecraft's incoherent way of writing (*Language and Revolution*, 98 ff.).

46   Mary Wollstonecraft, *A Vindication of the Rights of Woman*, ed. Carol H. Poston (New York / London: Norton, 1975), 10.

47   Cf. Michael Heyd, "The Reaction to Enthusiasm in the Seventeenth Century: Towards an Integrative Approach", *Journal of Modern History*, LIII (1981), 258–280.

The reason why Wollstonecraft spoke in favour of a spontaneous expression of emotions may have been that this set her above any suspicion of insincerity. If in the seventeenth century claims of factuality had been the distinguishing mark of the plain style, this was now replaced by an appeal to spontaneity and honesty. In both cases, a more "natural" way of speaking would be preferred before an "artificial" one.

Another passage shows the shifts and continuities between the two positions even more clearly. When Wollstonecraft argued against the use of "soft phrases" which concealed the heart, she had in mind an artificial "feminine discourse" which a dominating male society forced upon women. It was precisely because of her will "to render my sex more respectable members of society" that she tried to avoid that "flowery diction which has slided from essays into novels, and from novels into familiar letters and conversation".[48] Instead of cultivating "epithets of weakness", she argued, women should strive "to acquire strength, both of mind and body", thus referring to virtues which hitherto had been conceived of as "masculine".[49] In order to strengthen women's rights, it was necessary to refute the prejudices which a male-dominated society had cultivated over centuries. Rather than advocating a specifically feminine discourse, which would merely corroborate existing power structures, Wollstonecraft argued that gender characteristics were culturally constructed rather than naturally given.[50] In doing so, she attributed an entirely new meaning to characterizations which in the seventeenth century had still carried misogynist connotations. When, in 1667, Sprat had placed "Masculine Arts of Knowledge" above "Feminine Arts of Pleasure",[51] he had done so from the perspective of a male-centred culture which Wollstonecraft sought to overcome. It is worth remembering in this context that women were allowed to become members of the Royal Society no earlier than 1923.[52] The difference between Wollstonecraft and Sprat consists in the fact that Wollstonecraft protested against a social injustice which men like Sprat had taken for granted, namely to exclude women from the intellectual sphere.

---

48 Wollstonecraft, *A Vindication of the Rights of Woman*, 10.

49 *Ibid.*, 9.

50 Hodson equally observes that Wollstonecraft was interested in questioning gender-specific ways of writing rather than developing a specifically feminine style (*Language and Revolution*, 85).

51 Sprat, *The History of The Royal-Society*, 129.

52 G.S. Rousseau, "Science", in *The Eighteenth Century*, ed. Pat Rogers (London: Methuen, 1978), 153–207 (156).

Anti-rhetorical Romanticism

While writers such as Thomas Paine and Mary Wollstonecraft in many respects still represented the rationalist tradition of the seventeenth century, this does certainly not hold true for a romantic poet such as William Wordsworth. Nevertheless, it is striking that even in his poetry some commonplaces of the seventeenth-century debate are still discernible. In his preface to the *Lyrical Ballads* (1800), Wordsworth maintained that poets should try to detect the "primary laws of nature" in everyday events and that they should strive to express these in a simple, albeit emotional language.[53] The poetry he had in mind was to be shaped by the language of the ordinary people rather than by that of courtiers. In Wordsworth's view, a rustic style, which was "plainer and more emphatic" than that of the upper classes, represented a counterpart against the "poetic diction" of classicist authors.

Although there can be little doubt that Wordsworth's comments on the social implications of poetic styles were primarily inspired by the French Revolution which he had encountered first hand, they are, at the same time, reminiscent of Thomas Sprat. Like Sprat, Wordsworth believed that it was the language of ordinary people which was suited best to provide a path to nature. He also argued that this language was "more philosophical" than that of classicists who relished in their "arbitrary and capricious habits of expression".[54] Since Wordsworth wanted poets to act as representatives of the common people, he refrained from attributing to them a privileged social status. At the same time, however, Wordsworth departed from such an egalitarian idea when he stated the poet could act as a representative speaker only because he was endowed with special gifts. A poet, Wordsworth declared, is "a man speaking to men", not hesitating to add: "a man, it is true, endued with more lively sensibility, more enthusiasm and tenderness, who has a greater knowledge of human nature, and a more comprehensive soul, than are supposed to be common among mankind".[55]

That writers such as Sprat and Wordsworth pursued different aims is obvious. While Sprat had sought a convenient linguistic tool in the hands of scientists, Wordsworth thought of a poetic idiom suitable to celebrate the "common

---

53   William Wordsworth, "Wordsworth's Preface", in *Lyrical Ballads*, William Wordsworth and Samuel T. Coleridge, ed. W.J.B. Owen, 2nd ed. (Oxford: Oxford University Press, 1969), 153–179 (156).

54   *Ibid.*

55   *Ibid.*, 165.

man". Although he regarded nature as a primary source of inspiration, his poetry was to be contemplative rather than mimetic. In his view, individual perceptions mattered more than objective facts. Still, Wordsworth resembled Sprat in associating the preferred style with a vision of humanity's primordial stage. While Sprat had celebrated a "primitive purity ... when men deliver'd so many *things*, almost in an equal number of *words*", Wordsworth sought a poetic idiom which would revive the truthfulness of "a low and rustic life".[56] In both cases, language was regarded as an instrument to restore humanity to some alleged original place in nature.

Ironically, it is Wordsworth's poem *The Tables Turned* which most obviously reveals the author's unacknowledged indebtedness to early modern scientific rhetoric. Since it expresses the view that humanity has had "enough of science and of art",[57] it has rightfully been taken to illustrate Wordsworth's hostility towards the scientific tradition. In the poem, students are asked to lay aside their reading matter and to turn their eyes directly towards nature:

> Books! 'tis a dull and endless strife,
> Come, hear the woodland linnet,
> How sweet his music; on my life
> There's more of wisdom in it.[58]

While it is true that Wordsworth had in mind a meditation on the beauties of nature rather than a scientific investigation of its properties, it is equally true that the contrast he created between books, as a mediated form of acquiring knowledge, and a direct contact with the world of things represented a long-established commonplace. As early as 1667, Sprat had complained about "Bookish wise men" who believed in what they read more than in what they saw,[59] thus paraphrasing the Royal Society's motto "nullius in verba" ("on the words of no one"). The difference lay in the fact that Wordsworth did not have in mind any scientific methods when he pointed to nature as a "teacher". His line "we murder to dissect" explicitly repudiates the scientific practice of vivisection. Since in Wordsworth's view the bird's voice bears traces of a long forgotten "language of nature", it can act as a source of knowledge only if it stays alive.

---

56   *Ibid.*, 156.
57   *Ibid.*, 105.
58   *Ibid.*, 104.
59   Sprat, *The History of The Royal-Society*, 337.

The example of Wordsworth's poem demonstrates that by the end of the eighteenth century, anti-rhetorical postures had become so widespread that they could be employed even to criticize the scientific worldview. The contradictions of seventeenth-century anti-rhetoric did not vanish within the changed intellectual climate of the late-eighteenth century, but they took on a new guise. If some early modern scientific texts had been marked by a contrast between calls for brevity on the one hand and meta-communicative reflections on the other, *The Tables Turned* reveals a contradiction of its own sort. It may be true that romantic poets favoured the spoken word over the printed one, but this did not mean that they were independent of the constraints of the ever-increasing book market. When Wordsworth, like Sprat before him, rejected a "bookish learning" and dreamed of returning to some "primitive purity", he, like his seventeenth-century predecessor, was forced to do so within the confines of the printed page.

Works Cited

Bacon, Francis. *The Works of Francis Bacon*, edited by James Spedding, Robert L. Ellis, and Douglas D. Heath, 14 vols. London: Longman; rpt. Stuttgart, Bad Cannstatt: Frommann-Holzboog, 1961–1963 [1858–1874].

Boulton, James T. *The Language of Politics in the Age of Wilkes and Burke*. London: Routledge & Kegan Paul, 1963.

Boyle, Robert. *New Experiments Physico-Mechanical, Touching the Spring of the Air*. In *The Works*, Vol. 1. London: J. & F. Rivington; rpt. Hildesheim: Olms, 1965 [1772].

Burke, Edmund. *Reflections on the Revolution in France and on the Proceedings in Certain Societies in London*, 12th ed. London: Dodsley, 1793.

Carlyle, Thomas. *Past and Present*, edited by Richard D. Altick. New York: New York University Press, 1965.

Dear, Peter. "*Totius in verba*: The Rhetorical Constitution of Authority in the Early Royal Society". *Isis*, LXXVI (1985), 145–161.

Heyd, Michael. "The Reaction to Enthusiasm in the Seventeenth Century: Towards an Integrative Approach". *Journal of Modern History*, LIII (1981), 258–280.

Hinz, Manfred. "Systemgeschichte: Frühe Neuzeit". In *Rhetorik: Begriff, Geschichte, Internationalität*, edited by Gert Ueding. 118–131. Tübingen: Niemeyer, 2005.

Hobbes, Thomas. *The English Works of Thomas Hobbes*, edited by W. Molesworth, 13 vols. London: John Bohn; rpt. Aalen: Scientia, 1966 [1839–45].

Hodson, Jane. *Language and Revolution in Burke, Wollstonecraft, Paine, and Godwin*. Aldershot: Ashgate, 2007.

Hooke, Robert. *Micrographia: Or Some Physiological Descriptions of Minute Bodies Made By Magnifying Glasses With Observations and Enquiries Thereupon*. London: Jo. Martyn and Jo. Allestry, 1665; rpt. Bruxelles: Culture et Civilisation, 1966.

Hüllen, Werner. "The Royal Society and the Plain Style Debate". In *Fachsprachen / Languages for Special Purposes*, edited by Lothar Hoffmann et al. Vol. 2, 2465–2472. Berlin / New York: de Gruyter, 1999.

Jones, Richard Foster, et al. *The Seventeenth Century: Studies in the History of English Thought and Literature from Bacon to Pope*. Stanford, Cal.: Stanford University Press / London: Oxford University Press, 1969.

Locke, John. *The Works of John Locke*, 10 vols. London: Thomas Tegg et al.; rpt. Aalen: Scientia, 1963 [1823].

McKeon, Michael. *The Origins of the English Novel 1600–1740*. Baltimore / London: Johns Hopkins University Press, 1987.

Müller, Wolfgang G. *Topik des Stilbegriffs: Zur Geschichte des Stilverständnisses von der Antike bis zur Gegenwart*. Darmstadt: Wissenschaftliche Buchgesellschaft, 1981.

Nate, Richard. "The Interjection as a Grammatical Category in John Wilkins' Philosophical Language". *Historiographia Linguistica*, XXIII (1996), 89–109.

Nate, Richard. "Rhetoric in the Early Royal Society". In *Rhetorica Movet: Studies in Historical and Modern Rhetoric. In Honour of Heinrich F. Plett*, edited by Peter L. Oesterreich and Thomas O. Sloane. 215–231. Leiden: Brill, 1999; rpt. in *Rhetoric and the Early Royal Society: A Sourcebook*, edited by Tina Skouen and Ryan J. Stark. Leiden: Brill, 2014.

Nate, Richard. *Wissenschaft und Literatur im England der frühen Neuzeit*. München: Fink, 2001.

Nate, Richard. *Wissenschaft, Rhetorik und Literatur: Historische Perspektiven*. Würzburg: Königshausen & Neumann, 2009.

Nicolson, Harold. *The Age of Reason (1700–1789)*. London: Constable & Co, 1961.

Paine, Thomas. *Rights of Man, Being an Answer to Mr. Burke's Attack on the French Revolution*. London: Watson, 1836.

Paßmann, Dirk Friedrich. *"Full of Improbable Lies": Gulliver's Travels und die Reiseliteratur vor 1726*. Frankfurt a.M.: Lang, 1987.

Picciotto, Joanna. *Labors of Innocence in Early Modern England*. Cambridge, Mass.: Harvard University Press, 2010.

Plett, Heinrich F. (ed.). *Renaissance-Rhetorik / Renaissance Rhetoric*. Berlin / New York: de Gruyter, 1993.

Pope, Alexander. *The Major Works*, edited by Pat Rogers. Oxford: Oxford University Press, 2006.

Rousseau, G.S. "Science", in *The Eighteenth Century*, edited by Pat Rogers, 153–207. London: Methuen, 1978.

Skouen, Tina. "Science vs. Rhetoric? Sprat's *History of the Royal Society* Reconsidered". *Rhetorica*, XXIX (2011), 23–52.

Smith, Olivia. *The Politics of Language, 1791–1819*. Oxford: Clarendon, 1984.

Sprat, Thomas. *The History of The Royal-Society of London For the Improving of Natural Knowledge*. London: J. Martyn; rpt. edited by Jackson I. Cope and Harold W. Jones. St. Louis, Mo.: Washington University Press / London: Routledge and Kegan Paul, 1958 [1667].

Subbiondo, Joseph L. (ed.). *John Wilkins and 17th-Century British Linguistics*. Amsterdam / Philadelphia: Benjamins, 1992.

Swift, Jonathan. *Gulliver's Travels*, edited by Peter Dixon and John Chalker. Harmondsworth: Penguin, 1967.

Tuve, Rosemund. "Ancients, Moderns, and Saxons". *A Journal of English Literary History*, VI (1939), 165–190.

Vickers, Brian. "The Royal Society and English Prose Style: A Reassessment". In *Rhetoric and the Pursuit of Truth: Language Change in the Seventeenth and Eighteenth Centuries*, Brian Vickers and Nancy S. Struever. Los Angeles: William Andrews Clark Memorial Library, 1985.

Webster, Charles. *The Great Instauration: Science, Medicine and Reform 1626–1660*. London: Duckworth, 1975.

Wollstonecraft, Mary. *A Vindication of the Rights of Men*, 2nd ed. London: J. Johnson; rpt. edited by Eleanor Louise Nicholes, Delmar, NY: Scholars' Facsimiles & Reprints, 1960 [1790].

Wollstonecraft, Mary. *A Vindication of the Rights of Woman*, edited by Carol H. Poston. New York / London: Norton, 1975.

Wordsworth, William. "Wordsworth's Preface". In *Lyrical Ballads*, William Wordsworth and Samuel T. Coleridge, edited by W.J.B. Owen, 2nd ed. 153–179. Oxford: Oxford University Press, 1969.

CHAPTER 7

Reconnoitring and Recognizing: Modes of Knowledge in Shaftesbury's *Characteristicks*

Jorge Bastos da Silva

Abstract

Shaftesbury declared: "What I count True Learning ... is to know our selves". This study examines the strategies of argumentation expounded in *Soliloquy*, the essay in *Characteristicks* focused on self-knowledge. Shaftesbury experimented with several frames of reference because he was sceptical about the available templates for understanding human nature. His tentative stance betrays an epistemological predicament akin to observational science. This study will further explore the connection between the author's non-magisterial style, the codification of a culture of urban conviviality, and the way in which scientific inquiry was enabled by being encoded as gentlemanly behaviour within a culture of honour.

On 29 September 1694, Anthony Ashley Cooper, who was to become the third Earl of Shaftesbury, wrote a letter to his old tutor, the philosopher John Locke, in which he defined his own intellectual commitments as those of one who is primarily, if not exclusively, concerned with the problem of how men may become "the Honester or Better Creatures".[1] This long letter is remarkable in several ways. For one thing, it signals a turn away from empiricism, and therefore indicates the growing gap between the author's beliefs and pursuits and those of his one-time mentor.[2] Shaftesbury professes to be utterly disengaged from the pursuits of observational and experimental science, preferring to

---

1 E.S. de Beer, ed., *The Correspondence of John Locke. Volume 5: Letters Nos. 1702–2198* (Oxford: Clarendon Press, 1976), 151.

2 Shaftesbury's best biographer, Robert Voitle, submits that it was precisely after 1694 that "the intellectual rapport between these two men gradually dissolved". He further notes: "Until the day of Shaftesbury's death, his attitude toward Locke remained a classic example of real ambiguity: reverence for the man and all that he had done for him; detestation of Locke's ideas and their implications for society" (*The Third Earl of Shaftesbury 1671–1713* (Baton Rouge: Louisiana State University Press, 1984), 69–70, 230).

focus on the moral predicament of mankind instead. This position is founded upon a distinctively conservative stance which (in a fashion one might almost describe as anti-Enlightenment, were it not for the moral emphasis of British eighteenth-century thought as opposed to the more scientific orientation of the *philosophes*)[3] downplays the possible role of progress in the improvement of the life and conscience of human beings:

> for my part: I am so far from thinking that mankind need any new Discoverys, or that they lye in the dark and are unhappy for want of them; that I know not what wee could ask of God to know more then wee doe or easily may doe. the thing that I would ask of God should bee to make men live up to what they know; and that they might bee so wise as to desire to know no other things then what belong'd to'em, and what lay plain before them; and to Know those, to PURPOSE: and that all other Affectation of Knowledg Hee would preserve us from, as from a Desease:[4]

The terms in which Shaftesbury couches his critique of science deserve to be underlined, because they square with the general tenets of politeness which would come to be advocated by the author, and match the terms of the essay I intend to examine below. Science is an "Affectation of Knowledg" and a "Desease", he claims, thereby not only suggesting that it is misguided but also that it is presumptuous, and both symptomatic of, and conducive to, moral flaws.

In effect, this letter can almost be taken as a programme *in nuce* of the philosophical work Shaftesbury would eventually accomplish and publish under the general title *Characteristicks of Men, Manners, Opinions, Times*. In the letter, Shaftesbury asserts his conviction that it is humanistic pursuits rather than observational and experimental science which foster the cultivation of virtue:

> all the End to which my Studdyes, such as they are, have any leaning, or bent, is but to learn mee this one thing in short; how to Communicate every thing freely; how to bee more Sociable and more a Friend. how is itt possible that I should bee a Niggard here, and not impart all that I were able? Itt is not with mee as with an Empirick, one that is studdying of Curiositys, raising of new Inventions that are to gain credit to the author, starting of new Notions that are to amuse the World and serve them for

---

3   This point is underlined by Gertrude Himmelfarb in *The Roads to Modernity: The British, French, and American Enlightenments* (New York: Alfred A. Knopf, 2004), 18–19 *et passim*.

4   De Beer, *Correspondence*, 151.

Divertion or for tryall of their Acuteness (which is all one as if it were some new Play, a Chess, or a Game of cards that were envented.) Itt is not in my case as with one of the men of new Systems, who are to build the credit of their own invented ones upon the ruine of the Ancienter and the discredit of those Learned Men that went before. Descartes, or Mr Hobbs, or any of their Improvers have the same reason to make a-doe, and bee Jealouse about their notions, and DISCOVERY'S, as they call them; as a practizing Apothecary or a mountebank has to bee Jealouse about the Compositions that are to goe by his name. for if itt bee not a Livelyhood is aim'd; 'tis a Reputation. and what I contend for Reputation in, I must necessarily envy another man's possession of.[5]

Shaftesbury's disavowal of science has clear moral and social overtones. It suggests scientists are cunning impostors who, out of conceit and personal ambition, contrive idle notions deserving of suspicion and ultimately of ridicule. It also involves the imputation that scientists are not gentlemen but mere craftsmen, and, as such, jealous of the material benefits to be derived from their supposed discoveries or "Compositions". True philosophy, by contrast, is a genteel occupation which is carried out by those with a truly sociable character, driven by altruistic aspirations.

As if foreshadowing the "two cultures" debate of the twentieth century, but intersecting it with notions that resonate with the question of whether to accept or challenge received authority which is at the core of the neoclassical controversy of Ancients and Moderns, Shaftesbury points out – in a somewhat prejudiced vein, to be sure – that in science there is petty rivalry, victory and defeat; there is vanity and cupidity. Science is territorial: it aims at "possession".[6] By contrast, in moral speculation there is co-operation and improvement, there is progression without rejection – indeed, there is *conversation*, that key concept of the age, of which Shaftesbury has justly been hailed as a major proponent.[7]

---

5 *Ibid.*, 150–151.
6 Interestingly, the social and economic subtext of the letter combines allusions to both the landed interest and the moneyed interest, those contending forces of the period, as Shaftesbury also objects to scientists "build[ing] credit" (*ibid.*, 151).
7 The most influential study is Lawrence E. Klein, *Shaftesbury and the Culture of Politeness: Moral Discourse and Cultural Politics in Early Eighteenth-Century England* (Cambridge: Cambridge University Press, 2004 [1994]). It is interesting to notice that, while Shaftesbury impeaches the commonplace understanding of the development of science as a narrative of progress (thus pre-empting one of the abiding myths of modernity), his avowed opposition to the scientific spirit has clear political overtones: casting scientists as aggressive

This essay will maintain that it is inaccurate to assume a straightforward polarization between Shaftesbury's survey of the field of ethics and the practices of science. On the surface, however, his argument against the science and philosophy of the "Empiricks" who study "Curiositys" is consistent with his efforts at redirecting his inquiries towards human nature itself (an object, it will become apparent, that he approaches with significant reticence, under cover of an ostensible communicativeness), on behalf of sense, kindness and politeness. To quote once again from the letter to Locke, he declares in true classic mode:

> What I count True Learning, and all that wee can profitt by, is to know our selves; what it is that makes us Low, and Base, Stubborn against Reason, to be Corrupted and Drawn away from Vertue, of Different Tempers, Inconstant, and Inconsistent with ourselves; to know how to bee allways Friends with Providence though Death and many such Dreadfull Businesses come in the way; and to be Sociable and Good towards all men, though They turn Miscreants or are Injuriouse to us.[8]

The assumption that "True Learning ... is to know our selves" makes itself felt across the work of Shaftesbury and it obviously defines him as a moral philosopher first and foremost. But, as a basic statement of the nature of his pursuits, it also poses the problem of establishing what the intellectual procedures were by means of which Shaftesbury undertook his quest for "True Learning". We shall look into this problem by briefly examining some of the strategies of explanation and argumentation expounded in *Soliloquy: Or, Advice to an Author*, the essay in *Characteristicks* which most explicitly deals with the question of self-knowledge. Such strategies resort to a number of disparate frames of reference, and it is the purpose of this analysis to inquire into their consistency – and into the significance of their ultimate inconsistency.

Soliloquy was first published in 1710, towards the end of Shaftesbury's life, when he was already preparing *Characteristicks*, in which it was of course included in 1711. For the second edition, which came out in 1714, Shaftesbury took great care in commissioning illustrations that helped convey the import of his thought. The meaning of the emblem he devised for *Soliloquy* is worth

---

and unsociable types tacitly places them in the context of Shaftesbury's argument against Hobbes, and makes it possible to equate them with the attitudes traced by C.B. Macpherson as configuring an ethics of "possessive individualism". Cf. *The Political Theory of Possessive Individualism: Hobbes to Locke* (Oxford: Clarendon Press, 1962).

8   De Beer, *Correspondence*, 153.

mentioning. It shows two boys, walking in strikingly different landscapes, both holding a mirror in their hands. The two boys represent good and "evil conscience" (the phrase is from Shaftesbury's *Instructions* sent to Thomas Micklethwayte, the engraver).[9] The former, good conscience, is walking in daylight; he is looking at himself in the mirror in his right hand, and with his left hand he is pointing at his chest, apparently at his heart. The other boy, evil conscience, walks in the night; he holds a mirror in his left hand, but he disregards it completely. It shall be made clear that a binary perspective of this sort, all the more so as it is blatantly moralistic in conventionally pious terms, fails to do full justice to the complexity of Shaftesbury's argument in *Soliloquy*, the expression of which depends on several figurative devices and often subtly nuanced imagery, and on the whole amounts to a non-dogmatic, tentative approach to the issues it deals with. Insofar as the emblem introduces the motif of the mirror, however, it is indeed consistent with a central thematic component of the essay. Further, it reinforces the quote from Persius that the author chose to use as an epigraph: "Nec TE quaesiveris extrà", which translates as "You need not have looked beyond yourself".[10]

The main point of *Soliloquy* relates to the proviso that an author ought to be his own first critic, carefully examining his own thoughts and passions, and thereby grounding his authority upon virtue and sound sense. This is obviously relevant in and for an age when the emerging print market offered new opportunities for publishing and even for the professionalization of writing, and it is also significant that the stipulation of self-inspection applies to many different kinds of writers: it explicitly comprises poets, philosophers, orators, writers of memoirs and essays, and, with unmistakable irony, "*Saint*-Author[s]" or authors "of the *sanctify'd* kind".[11] The key method prescribed for introspection is one of colloquy with oneself: before pretending to engage in conversation with other people, especially when a prospective position of authority is at stake, a magisterial stance, one should engage in critical conversation with oneself.

As pertains to style, the most interesting feature of the essay lies in the diversity of images drawn upon by Shaftesbury to cast his thoughts. The line

---

9   Cf. Felix Paknadel, "Shaftesbury's Illustrations of Characteristics", *Journal of the Warburg and Courtauld Institutes*, XXXVII (1974), 307–308. On the emblem, see also Michael B. Gill, "Shaftesbury on Politeness, Honesty, and Virtue", *New Ages, New Opinions: Shaftesbury in his World and Today*, ed. Patrick Müller, assist. Christine Jackson-Holzberg (Frankfurt am Main: Peter Lang, 2014), 172, n. 9.

10   Anthony, Third Earl of Shaftesbury, *Characteristicks of Men, Manners, Opinions, Times*, foreword Douglas Den Uyl (Indianapolis: Liberty Fund, 2001) (3 vols), I, 95.

11   Shaftesbury, *Characteristicks*, I, 104.

of argument, as is often remarked of the author, is typically digressive, and it entails several different devices, from the quotation from classical sources through the aphorism to the allegedly historical anecdote (a diversity further supplemented by the *Miscellaneous Reflections* placed at the end of the collection). But merely to acknowledge the richness of the textual strategies in rhetorical terms – a richness which has not always found sympathetic readers (Shaftesbury's style of writing was criticized by the likes of Bernard Mandeville and Adam Smith for poor logicality)[12] – is not enough to comprehend what is at stake in the composition of *Soliloquy*. A passage of the essay in which Shaftesbury admits to the difficulty of the task of verbalization points to just this problem:

> One wou'd think, there was nothing easier for us, than to know our own Minds, and understand what our main *Scope* was; what we plainly drove at, and what we propos'd to our-selves, as our *End*, in every Occurrence of our Lives. But our Thoughts have generally such an obscure implicit Language, that 'tis the hardest thing in the world to make'em speak out distinctly. For this reason, the right Method is to give'em Voice and Accent. And this, in our default, is what the *Moralists* or *Philosophers* endeavour to do, to our hand; when, as is usual, they hold us out a kind of *vocal* Looking-Glass, draw Sound out of our Breast, and instruct us to personate our-selves, in the plainest manner.[13]

It is relevant to emphasize the phrasing: our thoughts, when we give them words, are "a kind of vocal looking-glass" and they "instruct us to personate ourselves". In other words, because we converse with ourselves we learn who we are and who we ought to be. Only as a result of this process are we prepared for conversation with others.

The meaning of the mirror motif would seem to be plain, but when combined with the topos of "personation" it becomes suggestive of hesitancy, of an uncertainty about the coherence of a subject who is not conceived of as unified but rather as double, as an individual who acts upon himself in order to become a better person. The subject is the object of his own will and of his power of self-inspection and self-instruction. Shaftesbury's precept of soliloquy implies a dynamic conception of human nature. While remaining fundamentally optimistic, this conception proves at the same time to be undermined by a permanent, ineradicable instability, if not outright indeterminacy, of the subject, which, as will be shown, is translated in the essay into images

---

12   Cf. Howard Caygill, *Art of Judgment* (Oxford: Basil Blackwell, 1989), 45 and 398 n. 6.
13   Shaftesbury, *Characteristicks*, I, 107–108.

of constant internal strife. This moral and psychological predicament at once empowers the individual – as the prime agent of his self-improvement and a collaborator in that of others – and makes him responsible for being the person he is and becoming the person he ought to be. *He* is the chief moral, social and cultural factor – not God, not Providence, not fate. The internalization of the moral injunction is in tune with the overall secularization of culture to which the Enlightenment contributed greatly.

It is presumably in keeping with his dual understanding of human nature as both dynamic and unstable, and perhaps even precarious, as well as with the avowed difficulty of finding words for thoughts that Shaftesbury reaches for several disparate frames of reference without ever succeeding in fully integrating them into a single, coherent whole. As a formal argument offering instruction in the sphere of ethics, *Soliloquy* is undoubtedly consistent, but if we read it not as an abstract piece of indoctrination but rather as a text composed of a web of imagery, we perceive that it can hardly claim to be a seamless unity, and the implications of its textural complexity are certainly worth investigating.

Of the several strains of imagery that can be identified throughout the essay, eight may be singled out as most significant. What follows includes an attempt to flesh out some of the implications of the conceptual apparatuses involved.

(1) *The idiom of medicine or physic*, as when Shaftesbury describes his propaedeutic programme as "the business of *Self-dissection*"[14] and professes to examine his topic "as a Case of SURGERY".[15] This places the would-be writer in the semantic field of health and disease – or, morally, of sanity and insanity. More interestingly, it relates the practices prescribed in the essay with the tradition of the compendia as "anatomies", from Philip Stubbs' *The Anatomie of Abuses* and Robert Burton's *The Anatomy of Melancholy* through Northrop Frye's *Anatomy of Criticism* (to mention a contemporary extension of the concept to the Humanities). Related images include "*Remedy*", "Perspiration", and "this Method of Evacuation".[16]

The metaphors related to pathology are an indication that *Soliloquy* shares common ground with Shaftesbury's letter to Locke quoted above. The term "Empirick" in the letter conjures up the picture of a medical practitioner who is deprived of the benefit of theory or formal training, hence an inferior or suspicious one.[17] The term carries a burden which the rise of "empiricism" would need to solve. It is a function of Shaftesbury's wish to set the mercenary

---

14   *Ibid.*, I, 100, in a paragraph to which we shall return.
15   *Ibid.*, I, 98.
16   *Ibid.*, I, 100–102.
17   Cf. Peter Burke, *A Social History of Knowledge: From Gutenberg to Diderot* (Cambridge: Polity Press, 2008 [2000]), 16–17, 205–206.

interest of the lower orders against the independence and liberality of the
gentility, who expect to be remunerated for their commitment to the liberal
arts only by a satisfaction which is fully compatible with disinterestedness. In
Soliloquy, however, Shaftesbury patently evokes medicine with the opposite
moral emphasis. Additional intersections between the letter and the essay are
ensured by the semantic field of drama, which as shall be seen is impressed
with a similar modulation (in the letter it refers to something gratuitous, like
chess or cards, that one engages in for the wrong reasons); by the problem of
being "Inconsistent with ourselves" (thus the letter); and by the topic of authorship, which of course is a central concern of the essay.

(2) *The political idiom of power to check subversive forces, and the legal idiom
of judging and passing sentence*, also combined with the topic of health, as in
the following passage:

> This indeed is but too certain; That as long as we enjoy a MIND, as long as
> we have *Appetites* and *Sense*, the *Fancys* of all kinds will be hard at work;
> and whether we are in company, or alone, they must range still, and be
> active. They must have their Field. The Question is, Whether they shall
> have it wholly to themselves; or whether they shall acknowledg some
> *Controuler* or *Manager*. If none; 'tis this, I fear, which leads to *Madness*.
> 'Tis this, and nothing else, which can be call'd *Madness*, or *Loss of Reason*.
> For if FANCY be left Judg of any thing, she must be Judg of all. Every-thing
> is right, if anything be so, because *I fansy it*.[18]

The intimation of a battle in the notion that the fancies will "have their Field"
if left unchecked gives sharpness to the understanding that the mind is torn
between physiological impositions (the appetites) and the faculty of judgment
(reason). The mind therefore exists in a state of perpetual strife, and reason
must be vigilant and triumph in order to preserve the subject from insanity.

(3) *The idiom of sovereignty versus party strife*, and, as it were, of Parliamentary debate:

> And here it is that our Sovereign Remedy and *Gymnastick* Method of
> SOLILOQUY takes its rise: when by a certain powerful Figure of inward
> Rhetorick, the Mind *apostrophizes* its own FANCYS, raises'em in their
> proper *Shapes* and *Personages*, and addresses'em familiarly, without the
> least Ceremony or Respect. By this means it will soon happen, that TWO
> form'd *Partys* will erect themselves *within*. For the Imaginations or Fancys

---

18   *Ibid.*, I, 198.

being thus roundly treated, are forc'd to declare themselves, and take party. Those on the side of the elder Brother APPETITE, are strangely subtle and insinuating. They have always the Faculty to speak by Nods and
Winks. By this practice they conceal half their meaning, and, like modern
Politicians, pass for deeply wise, and adorn themselves with the finest
Pretext and most specious Glosses imaginable; till being confronted with
their Fellows of a plainer Language and Expression, they are forc'd to
quit their mysterious Manner, and discover themselves mere *Sophisters*
and *Impostors*, who have not the least to do with the Party of REASON
and *good Sense*.[19]

Building on the notion of the self as an entity which is split by contending
factions, this passage expresses a concern with language that lies, with oratory
that distorts one's perception of reality. By the same token, the author declares
his reliance on "a certain powerful Figure of inward Rhetorick" amounting to a
sort of maieutic method capable of exposing the "mere *Sophisters* and *Impostors*" who are reason's adversaries.

On the other hand, it is worth noticing that an element of personal testimony also goes into the making of *Soliloquy*. In this widely evocative passage,
there is certainly sarcasm in the reference to the "modern Politicians" on the
part of the grandson of the great Whig leader who emerged in the later years
of Charles II's reign.

(4) *The idiom of intolerance and persecution*:

> As cruel a Court as the *Inquisition* appears; there must, it seems, be full as
> formidable a one, erected in our-selves; if we wou'd pretend to that Uni-
> formity of Opinion which is necessary to hold us to *one Will*, and preserve
> us in the same mind, from one day to another. Philosophy, at this rate, will
> be thought perhaps little better than Persecution: And *a supreme Judg* in
> matters of Inclination and Appetite, must needs go exceedingly against
> the Heart.[20]

The judicial imagery is here expanded to convey a more radical anxiety about
human nature. It is no longer simply a matter of pitting one aspect of the self
against another, as in (2) and (3) above, but of addressing an instability which
is so deeply constitutive of the subject that it amounts to a possibly inextricable uncertainty regarding the individual's very identity. What is at stake here

19   *Ibid.*, I, 117.
20   *Ibid.*, I, 116.

runs deeper and is potentially more disturbing than the psychological problem of constancy, of curbing "Inclination and Appetite". It points to the predicament of the subject as a (non-)continuous entity. Shaftesbury accordingly prescribes an "Operation" which "is for no inconsiderable End: since 'tis to gain him *a Will*, and insure him *a certain Resolution*; by which he shall know where to find himself; be sure of his own Meaning and Design; and as to all his Desires, Opinions, and Inclinations, be warranted *one and the same* Person to day as yesterday, and to morrow as to day".[21]

Shaftesbury's imagery of the court of law, and furthermore of a court which was notoriously intolerant, may be seen as one of the responses of the age to the difficulties posed by the primacy of sense perception in the philosophy of Locke (it is perhaps no accident that the word "Philosophy" stands in the passage). Locke's anthropology in *An Essay Concerning Human Understanding* assumed so thorough a dependence of mental life upon the experience of the senses that it effectively undermined the traditional category of the unified, continuous subject; the random quality of sense experience implied the transience of human identity.[22] Locke was reluctant to follow through to the inevitable logical conclusion, but Hume would eventually spell it out in *A Treatise of Human Nature*: "If any impression gives rise to the idea of self, that impression must continue invariably the same, thro' the whole course of our lives; since self is suppos'd to exist after that manner. But there is no impression constant and invariable".[23] The formulation of the basic tenets of a theory of aesthetic fruition hinging on the premiss that the practice and the enjoyment of art are beneficial for the subject necessitated a critique of the unstable and circumstantial character of the subject inherent in its connection with sense experience that is inevitably variable and contingent. Shaftesbury, together with other early eighteenth-century thinkers (such as Addison and Hutcheson), may be seen to be engaged in just such a critique.

(5) *The idiom of metaphysics*, alluding to a mode of explanation which is typically – and significantly, in view of the internalization of moral responsibility

---

21   *Ibid.*, I, 116.

22   See Jorge Bastos da Silva, "Exorcising Locke: Towards a Re-Appraisal of Addison's Literary Criticism", *Imitatio – Inventio: The Rise of "Literature" from Early to Classic Modernity*, ed. Mihaela Irimia and Dragoş Ivana (Bucureşti: Institutul Cultural Român, 2010), 309–312; Charles Taylor, *Sources of the Self: The Making of the Modern Identity* (Cambridge, Mass.: Harvard University Press, 1989), 159–176; Dror Wahrman, *The Making of the Modern Self: Identity and Culture in Eighteenth-Century England* (New Haven / London: Yale University Press, 2004), 189–197.

23   *The Philosophical Works*, ed. Thomas Hill Green and Thomas Hodge Grose (Aalen: Scientia Verlag, 1964) (4 vols.), I, 533.

highlighted above – revoked as abstruse and false, as when Shaftesbury re-
calls the antique conceit "That we have each of us *a Daemon, Genius, Angel,
or Guardian-Spirit*, to whom we were strictly join'd, and committed, from our
earliest Dawn of Reason, or Moment of our Birth". While granting that such
an "Opinion, were it literally true, might be highly serviceable, no doubt, towards the Establishment of our System and Doctrine", the author nevertheless
dismisses it, and corrects it by reference to two of the semantic fields already
examined, the idiom of physic and the idiom of party strife. Shaftesbury clari-
fies the matter in the following fashion:

> the very utmost the wise Antients ever meant by this *Daemon*-Compan-
> ion, I conceive to have been no more than enigmatically to declare, "That
> we had each of us a Patient in *our-self*; that we were properly our own
> Subjects of Practice; and that we then became due Practitioners, when by
> virtue of an intimate *Recess* we cou'd discover a certain *Duplicity* of Soul,
> and divide our-selves into *two Partys*".[24]

Shaftesbury seeks to replace metaphysics with psychology, and inspiration
with introspection. Interestingly, what this exercise reveals is the lack of vocabulary that is intrinsically psychological (as distinguished from the medical
connotations of "Practice" and the political resonance of "*Partys*"). Shaftesbury's wide range of metaphors is probably due more to the perceived insufficiency of the available intellectual frameworks than to a desire to seduce the
reader by showing an unusual degree of intellectual versatility or rhetorical
flourishes.

(6) *The idiom of drama and of teaching*, as in the following passage, which,
like the preceding quotation, also provides an example of how the several
strands of imagery may be intertwined:

> Accordingly, if it be objected against the above-mention'd *Practice*, and
> Art of *Surgery*, "That we can no-where find such a *meek Patient*, with
> whom we can in reality *make bold*, and for whom nevertheless we are
> sure to preserve *the greatest Tenderness and Regard*": I assert the contrary;
> and say, for instance, *That we have each of us* OUR SELVES *to practise
> on*. "Mere Quibble! (you'll say:) For who can thus multiply himself into
> *two Persons*, and be *his own Subject*? Who can properly laugh at *himself*,
> or find in his heart to be either merry or severe on such an occasion?"
> Go to the *Poets*, and they will present you with many Instances. Nothing

---

24   Shaftesbury, *Characteristicks*, I, 106.

is more common with them, than this sort of SOLILOQUY. A Person of profound Parts, or perhaps of ordinary Capacity, happens, on some occasion, to commit a Fault. He is concern'd for it. He comes alone upon the Stage; looks about him, to see if any body be near; then takes himself to task, without sparing himself in the least. You wou'd wonder to hear how close he pushes matters, and how thorowly he carrys on the business of *Self-dissection*. By virtue of this SOLILOQUY he becomes two distinct *Persons*. He is Pupil and Preceptor. He teaches, and he learns. And in good earnest, had I nothing else to plead in behalf of the Morals of our modern Dramatick Poets, I shou'd defend'em still against their Accusers for the sake of this very Practice, which they have taken care to keep up in its full force.[25]

By interweaving the imagery of physic with that of schooling and of drama, Shaftesbury conflates his apology of moral self-inspection with a defence of literature as an agent of edification. He effectively presents the poet as the paradigm of self-examination. More specifically, and treading boldly on the brink of paradox, Shaftesbury equates introspection with that most public of literary arts, the theatre, thereby replying to the criticism levelled at playwrights by numerous detractors of the stage, from the Puritans of the time of Elizabeth I to Jeremy Collier in the infamous *A Short View of the Immorality and Prophaneness of the English Stage* of 1698.[26] Once again, the argument of *Soliloquy* matches inherited and contemporaneous concerns pertaining to the dignity and the usefulness of literature. Authors, Shaftesbury contends, "are, in a manner, profess'd *Masters of Understanding* to the Age", capable today as of yore of "dictating Rules of Life, and teaching Manners and good Sense".[27]

(7) *Gendered language or imagery*, as when Shaftesbury mentions "the CORRECTRICE, by whose means I am in my Wits, and without whom I am no longer *my-self*". This is all the more noticeable as the paragraph following is insistent on the word "man", starting with the statement: "Every Man indeed who is not absolutely beside himself, must of necessity hold his Fancys under some kind of Discipline and Management".[28] The subject is almost invariably construed as male in *Soliloquy* (and the usage of pronouns throughout the present essay has been consistent with Shaftesbury's). To gender the controlling faculty

25   *Ibid.*, I, 99–100.
26   See Jonas Barish, *The Antitheatrical Prejudice* (Berkeley: University of California Press, 1981).
27   Shaftesbury, *Characteristicks*, I, 98.
28   *Ibid.*, I, 199.

as female appears to signal a dissociation of the components of the mind or
personality which is more pronounced than that obtained through other types
of imagery.

By a curious evaluative reversal, in a later passage of *Soliloquy* it is no longer
the positive faculty but rather the negative elements, like "the gayer Tribe of
Fancys" and "the gloomy and dark *Specters* of another sort", that are termed
"the encroaching *Sorceresses*".[29]

(8) Finally, *the idiom of the self divided*. Thus, the author confidently asserts:
"let my Senses err ever so widely; I am not on this account *beside my-self*: Nor
am I out of my own Possession, whilst there is a Person left within; who has
Power *to dispute* the Appearances, and *redress* the Imagination".[30] Similarly,
recollecting "the Antients", he explains "that celebrated *Delphick* Inscription,
RECOGNIZE YOUR-SELF: which was as much as to say, *Divide your-self*, or *Be
Two*".[31] And a character in a story recognizes the fact that

> I have in reality within me *two distinct separate Souls*.... There must of
> necessity be *Two*: and when *the Good* prevails, 'tis then we act handsomly;
> when *the Ill*, then basely and villanously. Such was my Case. For lately *the
> Ill* Soul was wholly Master. But now *the Good* prevails, by your assistance;
> and I am plainly a new Creature, with quite another *Apprehension*, an-
> other *Reason*, another WILL.[32]

In this case Shaftesbury does not avoid the language of metaphysics, either, it
may be inferred, because the reader could be trusted to identify the term "soul"
with Christian belief (regardless of the unorthodox notion of two souls in one
person), or because, differently from concepts like "*Daemon*" and "*Angel*" under (5) above, it did not clash with the propositions of deism he himself held.[33]

The notion of the subject as a disjointed entity on the verge of chaos (con-
veyed by imagery suggestive of disease, madness, political turmoil and war)
and in constant need of an instance of surveillance and control (curbing the
appetites or fancies in the name of reason or common sense, or at a deeper

---

29   *Ibid.*, I, 201.

30   *Ibid.*, I, 200.

31   *Ibid.*, I, 107.

32   *Ibid.*, I, 115.

33   It will be noted that in the letter to Locke, written a decade and a half earlier, Shaftesbury
      mentions his desire to be "allways Friends with Providence" – a vague phrasing which
      points to genial resignation, or the state of being reconciled to, while remaining some-
      what noncommittal towards the notion of God's interference in the affairs of this world.

level on behalf of the integrity of the self) may be seen as the overarching motif of *Soliloquy*. It arguably encompasses the disparate strains of imagery, fore-
grounding the assumption of a hierarchy of the faculties which is the common
denominator of the several explanatory templates adduced.[34] *Soliloquy* therefore calls on the reader at once to recognize that central thesis and appreciate
the significance of the *convergence* of discrepancies in the *tentative* submission
of an argument which aspires to cogency and consistency.

As the modern theorist of science John Ziman remarks, "scientific knowledge is distinguished from other intellectual artefacts of human society by
the fact that its contents are *consensible*.... The goal of science, moreover, is
to achieve the maximum degree of *consensuality*". Ziman accordingly adds
that "consensibility is a necessary condition for any scientific communication,
whereas only a small proportion of the whole body of science is undeniably
consensual at a given moment".[35] This distinction may be applied to the author
of *Characteristicks*, regardless of how keen he was to exclude himself from the
sphere of science. Shaftesbury's investment in a variety of co-existing idioms
of consensibility betokens the intrinsic fallibility of one-sided approaches to
reality. It betrays a form of scepticism which manifests itself as a difficulty in
achieving consensuality while, paradoxically, it seeks to remedy precisely such
difficulty by experimenting with a gamut of languages of assent.

To resort once more to Ziman, it is possible to say that, if *Soliloquy* falls
short of the certainty of a consensus, it nevertheless abounds in "*consensible*
message[s] with the *potentiality* for eventually contributing to a consensus".[36]
Shaftesbury tries to fit his data into a pattern, and then another and yet another.
He attempts to channel his points through recognizable structures of thought,
such as the body-mind analogy (physiological distempers are the equivalent of
madness) and the correspondence between microcosm and macrocosm (an
upsetting of the faculties parallels social upheavals). He is unquestionably certain of the moral points he wishes to make, but he spins hypotheses regarding
human nature; he has clear answers to offer in the field of ethical and psychological problems, even if man obviously defies categorization.[37] This tentative

---

34   Such hierarchy has recently been described as "a symmetry of the affections" in a discus-
      sion of Shaftesbury's "aesthetic realism" (Karl Axelsson, "A Realised Disposition: Shaftes-
      bury on the Natural Affections and Taste", *New Ages, New Opinions*, ed. P. Müller, 31).

35   John Ziman, *Reliable Knowledge: An Exploration of the Grounds for Belief in Science* (Cam-
      bridge: Cambridge University Press, 1996 [1978]), 6.

36   *Ibid.*

37   A comparable diffidence is found in Shaftesbury's vigorous opponent, Berkeley, who
      noted down: "Mem[orandum]: Carefully to omit defining of Person, or making much
      mention of it" (in *Philosophical Commentaries*, c. 1708; *apud* Wahrman, xi). At any rate,

stance may be rooted in a distrust of the "truths" warranted by the disciplines of the age, such as the philosophical psychology of Locke and science proper. He therefore experiments and explores. Yet this does not mean that *any* conceptual apparatus is potentially valid. Shaftesbury's dismissal of supernatural companions – see (5) above – makes it clear that, although different assumptions and explanatory frameworks may be entertained as conceivable, sanction is not to be indiscriminately extended to all and any possible epistemologies. This overthrow of what Sir Thomas Browne branded *pseudodoxia* is also revealing of the fact that for some of Shaftesbury's contemporaries that particular language of consensibility was still not entirely discredited.

Drawing on Ziman's work helps us realize that, no matter if Shaftesbury was fond of distancing himself from the endeavours of science, he found himself, to an extent, faced with epistemological problems which were akin to the practices of science. Indeed, throughout *Soliloquy* Shaftesbury adopts an inferential stance directed by empathy and intuition. The reader is confronted with the probative value of the author's insights as the essay progresses undogmatically by trial and error, tendering knowledge that never becomes fully naturalized. Frameworks and explanations are put forward which are accepted as authoritative – but only provisionally. The argument is fine-tuned in a fashion similar to Defoe's "realism" by approximation and particularization in *Robinson Crusoe*, a literary development which is itself suffused with Lockean assumptions, according to Ian Watt's classic study of the rise of the novel.[38] It is clear that Shaftesbury, the former pupil of Locke, did not miss out on the lesson of empiricism.

Umberto Eco has suggested that, when faced with "something that eludes our capacity for control and denomination", we are unable to resort to closed forms of representation. Eco focuses on modes of artistic depiction which have to do with what he calls the "topos of ineffability", but the point is equally pertinent beyond the bounds of art. When people are unable to make sense of

---

Shaftesbury's very insistence on relating inwardness to body and body to body politic (or, in other words, on positing innate predispositions, and on approaching morality, politics and aesthetics as interrelated spheres) proves he was far from being a subjectivist of Berkeley's temper.

38   Watt connects the new genre's particularized depiction of character, time and space with philosophical realism, in which context Locke figures prominently: see *The Rise of the Novel: Studies in Defoe, Richardson and Fielding* (Berkeley: University of California Press, 1957), 11–30. See also Ilse Vickers, *Defoe and the New Sciences* (Cambridge: Cambridge University Press, 1996), especially 65–69 and 99–131, which stress the importance of the Baconian spirit embodied in the Royal Society for *Robinson Crusoe* as well as Defoe's nonfictional works like *The Storm*.

things, and are therefore incapable of imposing a definite form on perceived or imagined data, they produce lists or catalogues. Eco ventures that a definition by properties (or, to be more precise, a *description* by properties) is typical not only of "a primitive culture that has still to construct a hierarchy of genera and species" but also of "a mature culture (maybe even one in crisis) that is bent on casting doubt on all previous definitions".[39] This, I submit, is precisely the situation that underlies Shaftesbury's *Soliloquy*, only instead of making a list of the things he wants to talk about he focuses on a single topic – man, viewed from a specific perspective – and resorts to a wide inventory of images. A trope of virtual inexhaustibility betrays a condition of unknowability, or of ignorance at least: the superabundance of approaches seeks to compensate for, and hopefully overcome, a cognitive and epistemological insufficiency.

Shaftesbury's eclectic, non-reductionist standpoint produces a kind of palimpsest which epitomizes both the defining communicative qualities of his work and the proper range of his analytical efforts. The first aspect entails the appositeness of the conversational as opposed to the magisterial style. Shaftesbury's preference for what has been described as a "rhapsodic and dialogical form"[40] is not only rooted in the character of the relationship between author and reader as one dictated by rules of urban conviviality; as evinced by a close reading of *Soliloquy*, it also derives from the very conditions of knowledge underlying his writing, i.e. the relationship between author and subject-matter. Shaftesbury himself had no qualms about defending his style. In the opening paragraph of *Miscellaneous Reflections* he praises the unnamed "charitable and courteous Author" who introduced "the ingenious way of MISCELLANEOUS

---

39   *The Infinity of Lists*, trans. Alastair McEwen (New York: Rizzoli, 2009), 117, 49, 218.

40   Caygill, *Art of Judgment*, 44. Lawrence E. Klein also remarks: "While *Characteristicks* was a collection its composite and digressive character was also a matter of design. The miscellanies, written specifically for the collection, were the most digressive of all the components and declared the cognitive value of the lack of system. This lack supported the philosophical, political, and cultural goals of the work by providing a textual embodiment of diversity, open-endedness and freedom" ("Cooper, Anthony Ashley, third earl of Shaftesbury (1671–1713)", *Oxford Dictionary of National Biography*, ed. H.C.G. Matthew and Brian Harrison (Oxford: Oxford University Press, 2004), XIII, 221). One may object to Manfred Geier's implication that the tone of Shaftesbury's writings (as compared to Locke's) is "eher ästhetisch als erkenntnistheoretisch" – for it is one *insofar* as it is the other (*Aufklärung. Das europäische Projekt* (Reinbek bei Hamburg: Rowohlt Taschenbuch Verlag, 2013), 74). On such matters see also Lawrence E. Klein, "Introduction" to Anthony Ashley Cooper, Third Earl of Shaftesbury, *Characteristics of Men, Manners, Opinions, Times*, ed. Klein (Cambridge: Cambridge University Press, 1999), x–xv; Patrick Müller, "'The Able *Designer*, who Feigns in Behalf of *Truth*': Shaftesbury's Philosophical Poetics", *New Ages, New Opinions*, ed. P. Müller, 239–258, and the profuse bibliographical references therein.

Writing": "It must be own'd that since this happy Method was establish'd, the Harvest of Wit has been more plentiful, and the Labourers more in number than heretofore", he submits.[41]

The relaxed but nonetheless impeccable style contributes to the fashioning of writing as a mediator in a mode of communication which seeks to preserve the character of polite personal interaction. Its qualities "confirm the freedom of the reader in relation to the text".[42] The reader is encouraged not to take truth claims for granted, given their virtual incompatibility; but, on the other hand, the fact that the text is also a performance of self (it hinges on the self-display of an author possessed with an authority which is conspicuously derived from the self-appointed criterion of self-examination) goes a long way towards crediting his assertions. A relatively unassuming pose converges with the avoidance of dogmatism and pedantry, two faults routinely attributed to scholasticism by the men of the Royal Society.[43] By contrast, as historians of science Steven Shapin and Barbara Shapiro have shown, scientific inquiry was enabled and problems of credibility were resolved by being encoded as gentlemanly behaviour within a culture of honour and rank in the seventeenth century.[44] Viewed

---

41   Shaftesbury, *Characteristicks*, III, 3. In this respect, it is not inapposite to recollect the importance of the dialogue as a genre for the discussion and dissemination of philosophical learning and scientific knowledge, in the case of Garcia de Orta, Galileo, Berkeley, Fontenelle and many other authors. For a study focused on Shaftesbury and other British authors of the eighteenth century, see Michael Prince, *Philosophical Dialogue in the British Enlightenment: Theology, Aesthetics and the Novel* (Cambridge: Cambridge University Press, 1996).

42   Klein, *Culture of Politeness*, 114. One is reminded of Sir Francis Bacon's discussion of the methods for the delivery of knowledge in *The Advancement of Learning*, and specifically of his regret that the "magistral" method has come to prevail over the method "of probation": "The latter whereof seemeth to be *via deserta et interclusa*. For as knowledges are now delivered, there is a kind of contract of error between the deliverer and the receiver. For he that delivereth knowledge, desireth to deliver it in such forms as may be best believed, and not as may be best examined; and he that receiveth knowledge, desireth rather present satisfaction, than expectant inquiry; and so rather not to doubt, than not to err: glory making the author not to lay open his weakness, and sloth making the disciple not to know his strength" (*The Advancement of Learning and New Atlantis*, ed. Arthur Johnston (Oxford: Clarendon Press, 1974), 134).

43   Cf. Steven Shapin, *Never Pure: Historical Studies of Science as if it Was Produced by People with Bodies, Situated in Time, Space, Culture, and Society, and Struggling for Credibility and Authority* (Baltimore: Johns Hopkins University Press, 2010), 161–162.

44   Cf. Steven Shapin, *A Social History of Truth: Civility and Science in Seventeenth-Century England* (Chicago / London: University of Chicago Press, 1995 [1994]), 65–119 *et passim*, and Shapin, *Never Pure*, 142–181; Barbara J. Shapiro, *A Culture of Fact: England, 1550–1720* (Ithaca / London: Cornell University Press, 2003 [2000]), 139–167.

against this backdrop, Shaftesbury's self-presentation vouches for his identity as a gentleman, and this is tantamount to an entitlement to intellectual authority. The literary self-depiction of the author as an instance of credibility is, however, not self-sufficient. The ascription of probity and veridicity requires an interlocutor: believability is finally contingent upon the validation of truth claims by the reader. It is ultimately up to *him* to redeem the speaker from the virtual disqualification from authority resulting from the discrepancies in the text. Compared to the fellows of the Royal Society, Shaftesbury turns out to be a special case: by dramatizing the construction, imparting and validation of knowledge as an aspect of conversation, his work crucially involves the *individual* reader – as distinguished from increasingly objective and impersonal protocols – in the interplay of conflicting rationales of knowledge.

The rhetoric of *Soliloquy* is made up of fine but far-reaching balances. The topos of (self-)examination colours Shaftesbury's speculative endeavours with the legitimacy of observational knowledge, subtly negotiating the borderlines between the domain of interiority and that of external realities. By making the boundaries permeable, this course of action avoids solipsism. Concurrently, the reader's *"Privilege of Turn"*[45] prevents the author from entirely disrupting the referentiality of language, also thereby keeping solipsism at bay.

Again, the conversational style fits Shaftesbury's avocation as a moral philosopher whose task is less to inquire into fundamentals (to ask the ontological, and perhaps the theological, question) than to consider the proper conduct of life in its various shapes and guises with a suitable degree of flexibility (notice the suggestion of topicality inscribed in the plural forms in the title of his *magnum opus*). Unlike science, on the other hand, ethics is a primarily operative discipline which does not deal with tangible objects; it therefore does not fare ill in the realm of the argumentative and the fictive where hypotheses are entertained. This openness to a plurality of conjectured explanations serves Shaftesbury's method of induction well.

His strictures against science and men of science in the letter to Locke notwithstanding, Shaftesbury's procedures in *Soliloquy*, and indeed in *Characteristicks* as a whole, also prove to be observational and experimental, as evidenced by the unsystematic overall shape of the collection. It is therefore

---

45   Deploring "Violation[s] of the Freedom of publick Assemblys" by those who disregard the principle that "what is contrary to good Breeding, is ... contrary to Liberty", Shaftesbury declares in *Sensus Communis*: "'Tis a breach of the Harmony of publick Conversation, to take things in such a Key, as is above the common Reach, puts others to silence, and robs them of their *Privilege of Turn*" (Shaftesbury, *Characteristicks*, I, 49). The freedom of the reader in relation to the text is a literary counterpart to such rights of spoken conversation.

not inadequate that he should protest at the outset of *Soliloquy*: "My Science, if it be any, is no better than that of *a Language-Master*, or *a Logician*".[46] There is modesty in such a statement, but there is also the significant claim that what he is doing is a legitimate form of "Science", a species of knowledge; and he stipulates a focal point which has to do with the proper use of language and the correct modes of thinking – what Locke called "the conduct of the understanding".

Shaftesbury's method may appear to produce a strange mélange if viewed through over-analytical eyes – but this is only because *it is itself over-analytical*, without, however, possessing the *esprit de système*. To compound an argument of very diverse and virtually contradictory elements is potentially self-defeating. An essay like *Soliloquy* pits the strength of the author's moral conviction against the inconsistency of his ontological assumptions. The outcome is fragile and heterogeneous, but it is never purely rhetorical in the sense of indulging in gratuitous wordiness. Shaftesbury is an observer of human behaviour and states of mind who brings to bear a number of frames of reference in an attempt to conceptualize his data: disparate idioms are his tools. More than merely deploying strategies of persuasion and illustration, the formal heterogeneity of his style constitutes a medium of discovery, an inflected hermeneutics of reality. He drives his points home and explores possibilities of knowledge at one and the same time. He expects cognitive breakthroughs to be generated by the interplay of language and concepts. He is the denizen of a configuration of awareness in which – to paraphrase a title by Anthony Grafton – words make worlds.[47] As he seeks to extract both truth and meaningfulness from his scrutiny of himself and others, he commits himself to the business of reconnoitring, not simply recognizing what others have found or laid out.

The ostensible looseness and calculated spontaneity of Shaftesbury's thinking and writing style are therefore vectors of an approach which in the vocabulary of our own time we have learned to label "constructivist". In this respect, it is illuminating to contrast Shaftesbury's methodology with that of another major Augustan writer, Alexander Pope, who, as it happens, did not shrink from acknowledging his interest in the sciences and in fact blended it with his faith and ethical concerns under a general spirit of theodicy. In *An Essay on Criticism* Pope placed a list of "Contents" before the poem. In *An Essay on Man* and the *Epistles to Several Persons* each of the epistles is introduced by an "Argument".

---

46   Shaftesbury, *Characteristicks*, I, 98.
47   Anthony Grafton, *Worlds Made by Words: Scholarship and Community in the Modern West* (Cambridge, Mass. / London, England: Harvard University Press, 2009).

The presence of a synopsis, especially if it includes headings and subheadings, immediately suggests a high degree of expository order and exhaustiveness; it bespeaks the precision and closure, and hence inculcates the authority, of a formal treatise. As the synopsis and the poem stand successively on the printed page, the implication arises that the substance of the work is contained in the former and that the message is but glossed into verse. Although this does not mean that such was the actual order of writing (we know little about Pope's methods of composition, but it is evidently unlikely that the poems were written on the basis of abstracts which as a matter of principle were never subject to revision),[48] the end result points to a chronology and a hierarchy: thinking comes before poetic elaboration. This applies to the creation of the work as well as to the reader's experience of it, and it agrees with Pope's definition of wit:

> *True Wit* is *Nature* to Advantage drest,
> What oft was *Thought*, but ne'er so well *Exprest*,
> *Something*, whose Truth convinc'd at Sight we find,
> That gives us back the Image of our Mind:[49]

The content precedes the poem, both formally and intellectually. It follows that Pope's images are explanatory, illustrative and persuasive. At their most typical, they are similes used for argumentative purposes and dependent on shared assumptions. Thus, the first instance of figurative language in *An Essay on Criticism* reads: "'Tis with our *Judgments* as our *Watches*, none / Go just

---

48   What we do know of Pope's methods involves a measure of contradiction. In a letter to William Walsh on versification, dated 22 October 1706, Pope appears to confirm that content takes precedence over expression when he maintains that "a good Poet will adapt the very Sounds, as well as Words, to the things he treats of" (George Sherburn, ed., *The Correspondence of Alexander Pope* (Oxford: Clarendon Press, 1956) (5 vols.), I, 22; the statement in repeated almost verbatim in a letter to Henry Cromwell dated 25 November 1710, *ibid.*, 107). In a conversation with Joseph Spence in 1743, too, Pope talked of a plan for an epic poem about Brutus which it should not take very long to write because "the matter is already quite digested and prepared" (Spence, *Observations, Anecdotes, and Characters of Books and Men, Collected from Conversation*, ed. James M. Osborn (Oxford: Clarendon Press, 1966) (2 vols.), I, 153, nr 343). However, the principles of versification laid out in the correspondence do not always square with the genetic evidence that can be extracted from the manuscripts. See, e.g., Robert M. Schmitz, *Pope's Windsor Forest 1712: A Study of the Washington University Holograph* (Saint Louis: Washington University, 1952), 51–55, 65–68.

49   Alexander Pope, *An Essay on Criticism*, lines 297–300. *Pastoral Poetry and An Essay on Criticism*, ed. E. Audra and Aubrey Williams (London: Methuen / New Haven: Yale University Press, 1961) (*The Twickenham Edition of the Poems of Alexander Pope*, gen. ed. John Butt, Vol. I).

alike, yet each believes his own".[50] The simile relies on the reader's recognition of the fact that individuals trust their respective watches implicitly (or, to remain within the thematic limits of the poem, uncritically), although they fail to make sure that their watches are keeping proper time. Pope's advice to distrust hastily-formed opinions is given in a manner which satisfies the requirements of his understanding of the role and nature of rhetorical devices. It is likewise noticeable that his writing does not presume to be exploratory, rather it is aimed at delivering an enhanced re-presentation of the familiar.

Shaftesbury's style is rhetorical too, but it is rhetorical in the more complex and ambitious sense that imagery is integral to and participates in the production of meaning, not simply in imparting it effectively. In Shaftesbury's case, expression is constitutive of thought, not a mere translation or, as Pope phrases it, "the *Dress* of *Thought*".[51] Whereas Pope draws upon the familiar to remind his readers of what may have become obscured or forgotten, Shaftesbury appears to be grasping for meaning, building it out of the fabric of language itself, taking advantage of the allusive qualities of language.[52] His project is adventurous, contentious and challengeable. It risks sinking as he navigates his way through imperfectly charted seas. What he does not purport to offer, in any case, is (to return to the text of his letter to Locke) a mere "Affectation of Knowledg", or "admirable Discoverys, which [are] nothing worth but to bee commended for their Subtility".[53] His intellectual honesty is above that.

Works Cited

Axelsson, Karl. "A Realised Disposition: Shaftesbury on the Natural Affections and Taste". In *New Ages, New Opinions: Shaftesbury in his World and Today*, edited by Patrick Müller, assisted by Christine Jackson-Holzberg. 27–44. Frankfurt am Main: Peter Lang, 2014.

---

50 Pope, *An Essay on Criticism*, lines 9–10.

51 *Ibid.*, line 318.

52 He is, in other words, bent on what Patrick Müller calls "the exploitation of language's semantic possibilities" – which, however, I do not see "as indicative of a stable, self-sufficient, and self-confident order which allows the imagination free rein" but rather as a response to a far more precarious philosophical context. I therefore agree with Müller that Shaftesbury's texts "are not so much concerned with fixing truths (that is, they do not aspire to be scientific in any modern sense of the word), but with the mental processes involved in the quest for truth" (Müller, "Able *Designer*", 249, 257) but see it in a different light.

53 Shaftesbury, *Correspondence*, 151.

Bacon, Francis. *The Advancement of Learning*, in *The Advancement of Learning and New Atlantis*, ed. Arthur Johnston. 1–212. Oxford: Clarendon Press, 1974.

Barish, Jonas. *The Antitheatrical Prejudice*. Berkeley: University of California Press, 1981.

Burke, Peter. *A Social History of Knowledge: From Gutenberg to Diderot*. Cambridge: Polity Press, 2008 [2000].

Caygill, Howard. *Art of Judgment*. Oxford: Basil Blackwell, 1989.

De Beer, E.S., ed. *The Correspondence of John Locke. Volume 5: Letters Nos. 1702–2198*. Oxford: Clarendon Press, 1976.

Eco, Umberto. *The Infinity of Lists*, translated by Alastair McEwen. New York: Rizzoli, 2009.

Geier, Manfred. *Aufklärung. Das europäische Projekt*. Reinbek bei Hamburg: Rowohlt Taschenbuch Verlag, 2013.

Gill, Michael B. "Shaftesbury on Politeness, Honesty, and Virtue". In *New Ages, New Opinions: Shaftesbury in his World and Today*, edited by Patrick Müller, assisted by Christine Jackson-Holzberg. 167–183. Frankfurt am Main: Peter Lang, 2014.

Grafton, Anthony. *Worlds Made by Words: Scholarship and Community in the Modern West*. Cambridge, Mass. / London, England: Harvard University Press, 2009.

Himmelfarb, Gertrude. *The Roads to Modernity: The British, French, and American Enlightenments*. New York: Alfred A. Knopf, 2004.

Hume, David. *The Philosophical Works*, edited by Thomas Hill Green and Thomas Hodge Grose. Aalen: Scientia Verlag, 1964. 4 vols.

Klein, Lawrence E. "Cooper, Anthony Ashley, third earl of Shaftesbury (1671–1713)". In *Oxford Dictionary of National Biography*, edited by H.C.G. Matthew and Brian Harrison. Vol. XIII, 217–223. Oxford: Oxford University Press, 2004.

Klein, Lawrence E. Introduction to Anthony Ashley Cooper, Third Earl of Shaftesbury, *Characteristics of Men, Manners, Opinions, Times*, edited by Lawrence E. Klein. vii–xxxi. Cambridge: Cambridge University Press, 1999.

Klein, Lawrence E. *Shaftesbury and the Culture of Politeness: Moral Discourse and Cultural Politics in Early Eighteenth-Century England*. Cambridge: Cambridge University Press, 2004 [1994].

Macpherson, C.B. *The Political Theory of Possessive Individualism: Hobbes to Locke*. Oxford: Clarendon Press, 1962.

Müller, Patrick. "'The Able *Designer*, who Feigns in Behalf of *Truth*': Shaftesbury's Philosophical Poetics". In *New Ages, New Opinions: Shaftesbury in his World and Today*, edited by Patrick Müller, assisted by Christine Jackson-Holzberg, 239–258. Frankfurt am Main: Peter Lang, 2014.

Paknadel, Felix. "Shaftesbury's Illustrations of Characteristics". *Journal of the Warburg and Courtauld Institutes*, XXXVII (1974), 290–312.

Pope, Alexander. *Pastoral Poetry and An Essay on Criticism*, edited by E. Audra and Aubrey Williams. London: Methuen / New Haven: Yale University Press, 1961. *The Twickenham Edition of the Poems of Alexander Pope*, general editor John Butt.

Prince, Michael. *Philosophical Dialogue in the British Enlightenment: Theology, Aesthetics and the Novel.* Cambridge: Cambridge University Press, 1996.

Schmitz, Robert M. *Pope's Windsor Forest 1712: A Study of the Washington University Holograph.* Saint Louis: Washington University, 1952.

Shaftesbury, Anthony Ashley Cooper, Third Earl of. *Characteristicks of Men, Manners, Opinions, Times,* foreword by Douglas Den Uyl. Indianapolis: Liberty Fund, 2001. 3 vols.

Shapin, Steven. *Never Pure: Historical Studies of Science as if it Was Produced by People with Bodies, Situated in Time, Space, Culture, and Society, and Struggling for Credibility and Authority.* Baltimore: Johns Hopkins University Press, 2010.

Shapin, Steven. *A Social History of Truth: Civility and Science in Seventeenth-Century England.* Chicago / London: University of Chicago Press, 1995 [1994].

Shapiro, Barbara J. *A Culture of Fact: England, 1550–1720.* Ithaca / London: Cornell University Press, 2003 [2000].

Sherburn, George, ed. *The Correspondence of Alexander Pope.* Oxford: Clarendon Press, 1956. 5 vols.

Silva, Jorge Bastos da. "Exorcising Locke: Towards a Re-Appraisal of Addison's Literary Criticism". *Imitatio – Inventio: The Rise of "Literature" from Early to Classic Modernity,* edited by Mihaela Irimia and Dragoş Ivana. 299–313. Bucureşti: Institutul Cultural Român, 2010.

Spence, Joseph. *Observations, Anecdotes, and Characters of Books and Men, Collected from Conversation,* edited by James M. Osborn. Oxford: Clarendon Press, 1966. 2 vols.

Taylor, Charles. *Sources of the Self: The Making of the Modern Identity.* Cambridge, Mass.: Harvard University Press, 1989.

Vickers, Ilse. *Defoe and the New Sciences.* Cambridge: Cambridge University Press, 1996.

Voitle, Robert. *The Third Earl of Shaftesbury 1671–1713.* Baton Rouge: Louisiana State University Press, 1984.

Wahrman, Dror. *The Making of the Modern Self: Identity and Culture in Eighteenth-Century England.* New Haven / London: Yale University Press, 2004.

Watt, Ian. *The Rise of the Novel: Studies in Defoe, Richardson and Fielding.* Berkeley: University of California Press, 1957.

Ziman, John. *Reliable Knowledge: An Exploration of the Grounds for Belief in Science.* Cambridge: Cambridge University Press, 1996 [1978].

CHAPTER 8

Readers of Nerves and Tears: From Plague to *Pamela*

Daniel Essig García

Abstract

Cultural studies deal with the "sentimental revolution", the "reading revolution" in the 1700s. This essay explores one theme – male sensibility making men more like women – in two novels: Daniel Defoe's *A Journal of the Plague Year*, as precursor to the revolution of sensibility, and Samuel Richardson's *Pamela*, the earliest best-seller of sentiment. In Defoe's *Journal*, we have a model of *reading*; not only reception and passion, but the *scene of reading*, which becomes the means for an epistemological critique of the circulation of information in the metropolis. *Pamela*, on the other hand, makes much of *a man crying*. In the visual arts, the "scene of reading" translated into the currency of paintings showing women reading. The scene of reading became a metaphor for the paradoxes of distance and privacy (including the theatricality of the reader reading readers).

•••

I do not know when it became "the thing" for Englishmen not to cry.

HARLEY GRANVILLE-BARKER

∵

The injunction to historicise, which has been hegemonic in cultural studies and literary criticism over the past thirty years, though seemingly unproblematic, is easier in principle than it is in practice; that is partly because it is often misunderstood. What we are called to look into when historicizing is not just – not mainly – the chronology and causation of political events, biography or the description of so-called "context", even less of pure intellect and fleshless debates; instead, it demands minute descriptions of sites and places, institutions, networks (all those eminently social; in Jorge Bastos da Silva and Miguel Ramalhete Gomes' more technical words in their introduction to this volume, "the dynamics and the morals of social interaction involved in [the] production and circulation [of literature and the sciences]"). It is also, at that most material level of the body itself – though still social – practices, gestures, "[the body's] palpitations and collapses", "the gestural force of feeling".[1] In that sense, historicizing is what Friedrich Nietzsche and, closer to us, Norbert Elias, Alexandre Koyré, Thomas Kuhn and George Rousseau taught us to do.

If genealogy – or, in a different language, "paradigms" – still poses a challenge to our normal modes of thinking, it is because of the question that subtends it: what can there be histories of? For the opening years of the eighteenth century, the point was made by George Rousseau in 1976: the mutual implication between culture, even entertainment, on the one hand, and, on the other, science and medicine.[2] To quote Bastos da Silva and Ramalhete Gomes again, "[Literature and science] are both linked to, and are indeed dependent on, issues of power and accountability".

Christopher Lawrence, more than forty years ago, specifically pointed out the connection between medicine and cultural history: "when the nervous system is thought of as an artefact, as something made historically within a specific form of physiological discourse, it is quite clear that it only came into existence at the end of the seventeenth century".[3] More generally, historians and literary critics have taught us to be attentive to "the trouble with the Enlightenment"; or rather, "troubles", according to Michel Foucault, Roy Porter, George Rousseau or Anne Vila (with the resonant title of her 1998 book, *Enlightenment and Pathology*).

My chapter will be paying attention to two examples of a cultural practice, so-called "sentimental reading" or "the reading of sensibility", whose essence is appropriately captured by Anne Jessie Van Sant: "If readers read for sensation (in order to be thrilled or to have their fibers shaken), the evidence of a writer's talent lies in the reader's body ... the signs of a writer's ability [are] located in the physiology of the reader".[4] Two novels will be compared, Daniel Defoe's *A Journal of the Plague Year* (1722) and Samuel Richardson's *Pamela*

---

1 John Mullan, *Sentiment and Sociability: The Language of Feeling in the Eighteenth Century*, (Oxford: Clarendon Press, 1988), 16, 201.

2 George Rousseau, "Nerves, Spirits and Fibres: Towards the Origins of Sensibility", *Blue Guitar*, 2 (1976), 125–133. Reprinted in *Nervous Acts: Essays on Literature, Culture and Sensibility* (Basingstoke: Palgrave Macmillan, 2004).

3 Christopher Lawrence, "Making the Nervous System", review of Max Neuberger, *The Historical Development of Experimental Brain and Spinal Cord Physiology before Flourens*, and Renato G. Mazzolini, *The Iris in Eighteenth-Century Physiology*, *Social Studies of Science*, XIV/1 (1984), 153–158.

4 Anne Jessie Van Sant, *Eighteenth-Century Sensibility and the Novel* (Cambridge: Cambridge University Press, 1993), 117.

(1740). The latter was, indeed, a trend-setter, the prototype of the genre. One claim of this chapter will be that Richardson's motif is *reading and writing like a woman*. The narrator-memorialist of my first example, Defoe's *Journal*, is not a woman; consequently, literary history has been fainthearted in approaching Defoe as a writer of sensibility, and understandably so. Yet Defoe's novels precede Richardson's by only twenty years. It is my claim that the exquisitely crafted narrator of *A Journal of the Plague Year* is better understood against the backcloth of the reading and writing of women, and that Defoe with his H.F. was anticipating the classical examples of sentimental characters such as Pamela or Clarissa.

The overarching thesis of this chapter will thus be that the development of sensibility and the feminization of culture in 1720–1770 were linked to a new spatial experience and phenomenology of intimacy and interiority; in novels published in the wake of *Pamela*, and until the last decade of the eighteenth century, that experience came to include tearful outbursts of emotion and lachrymose displays and identification. The middling sorts were no longer excluded from such experiences, which typically were associated with reading and writing.

Central to that practice – and present, in this case, both in Defoe and Richardson – is the seamless alternation between reading and writing, which cannot be adequately captured by the binary intensive vs. extensive reading.[5] The avid reader/writer cannot *write* outside – he or she will, on the other hand, indeed *read* outside – but much happens outdoors which needs to be pondered on, edited or written about. In short, material conditions – among the middling sorts, conspicuously so in terms of the architectural dialectic of inside/outside – influence reading and writing. That is evident, concerning the availability of materials for writing, namely ink and paper, in *Robinson Crusoe* or *Pamela*. In the case of *A Journal of the Plague Year*, in an epidemic of plague, it translates as the inevitability of long periods of enforced leisure or idleness and solitary reflection in middling-sort homes. Furthermore, the discourse of natural philosophy, that is, Science, to which the narrator of Defoe's *Journal*

---

5 "Drawing on sources taken from the Protestant north and middle regions of Germany, Rolf Engelsing has described a process by which the intensive reading of a small collective canon of texts, mostly of a religious kind and primarily the Bible, that were familiar, normative and repeatedly recited, was replaced with an extensive form of reading. In a modern, secularized and individual way, extensive reading was characterized by an eagerness to consume new and varied reading materials for information, and for private entertainment in particular". Reinhard Wittmann, "Was there a Reading Revolution at the End of the Eighteenth Century?", in *A History of Reading in the West*, ed. by Roger Chartier and Guglielmo Cavallo (Oxford: Polity, 1999), 285.

is delicately responsive, is also a *feminized* language, with the amalgamation of wonder and curiosity as its founding element.

I

Even a mere glance at the cultural history of the long eighteenth century brings forth some interesting paradoxes. For one, how is it that medical theory and practice dealt with conditions which people did not want to be cured of? Certain illnesses, which today fall in the province of psychiatry, were known as "nervous illnesses" and firmly associated with class and status between *c.* 1650 and *c.* 1800. Nerves and their quality or state were described along an axiological scale running from very lax or loose to very taut or tight, and, given that supposedly taut nerves were more susceptible or responsive, and that such reactivity was constitutive of *sensibility* – itself a mark of gentility –, tautness of nerves, indeed, came to be seen as desirable. Graham Barker-Benfield, and more recently Sean Quinlan, put it succinctly yet resoundingly: "Given the eighteenth-century connotations of 'degree', the quality of sensibility could be seen as a badge of rank";[6] "degrees of sensibility, then, betokened both social and moral status. Paradoxically, however, an innate refinement of nerves was also identifiable with greater suffering, with weakness, and a susceptibility to disorder";[7] "capitalist enterprise problematized traditional associations; self-interest and consumption threatened the (imaginary) domestic economy, once frugal and prudential ... As a result, excess – that point where 'sensibility and prudence' diverged – remained a chronic anxiety".[8] So, patients naturally did suffer from tautness of nerves, and demanded treatment. What was, then, the purpose of such treatment?

Among other marks of gentility, one that commentators in the early modern period firmly emphasized was *leisure*. Leisure, however, came to be troublingly linked with luxury. The leisure of the elites, in principle gendered masculine, was expected, precisely for that reason, to be associated with "the main ethic of the new sensibility [which] led to aesthetic refinement and civic responsibility",[9] and with tautness of nerves. But luxury, which was commonly

---

6   Graham Barker-Benfield, *The Culture of Sensibility: Sex and Society in Eighteenth-Century Britain* (Chicago: Chicago University Press, 1992), 8.

7   Barker-Benfield, 9.

8   Sean Quinlan, "Sensibility and Human Science in the Enlightenment", review, *Eighteenth-Century Studies*, XXXVII/2 (2004), 296–301 (297).

9   George S. Rousseau, *Nervous Acts: Essays on Literature, Culture and Sensibility* (Basingstoke: Palgrave Macmillan, 2004), 15.

considered a component of leisure, complicates the equation: that is, tautness of nerves should, implausibly, be compatible with both leisure and luxury. Such a claim ran counter to everything medicine and ethics – even literature, notably in satire – had been claiming from Western Antiquity to the Renaissance: in his pioneering work on the genealogy of luxury, John Sekora makes that point in a reference to Hellenistic philosophy: "Antisthenes, Crates, Zeno, Diogenes Laertius, Chrysippus, and Panaetius saw the great majority of men enfeebled by luxury, a multitude that, lacking moral discipline, could not conceivably achieve virtue and rationality".[10]

And the theme is vital for the greatest Roman writers:

> Cicero represents one of the Roman contributions to the history of luxury, the impulse to purge the disorder ... from every phase of Roman life, a practical approach that preoccupied most European nations until the middle of the eighteenth century. The wit and invective of the literary attacks by Horace and Juvenal represent another. In the most important, historians of the late Republic treated luxury not as object but as subject, discovering in it an essential, causative factor in the narrative of national calamity they were obliged to impart.[11]

Gender introduces another twist: with the advent of politeness in the age of Shaftesbury and Addison, culminating the advance of Norbert Elias' "civilizing process", women would be described as being particularly endowed with sensibility. But at that point one question arises, which has plunged historians in profound perplexity: were their nerves, the nerves of women, supposed to be taut, or lax? The tradition of moral discourse on nerves and fibres emphasized that the active life, gendered masculine, made nerves strong. But *responsiveness, sympathy, sociability* required delicacy in nerves. And as long as it was not clear that treatment, exercise and diet making nerves stronger did not carry with them a loss in delicacy, it could hardly be clear what the aim of treatment, by people like the physician George Cheyne, could be:

> Cheyne's approach to mental anguish and disordered emotions thus appears, at first sight, rather paradoxical. Precisely because he would not countenance the notion that such disturbances of the self as lowness of spirits, the horrors, and agitation were authentic diseases of the

10   John Sekora, *Luxury: The Concept in Western Thought, Eden to Smollett* (Baltimore: Johns Hopkins University Press, 1977), 33.

11   Sekora, 36.

mind – they were rather caused by defective nerves – those very disorders could ironically assume a certain legitimacy, even an aura. It might be considered a badge of distinction to be seen to be suffering from the English malady, because it was, by definition, exclusively a top people's disease.... In all those senses, it proved a tailor-made "fashionable disease", just what the doctor ordered.[12]

John Mullan, in a pithy reference to Richard Blackmore and George Cheyne, spots in many nervous illnesses "symptoms of a peculiar privilege, of heightened faculties or unusual intelligence. It is this appearance of weakness and strength together – of special faculties that are manifested in illness – which is the most important description common to the medical text and the novel of sentiment".[13]

The second paradox refers to the fact that, in the same period, discourse in a polity dominated by men started associating reading with passivity, and consequently was desperately bound to identify a practice which could alternatively, legitimately be vindicated, without oxymoron, as *active reading*. Advance toward that category can be tracked mainly in the second half of the eighteenth century. The first two decades of that century, on the other hand, witnessed the triumph of *apologies of the passive*, as explained by Scott Paul Gordon.[14] Later in this chapter attention will be paid to passivity associated with wonder and curiosity, as a component of the language of natural philosophy.

Originally detached from the system articulated by passion and passive, and from those shifts in the norms of gentility, civility and politeness, an influential discourse, which can be identified, in different ways, in Hobbes and Cervantes, insisted on passions and pathologies of reading: an inescapable connection between reading and, on the other hand, mental illness and moral disorder. Towards the end of the eighteenth century, the theme found expression in thinkers like Johan Adam Bergk, Immanuel Kant, and Samuel Auguste Tissot. Bergk's formulation is candid and memorable:

> Since [obsessive readers] choose only works that do not require much reflection and that are full of improbabilities and unnatural events and are worthless and tasteless, they forget the laws of nature ... and fall prey

---

12   George Cheyne, *The English Malady*, ed. by Roy Porter, Tavistock Classics in the History of Psychiatry (London: Routledge, 1991) [1733], xxxviii.

13   Mullan, 205.

14   Scott Paul Gordon, *The Power of the Passive Self in English Literature, 1640–1770* (Cambridge: Cambridge University Press, 2002), 119–181.

to countless errors and transgressions because they can no longer hear their own inner warnings. They make demands on people that cannot be met ...; they want positions in life which morality forbids us to aspire to; they kill all desire for activity and work and all love of freedom. They become moody, peevish, presumptuous, impatient. They become extraordinarily susceptible to every impression, which they are unable to muster inner powers to oppose.... The consequences of such tasteless and mindless reading are thus senseless waste, an insurmountable fear of any kind of exertion, a boundless bent for luxury, repression of the voices of conscience, ennui, and an early death.[15]

The modern scholar Anne Vila mentions that "Tissot devoted most of this treatise to scholars' nervous maladies and digestive disorders. He also addressed what he saw as the 'castration effect' of intense reading and meditation".[16]

Reading, thus, can be a *cause* (in Cervantes), but also in the age of sentiment, it can be a *consequence* of, taut as well as lax nerves. There are, then, conditions from which it is not dishonourable not to be cured, and which make *some* men read like *some* women.

In summary, culture came to be pervaded by the theme of nerves and nervous illnesses; this is at the centre of George Rousseau's argument in *Nervous Acts*. Quite independently, a shift came about in the discourse of fashion (in the sense both of "fashionable discourse", and "discourse which has fashion as its object"). There had for a long time been a connection between that discourse and social mobility and emulation, as in the case of sumptuary laws. The change which came about in the final decades of the seventeenth century, largely as a result of Dutch influence, was the publication of a number of moral and philosophical defences of luxury and consumption (not just Mandeville's (in)famous *The Fable of the Bees*, but also several works by Nicholas Barbon between 1685 and 1696).[17] To that, of course, one should add a straightforward

---

15   Johann Adam Bergk, *Die Kunst, Bucher zu lesen. Nebst Bemerkungen uber Schriflen und Schriflsteller* (Gena: In der Hempelschen Buchhandlung, 1799), 411–412. Quoted in Martha Woodmansee, "Toward a Genealogy of the Aesthetic: The German Reading Debate of the 1790s", *Cultural Critique*, XI (1988–1989), 203–221. The translation is Woodmansee's.

16   Anne C. Vila. "Sex, Procreation, and the Scholarly Life from Tissot to Balzac". *Eighteenth-Century Studies*, XXXV/2 (2002), 239–246 (240).

17   On the renewed interest in the modern controversy about luxury, interest, and sociability (including "politeness" and fashion), and notably the importance of Bernard Mandeville's thought and writings, see Christopher Berry, *The Idea of Luxury: A Conceptual and Historical Investigation* (Cambridge: Cambridge University Press, 1994); Maurice Marks Goldsmith, *Private Vices, Public Benefits: Bernard Mandeville's Social and Political Thought*

fact: books were, in 1705 or 1720, one of the most important symbols of wealth as well as materials for consumption, notably for the middling sorts. The theatre where those developments are most evident – to which books are central – is that of family intimacy and domesticity. Nervous illnesses became fashionable, a reason why upwardly mobile people were not necessarily impatient for nervous doctors to cure them.

Charles Webster and Margaret Pelling have described and explained how the new prestige of luxury and consumption in the period of the Enlightenment had been preceded by the gradual improvement in the status and position of physicians in the late seventeenth century.[18] Doctors occupy a privileged place in the story of the development of the modern professions. Here again, a substantive and visible convergence can be tracked between fashion and luxury. For the market of medicine, one crucial driving force was provided by nervous illnesses. Some physicians working with "nervous patients" even achieved in the 1730s and 1740s what appears to be beyond the reach even of luminaries in modern medicine: combining substantial practices for the rich with an active role in medical research and theory. Such is, famously, the case of the ailing George Cheyne, the celebrated author of *The English Malady*. One vital feature in the deontological code of practitioners which would shock us today is the reliance, for diagnosis and treatment, on a feeling of sympathy between doctor and patient: in the 1700s, conspicuously so among nervous specialists, the physician not only shared in his patient's symptoms and ailments, but actually based his therapy on mutual confession and on a current of sympathy between them. Much of that took place by letter,[19] that is to say, at a distance. A famous pair is Cheyne himself and his patient Samuel Richardson.

(Cambridge: Cambridge University Press, 1985); Maurice Marks Goldsmith, "Liberty, Luxury and the Pursuit of Happiness" in *The Languages of Political Theory in Early-Modern Europe*, ed. by Anthony Pagden (Cambridge: Cambridge University Press, 1987).

18   Margaret Pelling and Frances White, *Medical Conflicts in Early Modern London: Patronage, Physicians, and Irregular Practitioners* (Oxford: Clarendon Press, 2003), 1–24; Margaret Pelling, "Politics, Medicine, and Masculinity: Physicians and Office-bearing in Early Modern England", in *The Practice of Reform in Health, Medicine, and Science, 1500–2000: Essays for Charles Webster*, ed. by Margaret Pelling and Scott Mandelbrote, 81–105 (Aldershot: Ashgate, 2005); Charles Webster, *The Great Instauration: Science, Medicine and Reform 1626–1660*, 2nd ed. (Bern: Peter Lang AG, 2002), 250–273.

19   One typical persona of eighteenth-century literate culture is the woman reading and writing the self, for instance journals and letters (also in portraiture). I say "persona" because that does not mean that men were not also thoroughly epistolary. In fact, Daniel Defoe's manual *The Complete Tradesman* is organised on the basis of the importance of letters (Chapter Two in the manual bears the title "The Tradesman's Writing Letters").

II

Before analysing Richardson's first novel, I will be looking at Daniel Defoe's *A Journal of the Plague Year* (1722). A suggestive question comes to mind: is there any way in which Defoe's hero and narrator, H.F., the citizen of London, might be said to read like a woman? Could the *Journal* be read as a text of sensibility, riddled with the incongruities and paradoxes of reading and writing proper to the age of sentiment?

In many canonical sentimental texts, tears come in as signifiers of communication between protagonist and reader. As such, in the most immediate sense tears stand for sociability (thence, for sympathy and compassion); another, older, indicator of intimacy was the practice and activity of solitary reading. Admittedly, and very importantly, there are no tears or crying in *A Journal of the Plague Year*: it is a moot question precisely when – and whether – readers in the early 1720s cried while reading Defoe's harrowing report of the 1665 plague;[20] the narrator-memorialist, at any rate, does not mention tears.

---

20   The chronology of tears and crying has a bearing on how literary history is written: the question is difficult but illuminating because, if crying was indeed a cultural fashion, it was, for many reasons, more than a fashion (as the complication of the changes of attitudes towards tears makes clear; when, for example, would the fashion have appeared? When and how did it wane?). An important and ambitious text by Thomas Dixon throws some light on those questions. Most centrally, Dixon introduces two points: the connection between tears and religion in the case of Methodism in the period from 1735 to 1760 and what he very suggestively refers to as "the association between weeping and national identity", which he traces to the 1790s. To that useful focus on burgeoning nationalism, in my opinion, an attention to class should be added (evident already in Dixon's sources, as the examples of Methodism and the accounts of executions at Tyburn show). This is not trivial, because social and cultural historians have long challenged the propriety of the category "class" in periods prior to the late eighteenth century: the perplexing issue of the origin and nature of popular culture is only one particularly tricky implication of that. Now if one can speak of working-*class* culture in the period 1780–1830, the question of the impropriety of tears and weeping is surely relevant. That the question is extraordinarily complex is made evident by Dixon's difficulties in presenting his argument in the final section of his article. Very different case-studies are introduced: Wollstonecraft and Paine on Burke's tears over Marie Antoinette; but also the question of insincere crying ("crocodile tears") in politicians sympathetic to the early phases of the French Revolution. It became normative that Englishmen did not cry, whereas the French did; and yet what the evidence shows is the reactions of British observers to events in France; the supposed tearful behaviour of the French Jacobins is not the issue; on the other hand, the readership of counter-revolutionary pamphlets in English, characteristically non-elite, was expected to shed tears. A more general – and speculative – point, which suggests a possible

On the other hand, scenes where characters and readers alike fall into tears are common in Richardson's novels; and that will prove central to my argument in Section III. (However, even in Richardson, tears and crying do not function in the void, autonomously, as they do in Laurence Sterne's *Tristram Shandy*.)[21]

What we do have in Defoe, what delineates a space of intimacy, is obsessive and concentrated reading and writing, *a scene of reading and writing*; concentration thus preparing for absorption. To begin with, H.F. spends much time indoors because that is obviously the safer thing to do (although most readers are apt to remember H.F.'s apparent censure of the practice of home quarantine, Defoe in his other 1722 work on plague, *Due Preparations for the Plague*, insists on the desirability of locking oneself up at home as a defence against plague; H.F., indeed, is shown doing precisely that over and over again).

The word "scene" is an appropriate one to refer to theatricality and interior architecture, to the combination of interiority and concentration in the *Journal*; scene is at once context and ornament or decoration, and thus ancillary, but also body and gesture. Some light is thrown on that by Sean Quinlan, in his review of David Denby's *Sentimental Narrative and the Social Order in France, 1760–1820*, where he uses the word "tableau" (said by Denby to have as "its function ... to freeze narrative, to suspend temporal progression so that the set of forces which the narrative has brought together in a particular moment may be allowed to discharge their full affective power"):[22]

Denby's analysis encompasses beautifully crafted readings of sentimental writers such as Baculard d'Arnaud, Jean-Claude Gorjy, François

---

bridge between the two periods, is the analytical category of *generation* and generational gap in descriptions of revolutionary political change; for example, generation is pivotal for an understanding of the reception of *Tristram Shandy* and *The Man of Feeling* (on generation, see Roy Foster's work on early twentieth-century Irish history); Thomas Dixon, "Enthusiasm Delineated: Weeping as a Religious Activity in Eighteenth-Century Britain", *Litteraria Pragensia*, XXII/43 (2013), 59–81; Roy Foster, *Vivid Faces: the Revolutionary Generation in Ireland 1890–1923* (London: Penguin, 2015).

21   As in: "I thank thee, Trim, quoth my uncle Toby. I never think of his, continued Trim, and my poor brother Tom's misfortunes, for we were all three school-fellows, but I cry like a coward. – Tears are no proof of cowardice, Trim. – I drop them oft-times myself, cried my uncle Toby. – I know your honour does, replied Trim, and so am not ashamed of it myself. – But to think, may it please your honour, continued Trim, a tear stealing into the corner of his eye as he spoke". (Laurence Sterne, *The Life and Opinions of Tristram Shandy, Gentleman* (Harmondsworth: Penguin, 1985)), 276–277.

22   David Denby, *Sentimental Narrative and the Social Order in France* (Cambridge: Cambridge University Press, 1994), 76.

Vernes, Jean Jacques Rousseau, *idéologues* Pierre Cabanis and Destutt de Tracy, and post-revolutionary thinkers such as Germaine de Staël. Denby first isolates the "meta-structure" of sentimental texts, identifying [some] major characteristics.... Sentimental texts included a pictorial, spatio-temporal dimension (of which J.B. Greuze's paintings provide a striking visual analogy). These so-called "tableaux" froze the sentimental narrative's climactic moment, providing a synecdoche that wrung out all possible sympathetic effect.[23]

In Denby's detailed description,

> One of the principal textual constituents of the tableau becomes explicit and visible: the constitution of a particular description as a tableau is dependent upon an explicit or implied relation of looking, on the setting up of a distance between observer and observed ... [a] remoteness which sometimes characterises the sentimental tableau, ... tableau, memory and narrative repetition all function within a logic of reception. Hence the sustained importance in the sentimental text of phrases which serve to introduce the reaction of a subject to fictive reality. Subjects are constantly described as reacting (usually with tears) "au récit de", "au souvenir de" or "au spectacle de" some moving act or segment of narration. This repetition, this process of internal quotation, has no sense outside the reception framework: it is the reaction of an observing subject which gives sense to the narrative. This activation of the narrative sequence may take various forms: if the most common form is the speechless homage of tears, the impact of narrative on the subject may also be to spur him to virtuous action, or indeed to produce another text.[24]

That synecdochal condensation and concentration appear in the guise of compassion, inarticulacy, elusiveness or sheer inadequacy of language. Starting with the centrality of sympathy, closer attention to that synecdoche should progress along four dimensions. First, *ethical*; with compassion and identification at its centre (in the case of Defoe's *Journal*, the innumerable tragic stories and anecdotes of London effectively besieged; in Tom Keymer's words, "[H.F.] go[es] out of [his] way to court the sympathy of [the] reader – or, in H.F.'s case, to arouse it for others. *A Journal of the Plague Year* presents a crisis so extreme

---

23   Quinlan, 297.
24   Denby, 77. As an alternative to "tableaux", Van Sant refers to "pathetic presentations" (Van Sant, xi).

that normal emotions and relations are in collapse").[25] Second, *linguistic and rhetorical*, the insistence on the non-utterable, on "inarticulateness", which, in Ann Van Sant's words, is "one of the features of sensibility narratives";[26] linked to that, the importance in plague narrative of the non-phonetic sound of human suffering (Paula McDowell points out to the "pervasive concern", in the *Journal*, "with sound, especially paralinguistic vocalizations such as 'dying Groans', 'dismal Shrieks', and 'lamentable Cries'"),[27] "[w]ith its faithful, even fussy transcription of an utterance pitched somewhere between elemental cry and grunting bathos";[28] in a word, the elusiveness of linguistic-communicative meaning. Third, *psychological-phenomenological*, constructing dynamically the experiences of interiority and exteriority, notably in H.F.'s hesitation between wanting to be alone indoors and wanting to shun claustrophobia and go out, in other terms, mobility, restlessness, fickleness. Fourth, (dubiously) *moral-psychological*, or *confessional*, the narrator-memorialist moved by morbid curiosity, if not sheer prurience.

The description of the scene of tears, and that of obsessive reading/writing provide a striking exploration and problematising of the boundary between the private and the public: falling into tears is not supposed to happen in public, it is a mark of privacy, but that is precisely what makes it resonant. The same happens with the dual practice of obsessive reading and writing. Crying is both invitation and recrimination: a reminder of the intrusiveness of readers, both extra- and intradiegetic; the partial occupation of a space which is enclosed and restricted. H.F. keeps crossing a similar boundary as he walks in and out, and gets to places where he should not go. Central to the *Journal of the Plague* is the sense of the secret and the concealed; tears, in turn, are basic signifiers of that in *Pamela* (including the male protagonist's tears, as will be discussed in Section III).

One way of approaching the issue empirically is by asking Defoe's text questions, beginning with the most obvious, its title, or rather, *the generic adscription the title claims and manifests*. So, (a) why should a continuous, undivided retrospective narrative falsely call itself a "journal"? Or, at the very least, if the journal format is to be jettisoned, (b) why not then adhere to a relatively strict sequential order, presenting a succession of events in a straightforward,

---

25   Thomas Keymer, "Daniel Defoe", in *The Cambridge Companion to English Novelists*, ed. Adrian Poole (Cambridge: Cambridge University Press, 2009), 14–30 (25).

26   Van Sant, 116.

27   Paula McDowell, "Defoe and the Contagion of the Oral: Modeling Media Shift in *A Journal of the Plague Year*", *PMLA*, CXXI/1 (2006), 87–106 (99).

28   Keymer, 14.

traditional manner? What we have, in effect, is a text constantly repeating itself, jumping ahead and then retreating, moving astray from chronological sequence and, even worse, a text calling the reader's attention to the fact of edition, specifically, *censoring* edition:

> Such intervals as I had I employed in reading Books and in writing down my Memorandums of what occurred to me every Day, and out of which afterwards I for [*sic*] most of this Work, as it relates to my Observations without Doors: what I wrote of my private Meditations I reserve for private Use, and desire it may not be made publick on any Account whatever.
>
> I also wrote other Meditations upon Divine Subjects, such as occurred to me at that Time and were profitable to myself, but not fit for any other View, and therefore I say no more of that.[29]

And, again underlined, there is the systematic suppression of (fictional) prior stages in composition. The most troubling of these evidences of possible tampering with eye-witness evidence is the excising of what H.F. puzzlingly calls "private Meditations" and "Meditations upon Divine Subjects". A more general and pervasive, but also striking, narrative technique is the meticulous avoidance of any indication of the lapse of time between the events narrated and the (fictional) writing of the narrative.

The cardinal tropes of *A Journal of the Plague Year* appear to be disordering, erasure, and concealment. Is this Defoe's carelessness as a (supposed) hack writer? Or, much more suggestively, is there a reason why, if one takes Defoe seriously, H.F. as narrator should be so incompetent?

In trying to account for that puzzling trait of H.F.'s narrative, the prevalence of suppression and concealment, it will be convenient to leave aside, after only a fleeting mention, the question of H.F.'s politics. All that is shrouded in mystery. He claims to be a member of the Church of England, but he defends Dissenters, radical Non-Conformists evicted from their parishes; he is strangely silent on the Cavalier Parliament and the Second Dutch War; on the other hand, he has a very hostile attitude to Providentialism. But, again, he has only approximately 400 words criticizing the monarchy, and not very heartfelt (notably, the *Court* is mentioned, not the King). The citizen's surprisingly low profile in his treatment of the Stuart brothers suggests moderation and

---

29   Daniel Defoe, *A Journal of the Plague Year*, ed. by Cynthia Wall (London: Penguin, 2003), 75. Further references to Defoe's *Journal* are given after quotations in the body of my text.

the desire for compromise – he is probably what Lord Halifax called a "trim-mer", a word which came into use in the late 1690s. In brief, it is reasonable to wonder whether H.F., when he is writing his account, which is not a diary but a memoir, has held political office, has a political career in the Corporation of London behind him, and possibly, greater ambitions in the period following the Revolution of 1689.

More significant for the thesis of this essay, in a description of compression and disordering, one should underline the coalescence, in an almost hysterical manner, of H.F. the reader with H.F. the writer. That is exactly what happens in the maelstrom of epistolary interchange (not only sentimental or erotic). H.F.'s reading, in the suspicion under which compulsive reading was held, is reading that dares not speak its name: the narrator-wanderer who keeps in-sisting both on his role as eye-witness and on the veracity of the reading of his written sources. He is a frenzied reader not only (justifiably) of Bills of Mortality, but more generally of disreputable pamphlets, almanacs, and tracts of all sorts. All this entails necessarily – and paradoxically – extreme mobility (to start with, he must find and buy those printed sources), a challenge for H.F. to become, in fact, a virtual reader, someone reading vertiginously what he claims and knows are reports – often conflicting ones – based on rumour and gossip. This in turn entails geographical mobility. A telling example is the epistemological critique he makes of the veracity of reports about alleged murders by nurses:

> They did tell me, indeed, of a Nurse in one place that laid a wet Cloth upon the Face of a dying Patient whom she tended, and so put an End to his Life, who was just expiring before: and Another that smother'd a young Woman she was looking to when she was in a fainting fit, and would have come to herself: some that kill'd them by giving them one Thing, some another, and some starved them by giving them nothing at all. But these Stories had two Marks of Suspicion that always attended them, which caused me always to slight them and to look on them as mere Stories that People continually frighted one another with (I.) that wherever it was that we heard it, they always placed the Scene at the far-ther End of the Town, opposite or most remote from where you were to hear it. If you heard it in *Whitechapel*, it had happened at *St Giles's*, or at *Westminster*, or *Holborn*, or that End of the Town. If you heard of it at that End of the Town, then it was done in *Whitechapel*, or the *Minories*, or about *Cripplegate* Parish. If you heard of it in the City, why, then it hap-pened in *Southwark*; and if you heard of it in *Southwark*, then it was done in the City, and the like. (82–83)

What is assumed here is the plurality of reports, at least two (from "this" and "that" end of town; at St. Giles and at Whitechapel): he has heard, personally, not just "St. Giles' version", but also that circulating in Whitechapel (which claims "[the murder] happened at St. Giles"). He has been to "the other end of the town" (the utmost recklessness in the time of plague; he has no calling to do so, as he admits, "One Day, being at that Part of the Town on some special Business, Curiosity led me to observe things more than usually, and indeed I Walk'd a great Way where I had no Business" (18)). H.F. is our reader of no fixed place, that is, *our mobile reader.* H.F.'s restlessness is surreptitiously gendered, and that gendered restlessness suggests why his text is iterative, vacillating, self-censorious; this is a reader guardedly attentive to the issue of female reading and communication (rumour, panic, gossip), who behaves in the way which misogynous legend has for centuries attributed to women, a reader who has initiated *the conversion of the narrative text into a text written by a woman reading* (even though the texts of women in the London of the plague are carefully excised by H.F.). All this originates with the old misogynous anxiety about the mobility, not only or mainly epistemological of course, of women.

Mobility and lability – themselves the marks of desire – keep shifting the ground under the readers' feet; that is, our feet, since we are no more, but no less, readers than is H.F. himself. We could call that the sleight-of-hand of half-truths in *A Journal of the Plague Year.*

Let us consider another focus of convergence where this deviousness meets ethical reflections, and early eighteenth-century concerns about gender: the question of *curiosity.*

> Business led me out sometimes to the other End of the Town, even when the Sickness was chiefly there; and as the thing was new to me, as well as to every Body else, it was a most surprising thing to see those Streets which were usually so thronged now grown desolate, and so few People to be seen in them, that if I had been a Stranger and at a Loss for my Way, I might sometimes have gone the Length of a whole Street (I mean of the by-Streets), and seen no Body to direct me except Watchmen set at the Doors of such Houses as were shut up, of which I shall speak presently.
>
> One Day, being at that Part of the Town on some special Business, Curiosity led me to observe things more than usually, and indeed I walk'd a great Way where I had no Business. I went up *Holborn*, and there the Street was full of People, but they walk'd in the middle of the great Street, neither on one Side or other, because, as I suppose, they would not mingle with any Body that came out of Houses, or meet with Smells and Scent from Houses that might be infected. (18)

Overt mentions of the word "curiosity" are not censored (there are eleven instances of its use), but there is an inescapable insistence that this is for H.F. a shameful motive for staying in London; it is one, however, which is consistent with his mobility. The passage about editing out what is "Private Meditation" from the memoranda, quoted above,[30] is preceded by a reference to H.F.'s efforts to dominate his lust to move:

> Terrified by those frightful Objects, I would retire Home sometimes and resolve to go out no more; and perhaps I would keep those Resolutions for three or four Days, which Time I spent in the most serious Thankfulness for my Preservation and the Preservation of my Family, and the constant Confession of my Sins, giving my self up to God every Day, and applying to Him with Fasting, Humiliation, and Meditation. Such intervals as I had I employed in reading Books and in writing down my Memorandums of what occurred to me every Day, and out of which afterwards I for [sic] most of this Work, as it relates to my Observations without Doors: what I wrote of my private Meditations I reserve for private Use, and desire it may not be made publick on any Account whatever. (75)

In the following quotation, H.F. longs for the simplicity of a "Poor Man", impervious to the prodding of curiosity:

> "Well, honest Friend", said I, "thou hast a sure Comforter, if thou hast brought thyself to be resign'd to the Will of God; He is dealing with us all in Judgement".
>   "Oh, Sir!" says he, "it is infinite Mercy if any of us are spar'd, and who am I to repine!"
>   "Sayest thou so?" said I, "and how much less is my Faith than thine?" And here my Heart smote me, suggesting how much better this Poor Man's Foundation was on which he stayed in the Danger than mine; that he had no where to fly; that he had a Family to bind him to Attendance, which I had not; and mine was mere Presumption, his a true Dependence and a Courage resting on God; and yet that he used all possible Caution for his Safety. (105)

H.F. shows an agonising awareness that there is something in his soul, a motive, which is worse than mere recklessness, an impulse both un-Christian and unmanly; that is, recklessness provoked by insatiable curiosity – ghoulishness, rather:

---

30   See Defoe, 75.

> I went all the first Part of the Time freely about the Streets, tho' not so
> freely as to run my self into apparent Danger, except when they dug the
> great Pit in the Church-Yard of our Parish of Aldgate. A terrible Pit it was,
> and I could not resist my Curiosity to go and see it'. (58)

In connection with the "pit" – that is, a mass grave – Defoe's choice of verbs
for his narrator-hero H.F. is revelatory: not only "I could not resist", but also
"Curiosity led me" and, after correcting himself, the verb "drive": "It was about
the 10th of *September* that my Curiosity led, or rather drove, me to go and see
this Pit again" (59).

   We are liable to be numbed into inattention by the role that *motivation* plays
generally in the novel, even in its epistemology. (For example, numbed into
misreading the extreme, quotational, duplicity in H.F.'s resort to *sortes bibli-
cae* in his "use" – his manipulation, really – of Psalm 91, which is supposed to
persuade him to remain in London despite the epidemic). Concealment goes
accompanied by the invitation to pay painstaking attention to small details
or "particulars". The design is apparent: to awaken the reader's curiosity; what
better idea for that than to superpose layers of concealment, which work re-
cursively and cumulatively both to suggest and conceal *the narrator's curiosity*
itself ("do as I did, but be as discrete and secretive, as prudent as I was and am
now that I'm writing, years later, about those events"). There is a *phenomenology* of curiosity in *A Journal of the Plague Year*: depicted absolutely, with no
consideration for its context, genesis, or evolution, without or outside history.
It is just an absolute of consciousness which does not, cannot, find more than
momentary closure. Appropriately the pit which prompts it most acutely is
alternatively closed by day and re-opened at night.

> It was about the 10th of *September* that my Curiosity led, or rather drove,
> me to go and see this Pit again, when there had been near 400 People
> buried in it; and I was not content to see it in the Day-time, as I had done
> before, for then there would have been nothing to have been seen but
> the loose Earth; for all the Bodies that were thrown in were immediately
> covered with Earth by those they call'd the Buriers, which at other Times
> were call'd Beaters; but I resolv'd to go in the Night and see some of them
> thrown in. (59)

Yet history will intrude. H.F.'s curiosity is early modern in that its very nature
is to be insatiable, and this does not happen in a phenomenological vacuum.
Even this most grievous among H.F.'s faults came to have, by the middle of
the seventeenth century and until *c.* 1750, a claim to respectability, by a

Copernican turn in Western culture which took place just before the age of
Enlightenment. In naïve terms, it is the irony of eye-witnessing: there can hardly
be eye-witnessing reports without a combination of mobility and curiosity.
Here, several central themes of misogyny are deflected and re-claimed: very
notably the Patristic or Augustinian reading of the Fall.

Lorraine Daston and Katharine Park have described a very brief period,
of maybe two or three generations, when "curiosity shifted from the neigh-
borhood of lust and pride to that of avarice and greed",[31] that is, acquisitive
passions. Augustinian misogyny had placed much opprobrium on inquisitive
passions and desire, related to libido and lust; curiosity, specifically, was linked
to narratives of the Fall, and the role of over-sexed Woman. Moreover, in a
world still founded largely on neighbourliness, the passion of curiosity went
hand in hand with an unquenchable desire to pry into the private and the secret ("curiosity was the morally ambiguous desire to know that which did not
concern one, be it the secrets of nature or of one's neighbors"),[32] to find causes
where causes are most indeterminable ("The causes of the hidden and the
secret, by definition obscure, thereby set in motion the sequence of wonder-
curiosity-attention").[33] To Patristic and Medieval theologians, curiosity is akin
to lust (it is "a species of lust"; it keeps "links with pride and lust"; an instance
of "concupiscence of the eyes", it is "closely akin to bodily incontinence").[34]
During the seventeenth century, curiosity, though, came to be associated with
acquisitive passions. One central, defining train of ideas connected curiosity
with greed, notably greed for luxury objects: the fact that it was *insatiable* (as
opposed to bodily lust). Curiosity was a *"perpetuum mobile* of the soul":[35] "In
this attraction-repulsion mechanics of the passions, curiosity was not merely
one of a host of desires, but rather the archetypal desire.... Always seeking,
never satisfied, its pleasures were never exhausted. In contrast to the desires of
the body, curiosity was pure desire".[36] Both in popular misogyny and in theology, curiosity was epitomized by Eve's sin, and the combination of curiosity,
pride, and lust were considered as the causes of the Fall.

Over the last third of the seventeenth century a paradoxical cultural re-
fashioning took place abstracting curiosity from its gendered context, at the

---

31   Lorraine Daston and Katharine Park, *Wonders and the Order of Nature* (New York: Zone
      Books, 2001), 305.
32   Daston and Park, 305.
33   *Ibid.*, 315.
34   *Ibid.*, 306.
35   *Ibid.*, 307.
36   *Ibid.*

same time associating a separate passion, that of wonder, with women writers and interpreters. Originally, moreover, wonder was not stigmatized: "Wonder sparked curiosity, shaking the philosopher out of idling reverie and riveting attention and will to a minute scrutiny of the phenomenon at hand",[37] reverting a tradition in which "the passions of wonder and curiosity had ... been ... remote from one another".[38] Soon, however, "they drifted [again] away from one another":[39] with that separation it was now wonder which was gendered female and stigmatized. But in the 1650s and 1660s, male natural philosophers were to a certain extent feminized, as women reading. Insatiable curiosity over a longer period is, after all, what feeds the practice of compulsive reading and writing (Rolf Engelsing's "extensive reading").

There is another interesting factor, linking curiosity with the cultural changes discussed in the preceding section: the convergence between curiosity and luxury; curiosity and commerce; mobility and commerce: "The rhythms of curiosity were those of addiction or of consumption for its own sake, cut loose from need and satisfaction";[40] "both the acquisitive and the inquisitive sought out the new, the rare, and the unusual, so that natural philosophy caught something of the prestissimo tempo of fashion".[41]

The following passage from the *Journal of the Plague* shows, as a striking manifestation of Daston and Park's scenario of change, a woman as the mouthpiece of wonder, or awe. H.F.'s attitude, on the other hand, is a type of curiosity: in its initial prompting, when H.F. is curious as to the gathering of the small crowd; in his reaction, that is, when he looks curiously at the sky; and, finally, when at the end he produces a psychological commentary on the delusions of supposed witnesses of "prodigies":

> One time before the Plague was begun (otherwise than as I have said in St *Giles*'s), I think it was in *March*, seeing a Crowd of People in the Street, I join'd with them to satisfy my Curiosity, and found them all staring up into the Air, to see what a Woman told them appeared plain to her, which was an Angel cloth'd in white, with a fiery Sword in his Hand, waving it or brandishing it over his Head. She described every Part of the Figure to the Life, shew'd them the Motion, and the Form, and the poor People came into it so eagerly, and with so much Readiness ... I look'd as earnestly as the

---

37   *Ibid.*, 304.
38   *Ibid.*
39   *Ibid.*
40   *Ibid.*, 307.
41   *Ibid.*, 310.

rest, but perhaps not with so much Willingness to be impos'd upon; and I said, indeed, that *I could see nothing* but a white Cloud, bright on one Side by the shining of the Sun upon the other Part. The Woman endeavour'd to shew it me, but could not make me confess that, I saw it, which, indeed, if I had, I must have lied. But the Woman, turning upon me, look'd in my Face, and fancied I laughed, in which her Imagination deceived her too; for I really did not laugh, but was very seriously reflecting how the poor People were terrify'd by the force of their own Imagination.[42]

The 1660s were a period of notable concern about wonders, or prodigies. And H.F.'s milieu is still responsive to them. H.F.'s very obsession about being unable to provide particulars reveals their importance. The example is, again, the angel in the sky. Curiosity awakened about particulars may as well refer, in that anecdote, not to the shapes of clouds but to the psychology of the "witnesses"; the woman herself is apparently free from curiosity about particulars.

III

With Defoe's H.F., in what can reasonably be called an antiquarian guise, we are offered, as a final account of the decades of seventeenth-century passionate reading (that of the wars of religion in Europe), a man reading like a woman, but circumventing women and women reading – who are conspicuously absent from *A Journal of the Plague Year*. Samuel Richardson's *Pamela* (1740), on the other hand, an inaugural text in the age of sensibility, does at no point move its focus from a woman reading and writing. Woman, after the late Stuart crisis, after John Locke and Mary Astell, must be introduced as subject or, rather, as *the* subject. In political argument concerned with families,[43] it might have been inevitable that sentimental novelists, notably Richardson in *Pamela* and *Clarissa*, had resort to that aging figure, the rake. Richardson's point appears to be this: the man (or perhaps "Man") as sexual aggressor can only be reformed by being taught to "read" (that is, read sentimentally, with compassion and identification; the failure of Lovelace's reformation in *Clarissa* does not invalidate the point; it just means that timing might go tragically wrong).

---

42   Defoe, 24.
43   Described in a captivating and thorough way in Rachel Weil, *Political Passions: Gender, the Family, and Political Argument in England 1680–1714* (Manchester: Manchester University Press, 1999).

The predator reading his victim inevitably implies another reading (here "another" functions ambiguously). The medium is, once again, private readings.

Writing and reading, as in Defoe, suppose place. The sense of place in sentimental novels can be paradoxical, as it is in *Pamela*'s externality of domesticity; the older country house, rakish and Stuart, has to be domesticated by means of English gardening, and the pond.

The pond in Mr B.'s Lincolnshire estate – his love nest – plays an important part in *Pamela*. Samuel Richardson's mastery in the use of place becomes crucial in the climactic pages of the novel: the characters and the action itself circulate around the pond which stands like an eye at the centre of B.'s estate. B., ex-rake, successfully reformed by Pamela, can triumphantly stake a claim to the new domesticity – about which Michael McKeon not long ago published a remarkable 900-page volume[44] – and open the doors of the family seat for the subjects of sensibility. In Richardson's novel of 1740, there are four occasions in which the pond is pivotal, four *scenes*. I will here pay particular attention to two of those, separated by some twenty pages, both described in entries of Pamela's "diary" (when she is kept in isolation in Mr B.'s love nest, restrained from communication with the world at large, the letters, which she manages to send in "pacquets" and only in a serendipitous way, in effect become a diary). Two scenes in the same week, a week that begins ominously with B. trying to goad himself into raping Pamela; separated by three days, the two scenes include declarations of love, the second, the man crying. Scene (a), on the Wednesday, a preparatory scene, is all theatre: rich and multi-layered dialogue, attention to diction *dynamically*, importance of stage directions in Pamela's account; scene (b), which takes place three days later, on the Sunday, is the turning point of the novel.

In (a), the comical-bathetic scene, Pamela, a victim of harassment by her master, Brandon, comes close to declaring, to *him*, her love *for* him. But he misses the point: interpreting the scene requires reading like a woman, reading *for* the body, and Brandon has not yet been taught to do so; expertise in reading three-dimensionally is still several steps away for him. We have left behind us gendered epistemology. True vs. not true is no longer the major point: only women can read the inarticulate neither-presence-nor-absence.

In (b), the final pond scene, on the Sunday, Mr B., the master, the claimant to sovereignty, or rather tyranny, is manipulated in a theatre of reading. Master and subject are again in the open, by the fateful pond. But now the master will

---

44   Michael McKeon, *The Secret History of Domesticity* (Baltimore: Johns Hopkins University Press, 2005).

be reading Pamela's writing, supposedly a screen but in effect working in the exact opposite way:

> He led me then to the Side of the Pond; and sitting down on the Slope, made me sit by him. Come, said he, this being the Scene of Part of your Project, and where you so artfully threw in some of your Cloaths, I will just look upon that Part of your Relation. Sir, said I, let me then walk about, at a little Distance, for I cannot bear the Thought of it. Don't go far, said he .... Why this, said he, my Girl, is a very moving Tale. It was a very desperate Attempt, and had you got out, you might have been in great Danger; for you had a very bad and lonely Way; and I had taken such Measures, that let you have been where you would, I would have had you.
>
> You may see, Sir, said I, what I ventur'd rather than be ruin'd; and you will be so good as hence to judge of the Sincerity of my Professions, that my Honesty is dearer to me than my Life. Romantick Girl! said he, and read on.
>
> He was very serious at my Reflections, on what God enabled me to escape [i.e. the suicidal fantasies]. And when he came to my Reasonings, about throwing myself into the Water, he said, Walk gently before; and seem'd so mov'd, that he turn'd away his Face from me; and I bless'd this good Sign, and began not so much to repent at his seeing this mournful Part of my Story.
>
> He put the Papers in his Pocket, when he had read my Reflections, and Thanks for escaping from *myself*; and he said, taking me about the Waist, O my dear Girl! you have touch'd me sensibly with your mournful Relation .... Then he most kindly folded me in his Arms; Let us, say I too, my *Pamela,* walk from this accursed Piece of Water; for I shall not, with Pleasure, look upon it again.[45]

What is proposed here prefigures dozens of portraits in the second half of the eighteenth century: the subject reading captures the onlooker's gaze, in this reading of readers opening up *the space of absorption,*[46] absorption meaning

---

45   Samuel Richardson, *Pamela; or, Virtue Rewarded,* ed. by Thomas Keymer and Alice Wakely (Oxford: Oxford University Press, 2001), 240. Further references to *Pamela* are given after quotations in the body of my text.

46   On that subject as it appears in portraiture, see Michael Fried, *Absorption and Theatricality: Painting and Beholder in the Age of Diderot* (Chicago: The University of Chicago Press, 1980); Norman Bryson, *Word and Image: French Painting of the Ancien Régime* (Cambridge: Cambridge University Press, 1981).

here both "absorbing" and "being absorbed". The master, would-be tyrant, or would-*not*-be tyrant, identifies with Pamela, and is identified with himself – *recognised* – as he is read by the passive female reader. This tactical move is not transcendent but immanent to the binary active/passive. Importantly, manipulation here must be understood as a *regulation* of distance and proximity; we cannot interpret the scene with resort to a metaphysics of presence vs. absence but as *remoteness* and *proximity*. Pamela is not merely present, for B.'s reading, private and intimate, confuses presence (she has had to "walk gently before", to make him less uncomfortable, she is moving somewhere in the outer reaches of his perceptual field); but neither is she simply absent when he is supposed to be reading, absorbed: she is still somehow hovering around; and in fact she is doubly present, she still manages to get meaning across to Mr B. in the form of theatrical cues in her writing. B. with her personal diary in his hands is cued by Pamela thus:

> When he came, as I suppose, to the Place where I mention'd the Bricks falling upon me, he got up, and walk'd to the Door, and look'd upon the broken Part of the Wall; for it had not been mended; and came back, reading on to himself, towards me; and took my Hand, and put it under his Arm. (240–1)

Three paragraphs later, he is cued again to shed tears as he is reading, in her diary, the very sentence "Then, thinks I [*sic*], will he, perhaps, shed a few Tears over the poor Corse [*sic*] of his persecuted Servant" (172–73); by the pond, indeed, he does exactly so. He is now enclosed in that remarkable bubble or aura which is unescapable in Michael Fried's absorbed subjects. Like thick silence.

The themes, or, why not, the *paradigms* operative here are, (a) the new paintings and portraiture of the eighteenth century;[47] (b) the concern with theatre and theatrical metaphors;[48] and, most importantly, (c) the nervous system and nervous illnesses. After 1730 in the work of Boerhaave, Haller and Whytt, the beginning of research and experiment in electricity were marked by the convergence between experiments in physics and medicine involving questions of *irritability* and sensibility, by fascination with the possibility of effect at a distance. The term "electric" had in fact come into use

---

47   See Jean Starobinski, *L'invention de la liberté* (Geneva: Skira, 1964). In English, see also Norman Bryson, *Word and Image*, as well as William Beatty Warner's article about portraits of readers, "Staging Readers Reading" *Eighteenth-Century Fiction*, XII/2 (2000), 391–416.

48   Notably in Michael Fried.

in educated, non-specialized contexts, as Ann Van Sant reminds us with reference to Anna Laetitia Barbauld's 1811 "An Essay on the Origin and Progress of Novel-Writing":

> We can see the results of this coincidence in the ways that readers describe their reading. In her survey of narrative fiction, Barbauld describes Sterne's special talents:
>
> > It is the peculiar characteristic of the author, that he affects the heart, not by long drawn tales of distress, but by light electric *touches* which *thrill the nerves* of the reader who possesses a correspondent *sensibility of frame*. (Emphasis added)[49]
>
> Barbauld incorporates the language of physiology in her report of reading. *Touching the heart* is now electric, and *affecting* it means in this case *thrilling the nerves*.[50]

The 1740s, as manifest in the correspondence between Cheyne and Richardson, provided an environment where innovative medical theory, which had parallels in literature and had filtered to the sphere of consumption, still coexisted with traditional therapeutics which went back to Renaissance readings of Galenic medicine.

If one were asked to produce a pocket dictionary definition of "sentimental reading", one should include two pivotal elements. It must be understood as:

> (a) a moral and didactic intervention by writers of fiction, aimed at reforming manners, notably the manners of men forming the elite; the consequence of that intervention was imagined as being effective in *reforming* those elite men by making them cry; that intervention operated on the nervous constitution of masculine characters who read the writings of women, and thus enhanced male sensibility;

and, at the same time, as

> (b) a cultural fashion in the central decades of the eighteenth century, related to new developments in the market for luxury items like books or implements for writing; a fashion which relied on the leisure and consumption patterns of the newly enriched classes, for example in the case of activities such as writing letters. Letter-writing was largely, but

---

49   *The Works of Anna Laetitia Barbauld*, 3 vols. (Boston: 1826), III, 134.
50   Van Sant, 94.

not exclusively, a female cultural practice; moreover, a large part of the readers of novels such as Richardson's *Pamela* and *Clarissa* would have been men. In short, sentimental reading is a cultural practice which developed between 1720 and 1760, one which was, in practice, linked to the medicine of nerves, and thus to diet.

If made into necessary conditions, those two features would leave out, among Defoe's novels, *A Journal of the Plague Year*: not only for strict historical reasons – it was published in 1722, whereas Richardson's first novel was published in 1740 – but more importantly, because Defoe's avid reader/writer H.F., the narrator of the *Journal*, is a man. However, male or female, the protagonist-narrators of the *Journal of the Plague* and *Pamela* are both of them characters who read and write avidly. In Richardson, that characterization is split into two: on the one hand, the female actor in the epistolary exchange, who both reads and writes, and thus dominates the novel, which is a collection of letters by her; on the other, her (fictional) reader, Mr B.

In Defoe's novel, female readers are conspicuously absent: as a consequence, avid reading and writing are elided. In the characterization of H.F., however, attention is called to two traits, curiosity and mobility, which are, at once, old components of traditional misogyny (and, for that reason, would give H.F., in the eyes of readers, female features), but also central elements of the new culture and institutions of natural philosophy (in other words, English and generally European science after 1660). H.F. is, at once, eyewitness and inquirer, insatiably curious and restless, obsessive writer and reader: the centre of a novel which is sentimental *avant la lettre*.

Works Cited

Barbauld, Anna Laetitia. *The Works of Anna Laetitia Barbauld*. 3 vols. Boston, 1826.

Barker-Benfield, Graham. *The Culture of Sensibility. Sex and Society in Eighteenth-Century Britain*. Chicago: The University of Chicago Press, 1992.

Berry, Christopher. *The Idea of Luxury: A Conceptual and Historical Investigation*. Cambridge: Cambridge University Press, 1994.

Bryson, Norman. *Word and Image: French Painting of the Ancien Régime*. Cambridge: Cambridge University Press, 1981.

Cheyne, George. *The English Malady*, edited with an introduction by Roy Porter. Tavistock Classics in the History of Psychiatry. London: Routledge, 1991.

Daston, Lorraine, and Katharine Park. *Wonders and the Order of Nature*. New York: Zone Books, 2001.

Defoe, Daniel. *A Journal of the Plague Year*. Edited by Cynthia Wall. London: Penguin, 2003.

Denby, David. *Sentimental Narrative and the Social Order in France*. Cambridge: Cambridge University Press, 1994.

Dixon, Thomas. "Enthusiasm Delineated: Weeping as a Religious Activity in Eighteenth-Century Britain". *Litteraria Pragensia*, XXII/43 (2013), 59–81.

Foster, Roy. *Vivid Faces: The Revolutionary Generation in Ireland 1890–1923*. London: Penguin, 2015.

Fried, Michael. *Absorption and Theatricality: Painting and Beholder in the Age of Diderot*. Chicago: The University of Chicago Press, 1980.

Goldsmith, Maurice Marks. *Private Vices, Public Benefits: Bernard Mandeville's Social and Political Thought*. Cambridge: Cambridge University Press, 1985.

Goldsmith, Maurice Marks. "Liberty, Luxury and the Pursuit of Happiness", in *The Languages of Political Theory in Early-Modern Europe*, edited by Anthony Pagden, 225–251. Cambridge: Cambridge University Press, 1987.

Gordon, Scott Paul. *The Power of the Passive Self in English Literature, 1640–1770*. Cambridge: Cambridge University Press, 2002.

Keymer, Thomas. "Daniel Defoe". *The Cambridge Companion to English Novelists*, edited by Adrian Poole, 14–30. Cambridge: Cambridge University Press, 2009.

Lawrence, Christopher. "Making the Nervous System", review of Max Neuberger, *The Historical Development of Experimental Brain and Spinal Cord Physiology before Flourens*, and Renato G. Mazzolini, *The Iris in Eighteenth-Century Physiology*, *Social Studies of Science*, XIV/1 (1984), 153–158.

McDowell, Paula. "Defoe and the Contagion of the Oral: Modeling Media Shift in *A Journal of the Plague Year*". *PMLA*, CXXI/1 (2006), 87–106.

McKeon, Michael. *The Secret History of Domesticity*. Baltimore: Johns Hopkins University Press, 2005.

Mullan, John. *Sentiment and Sociability: The Language of Feeling in the Eighteenth Century*. Oxford: Clarendon Press, 1988.

Pelling, Margaret. "Politics, Medicine, and Masculinity: Physicians and Office-bearing in Early Modern England", in *The Practice of Reform in Health, Medicine, and Science, 1500–2000: Essays for Charles Webster*, edited by Margaret Pelling and Scott Mandelbrote, 81-105. Aldershot: Ashgate, 2005.

Pelling, Margaret, and Frances White. *Medical Conflicts in Early Modern London: Patronage, Physicians, and Irregular Practitioners*. Oxford: Clarendon Press, 2003.

Quinlan, Sean M. "Sensibility and Human Science in the Enlightenment", review of David Denby, *Sentimental Narrative and the Social Order in France*, Wendy Motooka, *The Age of Reasons: Quixotism, Sentimentalism and Political Economy in Eighteenth-Century Britain*, Roselyne Rey, *Naissance et développement du vitalisme en France, de la deuxième moitié du 18e siècle à la fin du Premier Empire*, and Gillian Skinner,

Sensibility and Economics in the Novel, 1740–1800: The Price of a Tear, *Eighteenth-Century Studies*, XXXVII/2 (2004), 296–301.

Richardson, Samuel. *Pamela; or, Virtue Rewarded*, edited by Thomas Keymer and Alice Wakely. Oxford: Oxford University Press, 2001.

Rousseau, George S. *Nervous Acts. Essays on Literature, Culture and Sensibility*. Basingstoke: Palgrave Macmillan, 2004.

Sekora, John. *Luxury: The Concept in Western Thought, Eden to Smollett*. Baltimore: Johns Hopkins University Press, 1977.

Starobinski, Jean. *L'invention de la liberté*. Geneva: Skira, 1964.

Sterne, Laurence. *The Life and Opinions of Tristram Shandy, Gentleman*. Harmondsworth: Penguin, 1985.

Van Sant, Ann Jessie. *Eighteenth-Century Sensibility and the Novel*. Cambridge: Cambridge University Press, 1993.

Vila, Anne. *Enlightenment and Pathology: Sensibility in the Literature and Medicine of Eighteenth-Century France*. Baltimore: Johns Hopkins University Press, 1998.

Vila, Anne. "Sex, Procreation, and the Scholarly Life from Tissot to Balzac". *Eighteenth-Century Studies*, XXXV/2 (2002), 239–246.

Warner, William Beatty. "Staging Readers Reading". *Eighteenth-Century Fiction*, xii/2 (2000), 391–416.

Webster, Charles. *The Great Instauration: Science, Medicine and Reform 1626–1660*. 2nd ed. Bern: Peter Lang ag, 2002.

Weil, Rachel. *Political Passions: Gender, the Family, and Political Argument in England 1680–1714*. Manchester: Manchester University Press, 1999.

Wittmann, Reinhard. "Was there a Reading Revolution at the End of the Eighteenth Century?", in *A History of Reading in the West*, edited by Roger Chartier and Guglielmo Cavallo, 284–312. Oxford: Polity, 1999.

Woodmansee, Martha. "Toward a Genealogy of the Aesthetic: The German Reading Debate of the 1790s". *Cultural Critique*, XI (1988–1989), 203–221.

CHAPTER 9

Quackery, "Chymistry" and Politics in Eighteenth-Century English Fiction

Wojciech Nowicki

Abstract

Two eighteenth-century novels, Tobias Smollett's *Launcelot Greaves* (1760–61) and *The Philosophical Quixote* (1782), anonymous, drew on the figures of two contemporary scientists. Smollett represented John Shebbeare in the figure of a quack whose manipulative strategies metaphorise the cynicism and prolixity of contemporary politicians. *The Philosophical Quixote* gives in turn the portrait of an apothecary who dabbles in electricity, with dire results: explosion, shock or conflagration. The "explosive" scenes serve both as an equivalent of irresponsible experimentation among the scientists of the day and of the political explosiveness or radicalism, such as Joseph Priestley practised.

This essay touches on the representation of scientific madness in the eighteenth century, on the verge of epochs, when science was coalescing into a unified body of study, with specific targets and rigid methodologies. The theme of excessive study which brings about mental instability goes far back, even to the Bible,[1] and survives in the Renaissance bestseller *Das Narrenschyf* by Sebastian Brant (1494) and *The Anatomy of Melancholy* by Robert Burton (1621). Eighteenth-century iconography sustains Burton's connection between melancholy and learning. In a 1750 painting by Johann David Nessenthaler called *Melancolicus*, a scholar is touching his forehead with one hand (a traditional sign of insanity) and holding a knife in the other, a clear threat to all around (see Figure 9.1).

In eighteenth-century English fiction unbalanced scholars or projectors are best exemplified by Swift's academicians of Lagado, the protagonist of

---

1   In the Old Testament Ecclesiastes complains that "of making many books there is no end; and much study is a weariness of the flesh" (Eccl. 12:12); in the New Testament Festus attacks Paul as he defends himself before Agrippa, "Paul, thou art beside thyself; much learning doth make thee mad" (Acts 26:24).

FIGURE 9.1   *A depressed scholar surrounded by mythological figures;*
               representing the melancholy temperament. Etching by
               J.D. Nessenthaler after himself, c. 1750.

The Memoirs of Martinus Scriblerus (1741) and Sterne's Shandy brothers. Yet while these texts are primarily oriented towards a satirical portrayal of old speculative science, two novels from the second half of the century draw a parallel between scholarly, or rather pseudoscholarly, activity and political wrangling, namely *The Adventures of Launcelot Greaves* (1760–61) by Tobias Smollett and *The Philosophical Quixote, or Memoirs of Mr David Wilkins. In a Series of Letters* (1782), an anonymous text, never since republished. The two narratives drew on the figures of contemporary scientists – John Shebbeare (1709–1788) in the former case and Joseph Priestley (1733–1804) in the latter, both of them practitioners of "chymistry", the new science of the day. Smollett represented Shebbeare in the figure of Ferret, a quack who attempts to sell his medicament to an unsuspecting audience. His manipulative strategies metaphorise the cynicism and prolixity of contemporary politicians and the act of selling a fake product stands for the blatant treachery of the country by the Hanoverians.

The Philosophical Quixote gives in turn the portrait of an apothecary, Mr Wilkins, who dabbles in electricity, with dire results: explosion, shock or conflagration. The sheer preponderance of combustibles links the protagonist to Priestley, who also experimented with gases, often in peril of his life. The "explosive" scenes in Wilkins' laboratory serve in the novel not only as an equivalent of irresponsible experimentation but also indirectly represent political explosiveness or radicalism, such as Priestley himself practised.

Both novels are written in the "Quixotic" tradition, a vogue which began soon after Cervantes' *Don Quixote* reached England in the first two decades of the seventeenth century. The history of the early adaptation of *Don Quixote* on English soil came full circle: initially, the story of the Spanish don was read as a crude satire on chivalry and at the end of the eighteenth century the same tendency returned. Only in mid-century was there an attempt at a more original treatment of Cervantes' intertext. Henry Fielding's *Joseph Andrews* (1742) refurbished Don Quixote in the character of Parson Adams, attributing to him similar features such as nobility of mind, empathy and generosity on top of irascibility and naive fantasising. In his ignorance and benevolence Adams was pitted against a corrupt world which arrogated to itself its own twisted morality as the norm, simultaneously stigmatizing the priest as someone abnormal. Fielding adopted from Cervantes the idea of madness, but reversed it on ethical grounds rather than epistemological: while in Cervantes the hero suffers from delusions concerning his identity and these must be painfully corrected by those around him, in *Joseph Andrews* it is the world which fails to perceive the truth, this being of a moral nature rather than existential.[2]

---

2   Susan Staves, "Don Quixote in Eighteenth-Century England", *Comparative Literature*, XXIV (1972), 193–215; Brean Hammond, "The Cervantic Legacy in the Eighteenth-Century Novel",

Another successful imitation of *Don Quixote* was written by an admirer of Fielding a decade later. Charlotte Lennox's *The Female Quixote* (1752) is partly a satire on female reading tastes targeting the excesses of romances of love and adventure, especially such as were turned out in seventeenth-century France by La Calprenède and Mlle de Scudéry, and partly a romance in its own right. Arabella constantly imagines that she is the heroine of such a romance and therefore always expects to be abducted by a pining lover. She also demands from all prospective suitors, including her official fiancé, that she be properly courted according to the rules devised by herself on the basis of the French romances. In imposing this ridiculous code of chivalric conduct on her friends and family, Arabella comes very close to the original absurdities of the Spanish knight. Lennox, however, refuses to construct her protagonist to a simple pattern: Arabella is mad only in matters of love and in every other respect she acts with wisdom, charm and verve, ultimately emerging as one of the most engaging heroines of eighteenth-century English fiction. Following Fielding's and Lennox's novels, Quixotic adaptations became less refined and returned to the stale model of topical satire. Richard Graves (1715–1804) in his *The Spiritual Quixote* (1773) presents quixotic madness as a religious frenzy. Geoffry Wildgoose is a freeholder who becomes fascinated with Methodism and leaves home to propagate the new religion, just as his literary prototype sets out to succour the needy and oppressed. The chief analogy between the protagonists of *The Spiritual Quixote* and *Don Quixote* lies in the use of language. Whereas in Cervantes the hero is incapacitated in his verbal communication by constant reference to the discourse of chivalric romance, which is alien to his addressees, in Graves the eponymous character fails to reach his audiences because his preaching is overloaded with biblical metaphors and allegories. Wildgoose exhibits unbridled enthusiasm in his quest, an attitude which at least since the seventeenth century carried with it connotations of religious fanaticism but in time was transferred to an unrestrained devotion to an idea.[3] By the mid-eighteenth century enthusiasm and quixotism were often treated synonymously. *The Amicable Quixote; or the Enthusiasm of Friendship* (1788), an obscure narrative of tertiary quality, published anonymously, also foregrounds the idea of enthusiasm – even in the title itself. Its central character, George Bruce, appears as a naive aficionado of friendship whose excessive emotionality and

---

in *The Cervantean Heritage. Reception and Influence of Cervantes in Britain*, ed. J.A.G. Ardila (London: Legenda, 2009), 96–103; Eric J. Ziolkowski, *The Sanctification of Don Quixote: From Hidalgo to Priest* (University Park, Pa.: The Pennsylvania University Press, 1991).

3   Gerald R. Cragg, *The Church and the Age of Reason 1648–1789* (Harmondsworth: Penguin Books, 1970), 14–15, 141–156.

a gross manifestation of it seem to invoke satirically the practices of contemporary literary sentimentalism. At the threshold of the nineteenth century *The Infernal Quixote: a Tale of the Day* (1801) written by one Charles Lucas took as the subject of satire the so-called Jacobin novels, represented by such reformists of the day as William Godwin, Thomas Holcroft, Robert Bage and Mary Wollstonecraft. Anti-Jacobin literature opposed the radicalism of these writers and proclaimed the universal fall of morality whose outward symptoms were madness and suicide. Lucas' novel realizes this scenario: through adopting the philosophies of Voltaire, Diderot and Rousseau, the protagonist proceeds to commit treason, murder and satanism, until he is overpowered by hallucinations and commits suicide.[4]

The two novels under discussion here belong to the less creative among Cervantean imitations. Each chose science as a direct satirical subject and politics as an indirect one, though the first incidentally and the other deliberately.

Launcelot Greaves

Smollett's *Launcelot Greaves*, his fourth novel and one of the two weakest, also toys with the notion of a Quixote but very nearly fails in the execution of the scheme. The titular character, a Yorkshire gentleman, is thwarted in his amorous designs when his beloved Aurelia is abducted by her uncle. This induces madness, a kind of *furor amoris*, which ceases only with the happy recovery of the lady. The hero gains no sympathy, since his romantic quest and noble actions, such as helping the poor and punishing the unjust, are tainted by viciousness and malice. The author saves the day by according some comedy to minor characters, some of whom also resemble Don Quixote. The whole quixotic melange seems to expose the corruption reigning paramount in some English institutions, chiefly the legal system and political life. Smollett addresses the same issues as Fielding before him, but, instead of relying on a clear opposition between a moral paragon and an immoral society, he rather awkwardly employs abnormal (quixotic) individuals in order to criticize the abnormal state of English affairs.

---

4 Wojciech Nowicki, *Awatary szaleństwa. O zjawisku donkichotyzmu w powieści angielskiej XVIII wieku* [*Avatars of madness. On the idea of Quixotism in the English novel of the eighteenth century*] (Lublin: Wydawnictwo Uniwersytetu Marii Curie-Skłodowskiej, 2008), 139–186; M.O. Grenby, *The Anti-Jacobin Novel: British Conservatism and the French Revolution* (Cambridge: Cambridge University Press, 2004).

The role of the most virulent critic of English politics is given to Ferret, a political weathervane and a declared misanthrope. Though not a quixotic figure, Ferret is nevertheless involved in quixotic discourse from the start. We meet him at the outset of the narrative when the eponymous hero of the piece, dressed in full armour and exhibiting signs "that his reason was a little discomposed",[5] introduces himself as a knight-errant to a group of surprised guests gathered in the Black Lion on the road from York to London, determined "to honour and assert the efforts of virtue; to combat vice in all her forms, re-dress injuries, chastise oppression, protect the helpless and forlorn, relieve the indigent, exert my best endeavours in the cause of innocence and beauty, and dedicate my talents, such as they are, to the service of my country".[6] In keeping with his misanthropic nature, Ferret argues that a modern Don Quixote is completely out of place and out of time and that such a figure belongs in literature rather than reality: "What was an humorous romance, and well-timed satire in Spain, near two hundred years ago, will make but a sorry jest, and appear equally insipid and absurd, when really acted from affectation, at this time a-day, in a country like England".[7] Launcelot Greaves on the face of it offers logical and rational refutation of Ferret's attack – he is no imitator of Don Quixote and not mad since able to argue, as now; but he immediately contradicts himself by declaring that he will attack "foes of virtue and decorum";[8] in other words, the protagonist rejects the image of a Don Quixote but inadvertently assumes the aspect of a ridiculous knight-errant; he is literary-conscious but not self-conscious.

Ferret makes his major appearance following the scene of fraudulent country elections in which Sir Launcelot intervenes and which ends in a typical Smollettian farce, with the electioneering mob dispersed by the hero's lance. It is here that a forceful analogy is drawn between medical charlatanry and politics, ironically, by Ferret himself, who this time plays the part of a mountebank vending an elixir of life. Smollett had already portrayed quacks in some of his earlier novels, notably Cadwallader Crabtree in *The Adventures of Peregrine Pickle* (1751) and the eponymous antihero of *The Adventures of Ferdinand Count Fathom* (1753). Ferret's speech begins on the note of the deprecation of the qualified medical profession: "Very likely, you may undervalue me and my medicine, because I don't appear upon a stage of rotten boards, in a shabby

---

5   Tobias Smollett, *The Adventures of Launcelot Greaves* (London: Printed for J. Coote, in Pater-Noster-Row, 1762 [1760–61]), I, 27.

6   *Ibid.*, I, 28.

7   *Ibid.*, I, 28–29.

8   *Ibid.*, I, 30.

velvet coat and tye-periwig, with a foolish fellow in motley, to make you laugh by making wry faces: but I scorn to use these dirty arts for engaging your attention. These paultry tricks, *ad captandum vulgus*, can have no effect but on ideots, and if you are ideots, I don't desire you should be my customers".[9] The last sentence, characteristically for its author, mingles a bitter sarcasm with an implied invective, but its overall purpose seems to be entirely mercenary, for Ferret simply wants to sell his drug.

The continuation of the whole address contains the key metaphor of the oration, the parallel between false medicine and the corruption of the country:

> Take notice, I don't address you in the stile of a mountebank, or a high German doctor; and yet the kingdom is full of mountebanks, empirics, and quacks. We have quacks in religion, quacks in physic, quacks in law, quacks in politics, quacks in patriotism, quacks in government; high German quacks that have blistered, sweated, bled, and purged the nation into an atrophy. But this is not all: they have not only evacuated her into a consumption, but they have intoxicated her brain, until she is become delirious: she can no longer pursue her own interest; or, indeed, rightly distinguish it: like the people of Nineveh, she can hardly tell her right hand from her left; but, as a changeling, is dazzled and delighted by an ignis fatuus, a Will o' the Wisp, an exhalation from the vilest materials in nature, that leads her astray through Westphalian bogs and deserts, and will one day break her neck over some barren rocks, or leave her sticking in some H—n pit or quagmire.[10]

By claiming that he is not a quack, while circumstances show that he is, Ferret contradicts himself in precisely the same manner that Launcelot contradicted himself in the Black Lion. Ferret deftly switches between the image of the homeland as a sick body submitted to painful surgery by incompetent operators and the image of a personified England that treads on dangerous territory and is ultimately lost in it. In frequently referring to the German nationality of the medics Ferret alludes to the Hanoverian kings of Britain as chief predators, but his speech also testifies to the real presence of German doctors and quacks in contemporary England.[11]

---

9   *Ibid.*, I, 201.

10   *Ibid.*, I, 201–202.

11   On the history of quackery in post-Renaissance England, see Roy Porter, *Health for Sale: Quackery in England, 1660–1850* (Manchester and New York: Manchester University Press, 1989).

Ferret's feat of rhetorical cynicism is the employment of the idea of selling
in both its figurative and literal sense: "For my part, if you have a mind to betray
your country, I have no objection. In selling yourselves and your fellow-citizens,
you only dispose of a pack of rascals who deserve to be sold – If you sell one another, why should not I sell this here Elixir of Long Life, which if properly used,
will protract your days till you shall have seen your country ruined?".[12] By comparing the selling of the country to the selling of his substandard merchandise,
he aptly equates political with medical charlatanry, the ironic twist lying in a
piece of devious self-denial, for his "elixir" seems to promise a short life rather
than long, since the country is already in ruins or will be ruined soon enough.

In his extensive speech Ferret fully indulges in alchemical gibberish which
in substance conveys above all the speaker's malice:

> I shall not pretend to disturb your understandings, which are none of the
> strongest, with a hotch-potch of unintelligible terms, such as Aristotle's
> four principles of generation, unformed matter, privation, efficient and
> final causes. Aristotle was a pedantic blockhead, and still more knave than
> fool. The same censure we may safely put on that wise-acre Dioscorides,
> with his faculties of simples, his seminal, specific, and principal virtues;
> and that crazy commentator Galen, with his four elements, elementary
> qualities, his eight complexions, his harmonies, and discords. Nor shall
> I expatiate on the alkahest of that mad scoundrel Paracelsus, with which
> he pretended to reduce flints into salt; nor the *archæus* or *spiritus rector*
> of that visionary Van Helmont, his simple, elementary water, his *gas*, fer-
> ments, and transmutations; nor shall I enlarge upon the salt, sulphur, and
> oil, the *acidum vagum*, the mercury of metals, and the volatilized vitriol
> of other modern chymists, a pack of ignorant, conceited, knavish rascals,
> that puzzle your weak heads with such jargon, just as a Germanized m—r
> throws dust in your eyes, by lugging in and ringing the changes on the bal-
> ance of power, the protestant religion, and your allies on the continent;
> acting like the juggler, who picks your pockets while he dazzles your eyes
> and amuses your fancy with twirling his fingers, and reciting the gibber-
> ish of *hocus pocus*; for, in fact, the balance of power is a mere chimera; as
> for the protestant religion, nobody gives himself any trouble about it; and
> allies on the continent we have none; or at least, none that would raise
> an hundred men to save us from perdition, unless we paid an extrava-
> gant price for their assistance. But, to return to this here Elixir of Long
> Life, I might embellish it with a great many high-sounding epithets; but I

---

12   Smollett, *Launcelot Greaves*, I, 202.

disdain to follow the example of every illiterate vagabond, that from idleness turns quack, and advertises his nostrum in the public papers. I am
neither a felonious dry-salter returned from exile, an hospital stump-
turner, a decayed stay-maker, a bankrupt-printer, or insolvent debtor,
released by act of parliament. I did not pretend to administer medicines,
without the least tincture of letters, or suborn wretches to perjure themselves in false affidavits of cures that were never performed; nor employ
a set of led-captains to harangue in my praise, at all public places. I was
bred regularly to the profession of chymistry, and have tried all the processes of alchemy, and I may venture to say, that this here Elixir is, in fact,
the *chrusion pepuromenon ek puros*, the visible, glorious, spiritual body,
from whence all other beings derive their existence, as proceeding from
their father the sun, and their mother the moon; from the sun, as from a
living and spiritual gold, which is mere fire; consequently, the common
and universal first created mover, from whence all moveable things have
their distinct and particular motions; and also from the moon, as from
the wife of the sun, and the common mother of all sublunary things: and
for as much as man is, and must be the comprehensive end of all creatures, and the microcosm, he is counselled in the Revelations to buy gold
that is thoroughly fired, or rather pure fire, that he may become rich and
like the sun; as, on the contrary, he becomes poor, when he abuses the
arsenical poison; so that his silver, by the fire, must be calcined to a *caput
mortuum*, which happens, when he will hold and retain the menstruum
out of which he partly exists, for his own property, and doth not daily
offer up the same in the fire of the sun, that the woman may be cloathed
with the sun, and become a sun, and thereby rule over the moon; that is
to say, that he may get the moon under his feet. – Now this here Elixir, sold
for no more than six-pence a vial, contains the essence of the alkahest,
the archæus, the catholicon, the menstruum, the sun, moon, and to sum
up all in one word, is the true, genuine, unadulterated, unchangeable,
immaculate and specific *chrusion pepuromenon ek puros*.[13]

George Rousseau, in an essay intended as a contribution to the history of
quackery in Britain, emphatically confirmed the findings of earlier scholars
that Ferret was modelled on Smollett's personal enemy John Shebbeare (1709–
1788), a hack political author and a physician who may also have dabbled in
alchemy. Shebbeare earned Smollett's scorn after he had published his *Letters
to the People of England*, in which he virulently attacked the administration for

---

13   *Ibid.*, I, 203–207.

its policies from a consistently anti-Whig and anti-Hanoverian standpoint.[14] Rousseau argues that Smollett's violent response to Shebbeare's fifth *Letter* in a review published in his own periodical was the source of Ferret's portrait:

> That he may fill the poor gaping crowd with ideas of his own impor-
> tance, he begins with a furious and a railing harangue full of high sound-
> ing metaphors, in which, without any decency, he abuses his superiors,
> dictates to them in a swaggering magisterial manner, and at length con-
> cludes with assuring us, "that the nation is now agonizing at the last gasp,
> drained to the last drop by the miserable transfusion of the vital power
> of *England* into *Germany*". Miserable state! Nevertheless he says, take but
> his two shilling remedy, he offers to the public from mere disinterested
> motives, and all will be well.[15]

As Paul-Gabriel Boucé notes, the verbal ingenuity of the fake doctor is quite typical of his profession because it involves the use of quasi-medical lingo which is an end in itself; in other words, the real purpose of quackish discourse is to mask its vacuity rather than communicate knowledge. Ferret uses nega-tions and counternegations, followed by dynamic enumerations whose logic can be easily questioned even though they are skilfully linked by coordinat-ing clauses. On top of this syntactic adroitness he stuns his audience with ob-scure medical vocabulary, larded with phrases in Latin and Greek. When in turn he talks about medical authorities, he refers to them in disparaging terms, openly questioning their intelligence and sanity.[16] Ferret's address seems to be entirely self-oriented and can only be appreciated by someone of his own pro-fession. One person among the listeners, though, has taken in the tenet of the oration: Sir Launcelot "could not help admiring the courage of the orator, and owning within himself, that he had mixed some melancholy truths with his scurrility".[17] In his capacity as a street vendor of medicaments, Ferret excels in two things: invective and verbiage. Both have connotations with political life. By challenging his listeners' understanding and exposing their potential

---

14   George S. Rousseau, *Tobias Smollett: Essays of Two Decades* (Edinburgh: T. & T. Clark, 1982), 124–137; M. John Cardwell, "Shebbeare, John (1709–1788)", in *Oxford Dictionary of National Biography*, Oxford University Press, 2004. <http://www.oxforddnb.com/view/article/25282>, accessed 25 Feb 2012.

15   *Critical Review*, IV (August 1757), 274–275, quoted in Rousseau, *Tobias Smollett*, 129.

16   Paul-Gabriel Boucé, *The Novels of Tobias Smollett* (London and New York: Longman, 1976), 318–319.

17   Smollett, *Launcelot Greaves*, I, 207.

venality, he is metonymically challenging all politicians – after all the assembly consists of parliamentary electors. His verbosity stands for a similar prolixity of politicians, who effect nothing but incomprehension and frustration in ordinary citizens.

The Philosophical Quixote

The Philosophical Quixote in turn portrays a devotee of scientific experimentation. The principal character, Mr Wilkins, is defined already in the title, since being called a Quixote is tantamount to being called mad. That appellation is often attributed to him in the course of the story. The adjective "philosophical" historically matched our understanding of "scientific" and referred to *philosophia naturalis*, a discipline concerned with the study of the laws of nature, especially its physical properties, although the word "scientific" *was* then in operation and referred to a broad range of areas of knowledge including natural philosophy, mathematics and theology.[18]

The entire narrative is embedded within a statement from the "Editor", who pretends to be publishing without permission a manuscript containing a series of letters from Mr J. Harcourt to Mr Samuel Dennis in which the character of Wilkins is described. The convention of the manuscript found is upheld by apparent hiatuses in the text or blank spaces on the pages, which, according to a note, came about because of spilt ink.[19]

There are two protagonists: Harcourt (a journeyman apothecary with Mr Wilkins, in love with his daughter, also a dramatized narrator) and Wilkins – the subject of Harcourt's narrative and the object of ridicule. Generically then, we receive an extended character sketch with a stereotypical love story artificially welding the various disparate elements into an awkward whole. Yet the flimsy story is only a pretext for stitching together Wilkins' absurd experiments and his pseudolearned disquisitions. The novel ends when the lovers are reunited and rewarded with a period of premarital bliss, all couched in highly exalted terms. When Harcourt asks Wilkins for the daughter's hand, Wilkins

---

18   The most comprehensive discussion of the range of meanings offered by the contemporary idea of "science" and its derivatives can be found in *The Cambridge History of Science. Volume 4: Eighteenth-Century Science*, edited by Roy Porter (Cambridge: Cambridge University Press, 2003).

19   *The Philosophical Quixote; or Memoirs of Mr David Wilkins. In a Series of Letters*, Vol. 1, 2 (London: Printed for J. Johnson, in St. Paul's Churchyard, 1782), I, 125ff.

is about to speak but his consent is not given and the narrative terminates
abruptly.[20]

The description of Wilkins typifies the dire effects of long study:

> My master, Mr. David Wilkins, is of a middle stature, and about fifty years
> of age; though by his appearance, I should have taken him to be at least
> ten years older. This, as I since learn, is owing to his having of late years,
> greatly addicted himself to study, which indeed I conjectured on first see-
> ing him, from his pale countenance and retired absent look. In his dress
> he unites the plainness of a Quaker with the negligence of a philosopher.
> His temper appears to be good, though from his thoughts being continu-
> ally absorbed in study, he has even more than the usual share of English
> taciturnity .... Mr Wilkins appears to have had a good general education,
> at least of the modern kind. He speaks French fluently, and is pretty well
> acquainted with Latin and Greek; he has also made considerable profi-
> ciency in the mathematics. But his principal forte, and which he most
> values himself upon, is his knowledge in natural philosophy, particularly
> the chemical and medical branches of it, of which he is an enthusiastic
> admirer.[21]

The word "enthusiastic" is critical for the proper evaluation of the protagonist
since, as noted above, it connotes madness. In line with the modelling function
of Cervantes' intertext, this vocational mania is complemented with biblioma-
nia: Wilkins has a library which consists "chiefly of medical and philosophical
books, almost wholly modern; for the antients are held by him in the utmost
contempt".[22] Wilkins also possesses a huge laboratory, fitted out for all kinds
of experiments. In these he sometimes succeeds, especially when he ventures
into modern science; for instance, he practises effective inoculation through
the digestive system rather than through the blood and cures a fever through
overdosing traditional bark powder.[23] But he is not wholly modern, for he
also indulges in "alchemistic" experiments: among other things he attempts
to change water into earth, turn various substances into silver or gold, make
quicksilver solid, etc., all done for the good of mankind.[24] In following such
enterprises Wilkins calls himself "a NEWTON"[25] and this poses a problem: is

---

20   *The Philosophical Quixote*, II, 164.

21   *Ibid.*, I, 9–10, 12.

22   *Ibid.*, I, 90ff.

23   *Ibid.*, I, 97–101.

24   *Ibid.*, I, 15–16.

25   *Ibid.*, I, 29–30.

this an endorsement of modern science, since Newton was among the most respected public figures of the epoch, or is it an ironic twist, an attack, given the character who utters such a declaration? It seems that the latter is the true option, because Newton himself was easy game for any satirist of contemporary science. Newton was president of the Royal Society, an organization which among its purposes mentioned the disinterested popularization of experimental science, and he pursued this interest on a private scale by setting up a laboratory in the garden outside his room in Trinity. But, paradoxically, Newton wavered between the course of modern science and the attractions of alchemy. Around 1670 he wrote a treatise on "The vegetation of metals", attributing a biological function to inanimate matter.[26] Wilkins' chimeras are similar and include finding and extracting "a ferment or leven, capable of converting mineral substances into vegatable or animal, as yeast converts flour into dough, or must into wine".[27] The anonymous author of *The Philosophical Quixote* may have been targeting Newton also through a personal allusion to his profession of a mathematician, which is done in a Swiftian style: Wilkins is absent-minded "and frequently requires as much the assistance of a flapper, as the mathematicians in the flying island".[28] More generally, the text attacks the Royal Society by referring to the gullibility of "some whose names are foremost in the Republic of Science".[29] The publishing ventures of the Royal Society are satirized in the catalogue of absurd titles of pseudoscientific treatises that Wilkins proposes: air as the vital substance of bodies, the negative electricity of medicinal virtue, admitting mathematical and metaphysical reasoning into medicine, extracting sugar from potatoes, centrifugal force residing in phlogiston, etc.[30] The writer's attitude to learned societies emerges most conspicuously when Wilkins undertakes to found an academy based on mutual praise and obsequiousness.

Wilkins' special interest remains electricity,[31] or – to be precise – frictional electricity, which produces an electrostatic discharge between two surfaces. Surprisingly, the text offers a fairly reliable state-of-the-art theory on frictional

---

26   Richard S Westfall, "Newton, Sir Isaac (1642–1727)", in *Oxford Dictionary of National Biography*, Oxford University Press, 2004. <http://www.oxforddnb.com/view/article/20059>, accessed 2 March 2013.

27   *The Philosophical Quixote*, I, 34.

28   *Ibid.*, II, 57.

29   *Ibid.*, I, 46.

30   *Ibid.*, II, 78–82.

31   Electricity was the foremost branch of experimental physics at the time. See J.L. Heilbron, *Electricity in the 17th and 18th Centuries: A Study of Early Modern Physics* (Berkeley and Los Angeles: University of California Press, 1979).

electricity, a phenomenon known since antiquity and studied by Francis Hauksbee and Benjamin Franklin, among many others:[32]

> Bodies possessed of contrary electricities, rush together, or attract each other. But bodies mutually electrified, either plus or minus, are, on the contrary, repulsive. If therefore, a drop of rain be in plus, they will mutually repel each other; and if the electricity be sufficiently strong, the repulsion will be so great that the drop will be diverted from its perpendicular course, and turned away obliquely from the body. The same thing will happen if the electricity be strongly negative. Consequently a man thus charged, may walk through the heaviest shower of rain that ever fell, without being in the least wetted by it.[33]

However, there was a sufficient rift between theory and practice in eighteenth-century views on electricity for it to be pounced upon by a seasoned satirist like the author of *The Philosophical Quixote*, since, as R.W. Home reminds us, electricity "came during the eighteenth century to refer ... to a cluster of surprising and remarkable effects".[34] Wilkins' application of electrostatics invariably has dire effects, as exemplified by the invention of "electrical shoes" protecting one from rain:

> And as they had been strongly electrified indeed ... the shock which they felt in consequence thereof was terrible! They sprung aloft, with a loud scream, into the air; many of them, reft of sense; and loosing their self balance, fell forward on their faces, lying like breathless corpse on mother earth, which was stained red with the fluid issuing from their bloody noses. They who retained their senses, smarting from the violence of the shock, wet through, ... flew upon poor Wilkins in their rage, and would probably have demolished him, had he not happily been rescued by the better part of the company, and conveyed away in safety. On his electrical apparatus, however, they had no mercy, but considering it as infernal, instantly broke it piece-meal, burning the diabolical fragments.[35]

---

32   R.W. Home, "Mechanics and Experimental Physics", in *The Cambridge History of Science. Volume 4: Eighteenth-Century Science*, ed. Roy Porter (Cambridge: Cambridge University Press, 2003), 354–374.

33   *The Philosophical Quixote*, II, 31–32.

34   Home, "Mechanics and Experimental Physics", 368.

35   *The Philosophical Quixote*, II, 36–37.

Incidentally, even though the scene above is farcically overdrawn for satirical purposes, in contemporary practice electricity *was* occasionally put to serious uses. Lucy Inglis, while examining the activities of London hospitals in the eighteenth century, noted that a certain John Birch, a doctor working at St Thomas', applied electric shocks to his patients, among others to those suffering from nervous diseases. He passed the current through the body, sometimes directly through the brain, and achieved notable success in treating Bell's palsy and depression.[36]

The fascination with electricity links the protagonist to another scholar of the epoch, Joseph Priestley (1733–1804). Priestley was the author of *The History and Present State of Electricity* (1767), and also experimented with gases, often in peril of his life. He was a Newtonianist, if only because he believed in an internal force which regulates matter, somewhat akin to Newton's force of vegetation in metals. This meant ignoring the role of God in the scheme of things and flying in the face of conservatives, all the more so as Priestley defended the ideals of the French Revolution. As a result his house and laboratory were burned down by a mob, after which he emigrated to the United States. What is important in this context is that Priestley saw rhetorical value in chemistry and did not hesitate to use it in his political discourse. As Richard Yeo reminds us:

> Priestley explicitly linked the terminology of chemistry – gases, gunpowder, explosions – to talk about political upheavals. In a sermon of 1787 he declared: "We are ... laying gunpowder, grain by grain, under the old building of error and superstition, which a single spark may hereafter inflame so as to produce an instantaneous explosion". This presented Edmund Burke with a ready-made equation between chemistry and sedition, making Priestley an accomplice of the French chemists and *philosophes*....[37]

The fiery spectacles in Wilkins' laboratory were probably seen not only as a metonymy for irresponsible experimentation but also indirectly represented political explosiveness or radicalism, such as Priestley himself practised. Priestley's career extended over several decades, long enough for the

---

36   Lucy Inglis, *Georgian London: Into the Streets* (London: Viking Penguin Books, 2003), 275–276.

37   Richard Yeo, "Natural Philosophy (Science)", in *An Oxford Companion to the Romantic Age: British Culture 1776–1832*, ed. Iain McCalman (Oxford: Oxford University Press, 1999), 320–328 (323).

anonymous author of *The Philosophical Quixote* to note the connection between chemistry and sedition.

The Philosophical Quixote adds to the gallery of deranged scientists in the
eighteenth century, both with a difference, as when the melancholy scholar
from Nessenthaler's picture changes into its opposite, a burning enthusiast,
and with a similarity, as when it revives the Swiftian-Sternian experimenter.
But Swift and Sterne are only links in the anti-experiment tradition, which goes
back to the hostile reaction against Puritan attempts in the mid-seventeenth
century to reform university curricula and introduce experimental science
along the lines proposed by Francis Bacon, at the expense of humanistic subjects.[38] This was precisely the time when Puritan religious fervour began to
be perceived as enthusiasm and enthusiasm began to be associated with the
figure of Don Quixote. In the late eighteenth century the memory of Puritan
radical empiricism still survived, and so the idea of an experimenting Quixote
was all the more acceptable because it was grafted onto the idea of a religious
Quixote.

Works Cited

Boucé, Paul-Gabriel. *The Novels of Tobias Smollett*. London and New York: Longman,
    1976.
Cardwell, M. John. "Shebbeare, John (1709–1788)". In *Oxford Dictionary of National
    Biography*. Oxford University Press, 2004. http://www.oxforddnb.com/view/arti
    cle/25282, accessed 25 Feb 2012.
Cragg, Gerald R. *The Church and the Age of Reason 1648–1789*. Harmondsworth: Pen-
    guin, 1970.
Grenby, M.O. *The Anti-Jacobin Novel: British Conservatism and the French Revolution*.
    Cambridge: Cambridge University Press, 2004.
Hammond, Brean. "The Cervantic Legacy in the Eighteenth-Century Novel". In *The
    Cervantean Heritage. Reception and Influence of Cervantes in Britain*, edited by
    J.A.G. Ardila, 96–103. London: Legenda, 2009.
Heilbron, J.L. *Electricity in the 17th and 18th Centuries: A Study of Early Modern Physics*.
    Berkeley and Los Angeles: University of California Press, 1979.

---

38   R.F. Jones, "The Background of the Attack on Science in the Age of Pope", in *Eighteenth-
      Century English Literature. Modern Essays in Criticism*, ed. James L. Clifford (London:
      Oxford University Press, 1959), 68–83.

Home, R.W. "Mechanics and Experimental Physics". In *The Cambridge History of Science. Volume 4: Eighteenth-Century Science*, edited by Roy Porter, 354–374. Cambridge: Cambridge University Press, 2003.

Inglis, Lucy. *Georgian London: Into the Streets*. London: Viking Penguin Books, 2003.

Jones, R.F. "The Background of the Attack on Science in the Age of Pope". In *Eighteenth-Century English Literature. Modern Essays in Criticism*, edited by James L. Clifford, 68–83. London: Oxford University Press, 1959.

Nowicki, Wojciech. *Awatary szaleństwa. O zjawisku donkichotyzmu w powieści angielskiej XVIII wieku* [*Avatars of madness. On the idea of Quixotism in the English novel of the eighteenth century*]. Lublin: Wydawnictwo Uniwersytetu Marii Curie-Skłodowskiej, 2008.

Porter, Roy. *Health for Sale: Quackery in England, 1660–1850*. Manchester and New York: Manchester University Press, 1989.

Porter, Roy, ed. *The Cambridge History of Science. Volume 4: Eighteenth-Century Science*. Cambridge: Cambridge University Press, 2003.

Rousseau, George S. *Tobias Smollett: Essays of Two Decades*. Edinburgh: T. & T. Clark, 1982.

Smollett, Tobias. *The Adventures of Launcelot Greaves*. Vol. 1, 2. London: Printed for J. Coote, in Pater-Noster-Row, 1762 [1760–61].

Staves, Susan. "Don Quixote in Eighteenth-Century England", *Comparative Literature*, XXIV (1972), 193–215.

The Philosophical Quixote; or Memoirs of Mr David Wilkins. In a Series of Letters. Vol. 1, 2. London: Printed for J. Johnson, in St. Paul's Churchyard, 1782.

Westfall, Richard S. "Newton, Sir Isaac (1642–1727)". In *Oxford Dictionary of National Biography*, Oxford University Press, 2004. <http://www.oxforddnb.com/view/article/20059>, accessed 2 March 2013.

Yeo, Richard. "Natural Philosophy (Science)". In *An Oxford Companion to the Romantic Age: British Culture 1776–1832*, edited by Iain McCalman, 320–328. Oxford: Oxford University Press, 1999.

Ziolkowski, Eric J. *The Sanctification of Don Quixote: From Hidalgo to Priest*. University Park, Pa.: The Pennsylvania University Press, 1991.

Index